A RICH AND TANTALIZING BREW

## FOOD AND FOODWAYS

SERIES EDITORS:
JENNIFER JENSEN WALLACH
AND MICHAEL WISE

### OTHER BOOKS IN THIS SERIES

# A Rich and Tantalizing Brew

## A HISTORY OF HOW COFFEE CONNECTED THE WORLD

JEANETTE M. FREGULIA

The University of Arkansas Press
Fayetteville
2019

ISBN: 978-1-68226-086-9 (cloth)
ISBN: 978-1-68226-087-6 (paper)
eISBN: 978-1-61075-655-6

23   22   21   20   19      5   4   3   2   1


♾ The paper used in this publication meets the minimum
requirements of the American National Standard for
Permanence of Paper for Printed Library Materials Z39.48-1984.


Library of Congress Cataloging-in-Publication Data

Names: Fregulia, Jeanette M., author.
Title: A rich and tantalizing brew : a history of how coffee connected the
   world / Jeanette M. Fregulia.
Description: Fayetteville : University of Arkansas Press, [2019] | Series:
   Food and foodways | Includes bibliographical references and index. |
   Identifiers: LCCN 2018023706 (print) | LCCN 2018031020 (ebook) |
   ISBN 9781610756556 (electronic) | ISBN 9781682260869 (cloth : alk. paper) |
   ISBN 9781682260876 (pbk. : alk. paper)
Subjects: LCSH: Coffee—History. | Coffee—Social aspects. |
   Coffee industry—Social aspects.
Classification: LCC GT2918 (ebook) | LCC GT2918 .F74 2019 (print) |
   DDC 394.1/2—dc23
LC record available at https://lccn.loc.gov/2018023706

*For my daughter, Carmen*

# CONTENTS

The University of Arkansas Press Series on Food and Foodways explores historical and contemporary issues in global food studies. We are committed to representing a diverse set of voices that tell lesser-known food stories and to stimulating new avenues of interdisciplinary research. Our strengths are works in the humanities and social sciences that use food as a critical lens for examining broader cultural, environmental, and ethical issues.

Feeding ourselves has long entangled us in complicated moral puzzles of social injustice and environmental destruction. When we eat, we consume not only the food on the plate but also the lives and labors of innumerable plants, animals, and people. This process distributes its costs unevenly across race, class, gender, and other social categories. The production and distribution of food often obscures these material and cultural connections, impeding honest assessments of our impacts on the world around us. By taking these relationships seriously, the Food and Foodways series provides new critical studies that analyze the cultural and environmental relationships that have sustained human societies.

*A Rich and Tantalizing Brew* explores the history of coffee's centuries-long diffusion across the globe, from its origins as an indigenous plant of eastern Africa to its eventual ubiquity as a staple of modern culinary cultures worldwide. As Jeanette Fregulia demonstrates, tracing the drink's routes—from Africa to the Near east to other parts of Asia and Europe and eventually to the Americas—reveals how our historical conceptions of places themselves are implicated within culinary subjectivities that emerged alongside a spreading taste for coffee's stimulating, caffeinated properties. Written in a voice that is both scholarly and approachable, this book encourages readers to reflect on the alimentary sensations that constitute our perceptions of food and history. It is no simple accident of culture, for instance, that, for centuries, people curious about that past and other intellectual inquiries commonly indulged themselves with a warm and energizing beverage while reading a work of scholarship such as this. Physical sensations pertain to even the most academic tasks, a certainty generally acknowledged more readily by scholars during the ancient and early modern worlds than in our own, despite the fact that our own scholars consume far more coffee! Fregulia's contribution to the history of coffee therefore exceeds the boundaries of a modest empirical study of scholarly sources. It provokes new questions about the role of taste in the production of knowledge and does so in a light-handed manner that will please as well as arouse the curiosities of scholarly and popular audiences alike.

JENNIFER JENSEN WALLACH
MICHAEL WISE

# A Personal Journey to Coffee

The joys, and as it turns out, the perils, of reconsidering coffee's history came to me not simply from my love for the beverage itself but from years of trying to answer a series of nagging questions about how the connections and intersections of my research in the history of the early modern Mediterranean and my work in the history of the premodern and modern Middle East, primarily the Levant, might be integrated. Compounding my professional interests was an inability to extricate myself from the Italy of my family's past or from the lessons learned, and questions unanswered, that my professional and personal travels around the Mediterranean continue to inspire. In the cups of coffee enjoyed on both sides of that sea I found not only a remedy for years of discontent but also a product with a rich story that demanded a retelling.

If the history this book attempts to provide originated from scholarly frustration, the more immediate spark belongs to a love of chocolate. One semester some years ago, I was perusing the chocolate options at my local natural food store in search of the perfect antidote to an aggravating lack of inspiration for an upcoming guest lecture topic. As I moved through the aisles, thinking about what topic might engage students and demonstrate that history really does matter, the answer came to me. My students, my family, and my friends all know that my travel for work and for pleasure is really about something much more carnal, much more easily satiated—I leave home to eat and to drink. Whether for research or to replenish my soul, travel for me is always about exciting new tastes and for opportunities to reconsider the history conveyed in the bright green pesto of my father's family, a steaming bowl of harira, just the right amount of tahini in hummus, and the beloved anchovy, garlic, butter, and olive oil concoction of my mother's ancestors from the Piedmont region.

As I stood considering my fair-trade chocolate options it occurred to me that I wanted to talk to the students about more than just the history of food consumption, in this instance chocolate, or the ways people have endeavored to keep together body and soul. I wanted them to understand that in their favorite chocolate was an ocean of history, not just the present. I wanted to explore with them what food means to the history of the world and, just as importantly, to their own pasts. And so this book was born.

I still lecture on chocolate and on all sorts of other food and drink, grateful to all those with far more to say than I for providing the material that makes our discussions both scholarly and tasty. I am indebted to those who share my passion for all things edible. Without their inspiration, this project would simply not exist. Here begins a journey into the past of a beverage that is both ubiquitous and elusive.

# ACKNOWLEDGMENTS

No book comes to completion without the help, prodding, and dedication of others, and this project is no different. Indeed, it would still be just an interesting idea were it not for the enthusiasm and encouragement of the many to whom I owe no small debt of gratitude.

I begin at the University of Nevada, Reno. Dr. Kevin Stevens and Dr. Barbara Walker were guides, mentors, and necessary critics throughout my graduate education, and they have since become friends and colleagues. They, along with Dr. Martha Hildreth, taught me to think boldly, words of wisdom I try to bring to my work and words I use to try to inspire my students. I also thank Dr. Scott Casper, chair of the History Department during my doctoral work; I try to follow his example now that I am a department chair.

Over the years, friends and colleagues have patiently listened to my triumphs and lamentations. Heather Navratil and Zoe Ann Stoltz elevated picnics to an art form and reminded me that we all need to make time to break bread with others. I would be remiss if I did not mention my book club, the Reading Women, who are probably happy this project has ended so I can actually talk about the books at our monthly gatherings, and the members of my parish, Saint Mary Catholic Community, who nourish my soul.

I need to thank many at Carroll College. I thank the other two members of this History Department, Dr. D. J. Cash and Dr. Dean Pavlakis, for reminding me why history matters, and everyone outside the department, both faculty and staff, for reminding me that there is more to life than history. Thanks to Dr. Dan Gretch, Dr. Kyle Strode, and Dr. David Hitt in the Chemistry Department, who helped me have a few words to say about the science of taste. I am grateful to Virginia Cooper for proofreading and editing the first draft of this book. I also thank the Carroll College Faculty Development Committee for the financial support they award in support of faculty research and scholarship.

Much of the daily life of faculty at my institution is filled with students. Their struggles, triumphs, and probing questions gave me a reason to think about something other than this book. I thank them for their moments of levity, their curiosity, and their patience with all things coffee.

Friends and accomplished colleagues outside Montana reminded me that book projects do reach completion if we persevere; they have my sincerest thanks. In particular, I am grateful to Dr. Jennifer M. Brinkerhoff at the George Washington University Elliot School of International Affairs, who shared her knowledge of the current state of the Ethiopian coffee trade. Thank you also to friends on both sides of the Mediterranean Sea, and beyond, who helped turn travel for research into adventures of joy, at the end of which were always coffee and really great food.

I am indebted to a number of people at the University of Arkansas Press. David Scott Cunningham, editor in chief; Molly Rector, project editor; and Jennifer Vos, editorial assistant, shepherded this project to its completion with care and skill. I owe more than a word of thanks to Dr. Jennifer Jensen Wallach of the History Department at the University of North Texas and co-editor of the University of Arkansas Press's Food and Foodways series for believing in this book. I thank Dr. Wallach and Dr. Michael Wise for writing the preface. I extend my gratitude to the anonymous reviewers who took the time to read my manuscript; this book is far better for their time and comments. All errors are, of course, mine alone.

I want to thank an extraordinary copy-editor, Kate Babbitt, and also Rudy Leon for creating such a fine index. Finally, the staff at the Smithsonian Library assisted with the procurement of one of the images and permissions.

My family has my greatest thanks. My mother Deanna, my father Don, my sister Leah, my brother Donald, and my nephews Connor, Jamison, and Lorenzo, along with Jessica, Allan, and Gabe, who became family when they got caught up with the Fregulias, were there with their own unique forms of inspiration throughout this project. Two sets of grandparents, Paul and Antoinette Troglia and Mary and Edward Fregulia, are no longer with us, but I know they are raising a cup from heaven. I am blessed and grateful.

# A RICH AND TANTALIZING BREW

# One Bean, Many Histories

*A Taste of History O Coffee, thou dost dispel all care, thou art the object of desire to the scholar*
                                        —Anonymous Arabic poem, 1511[1]

*A very good drink . . . that is almost as black as ink and very good in illness . . .*
                                        —Leonhard Rauwolf, 1573[2]

*Fuma et arde il legume a te d'Aleppo guinto e da Mocap che, di milled Navi popolata mai sempre, insuperbisce.*
                                        —Giuseppe Parini, 1763[3]

*People love coffee because of its two-fold effect—the pleasurable sensation and the increased efficiency it produces.*
                                        —William Ukers, 1922[4]

*Coffee is not just a beverage, it is a cup of liquid sanity.*
                                        —Coffee Capsules Direct, February 2017[5]

An unknown Arab poet, a German physician, an Italian lyric poet, an American publisher, and a website devoted to coffee quotes, separated from one another by distance and time, together express the history of coffee as beverage, cure, and object of longing. The authors quoted above illuminate an enduring fascination with a bitter beverage that still, over 500 years after the first quote, inspires personal devotion and the avid attention of writers and their readers. The anonymous poet who wrote in early sixteenth century Arabia in the same year that the religious leader of Mecca attempted to ban the coffeehouses in his city; the German doctor, scientist, and traveler who reached Aleppo, Syria, in 1573 and would later be recognized as the first European (although not the first individual) to call attention to coffee in writing; the Italian poet who proclaims the pride both Aleppo and the port of Mocha in Yemen have in their beans; and the American whose journal, founded in 1901, is still published today also reveal that coffee binds together centuries of history that seem, at first glance, to have little connection to one another. Indeed, despite volumes of writing in medical treatises, in travel narratives, in contemporary commentaries on fair trade and equity for farmers, in instruction manuals for proper brewing, in observations on sociability in the public spaces of the coffeehouse, coffee is an unexhausted topic, demanding a fresh consideration of how a drink that still garners the unflagging devotion of many around the world, including 62 percent of people in the United States, cannot be understood outside the contexts of its many pasts and its contested present.[6] More wide-ranging than the story of coffee in one physical location during a particular historic time, this book reveals coffee and the coffeehouse as the threads that bring together the places, ideas, cultures, and eras through which it moved and the peoples—merchants, soldiers, consumers, members of religious communities, leaders, scientists, philosophers, travel writers, and others—whose lives they changed forever. In this new story, coffee and the coffeehouse become the lenses through which to reconsider the history of globalization. Proving the claim that the history of coffee and the coffeehouse are, in fact, the story of the globalization of both commodities and social life entails more than taking readers on a journey that starts with coffee's legendary beginnings and ends with the ethical questions of the present. It also means bringing forth evidence of that moment when the world went from being a landmass of entities separated by distance to a time of intentional connection, for it is in this moment that the foundation of coffee's story is laid.

## Coffee's Many Histories

Taking a moment to peer through the window of any coffeehouse, whether in early modern Venice, Italy, or present-day Helena, Montana, makes it possible to recognize the larger themes in which coffee's historic legacy is embedded. An important premise of this book is that coffee belongs simultaneously to the social, cultural, economic, political, legal, and religious histories of centuries of humanity. Coffee belongs first to the highlands of Ethiopia and Yemen, from which it moved out across the deserts of Arabia, through the Levant, into Turkey, across the Mediterranean Sea to Europe, and later into parts of Asia and to the Americas. At the intersections of the varied histories encountered in these pages, readers will find not just coffee but also the coffeehouse. Many voices enlivened the space of the coffeehouse, which invigorated even it as challenged public space. Those who praised their local shop encountered the cries of those who vociferously claimed that both the brew and the café would be the ruination of humanity.

Coffee is a part of the study of food and foodways. This multidisciplinary field is described by the discipline's leading journal, *Food and Foodways*, as "reflecting on the role food plays in human relations[,] . . . the powerful but often subtle ways in which food has shaped, and shapes, our lives socially, economically, politically, mentally, nutritionally, and morally. Because food is a pervasive social phenomenon, it cannot be approached by any one discipline."[7] Situated at the convergence of consumption, production, culture, tradition, and—most important for this book—history, coffee is a striking example of how the study of food and drink, which begins with the items that have graced the tables of our ancestors, opens wide larger windows into what people do not eat and drink and the reasons for such prohibitions, how people eat and drink, and where and with whom people pursue these life-sustaining activities, thereby illuminating what and who people value and the reasons behind these choices. Foodways also offers insight into the patterns of people's daily lives, what they find pleasing or displeasing in taste, and how all of these matters have changed over time, sometimes as the result of contact with people from outside their cultural group and other times because of catastrophic events that make traditional foods less available. Finally, the history of one food is at times narrated through that of another food or drink. Such is the case with coffee, as its arrival in Europe coincided with the arrival of several other new edibles, most notably chocolate from the Americas, tea from India, and sugar from the Levant.[8]

The history of coffee is about place and is therefore deeply embedded in the regional histories of eastern Africa, Arabia, the Levant, the Ottoman Empire, Europe, and later the Americas and parts of Asia. The spatial history of coffee is not just linked to specific territories but also to the arteries that connected them, in particular the Mediterranean Sea and the Silk Road. This geographical history of coffee is tricky, as the geopolitical structure of the world today is the result of centuries of shifting boundaries, sometimes instigated by humans, sometimes by nature. It is important to keep in mind, therefore, that the idea of region is not straightforward but is rather "something that is politically constructed through spatial metaphors and ways of knowing the world" and is therefore constantly shifting.[9] For example, in eastern Africa and the Middle East, where coffee originated, and the regions where non-indigenous coffee plantations later appeared, the territorial demarcations accepted today are the result of colonialism, imperialism, and greed, constructed at various times in history to accommodate the desires of foreigners. Recognizing these challenges, I have tried to be as specific as possible when making references to geographical space in the text. I have also included maps.

Coffee has a commercial history. Along the peaks and valleys of the Silk Road, across the deserts of Arabia, and around the shores of the Mediterranean, also known as "the great sea," flowed a dazzling array of products accompanied by equally vibrant cultural exchanges.[10] The spread of coffee beyond its original borders owes much to the trading ambitions of such ancient civilizations as the Greeks, Phoenicians, Romans, Chinese, and Arabs, all of whom developed profitable global ties to one another, importing and exporting everything from spices and elegant textiles to artistic and architectural motifs, medical tracts, and technologies useful in warfare and navigation. Commerce in coffee remained exclusively part of the business ties between the eastern and western sides of the Mediterranean Sea until the mid-eighteenth century, when the coffee plants that had always been under the proprietary control of people in the highlands of Yemen were smuggled out by an enterprising Portuguese merchant and planted in parts of India, South and Central America, Indonesia, and elsewhere. The coffeehouse also has a share in this mercantile history, as the coffeehouses Italian merchants and traders likely frequented during their travels to cities all over the eastern Mediterranean became the model for those that sprang up elsewhere.

The commercial history of coffee as an expensive luxury good belongs with the related field of the histories of the Renaissance and early modern consumerism and acquisitiveness, participation in what Richard Goldthwaite calls a "world of goods."[11] Evelyn Welch explored Goldthwaite's idea in her work on shopping during this age and a number of scholars have reconsidered the concept, including the contributors to Frank Trentmann's edited collection *The History of Consumption*. Europeans' desire for the rare, which had begun centuries before as the

Roman Empire expanded east, grew throughout the Middle Ages and intensified during the Renaissance, when consumer demand for physical adornments, oddities for display, and new tastes for their tables increased. The goods that traveled the longest distances are of particular interest because for early modern Europeans of sufficient means, a general requirement was that the goods they bought had a foreign provenance.

The coffeehouse is part of this history of acquisition and consumption, as it was merchants who forged the path the coffeehouse would travel. These traders, who facilitated the continuous flow of material and cultural encounter, proved themselves to be influential conduits for information about coffee and the coffeehouse, accomplices in the production of western curiosity about those who lived in the land where coffee originated, and tellers of the anxieties and controversies that surrounded coffeehouses of the Muslim world, fears that manifested everywhere coffee moved.

As news of coffee spread, it joined the Renaissance universe of the marvelous.[12] Much of this interest fed by the written word, and thus coffee has a literary and artistic history. It appeared not just in the accounts of merchants but also in the musings of those moving east in quests to study the flora and fauna of foreign landscapes, religious pilgrims, conquerors, or just restless adventurers, seeking to both inform and to entertain their reading and listening audiences back home with tales of adventure, hardship, and spiritual enlightenment. Indeed, information about coffee often preceded its actual arrival. In the case of the West, people first learned of coffee in the narratives of exploration and encounter that shaped evolving ideas about all who were different from themselves. While they were less common, non-European writers also produced accounts of their journeys; the Moroccan Muslim scholar Ibn Battutah (1304–1377) is among the most notable. Battutah, who originally set out to make a hajj, or pilgrimage, to Mecca, continued far beyond the holy city and did not return home to stay for twenty-nine years. His wanderings took him as far as China, and his account of his voyage provides a necessary counterpoint to the more common Eurocentric narratives.[13]

At a time when the world was becoming increasingly connected, early modern notions of acquisition joined with travel literature to produce both an intensification of interest in compelling others and the vigorous colonial expansion of the English, Dutch, Spanish, and Portuguese. These acts brought coffee drinking and coffee production into the Americas and parts of Asia. Coffee and coffeehouses are part of the literature of travel and are visible in the art and architecture of such places as the Doge's

Palace and the Basilica of Saint Mark in Venice. Arriving in Europe at a time when a drive to recover the ideas, languages, and philosophies of antiquity, they collided with a craving for the new that, in the case of coffee, meant both an unfamiliar taste and a novel way of socializing in public space.

Coffee also belongs with legal and religious histories. Members of the mystical sect of Islam, the Yemeni Sufis, drank coffee as an aid to wakefulness in religious rituals that might last most of the night. Not all religious leaders similarly embraced coffee, and as elaborated in a later chapter, secular and religious leaders and scholars exhibited some anxiety about coffee. For Islamic leaders, coffee attracted unwanted attention both because it altered human chemistry and was therefore sometimes categorized with the other intoxicating beverages forbidden to followers of Islam, and because it took men away from prayers. In addition, wherever coffeehouses arose, accusations swirled that the men inside were conspiring to plot treason and revolution, prompting rulers and spiritual officials to make legal pronouncements about them. As it turns out, objections to coffee help explain why the public coffeehouse was initially slow to take hold even in the region where it had likely been consumed in domestic space for centuries.

Coffee also finds a home in the history of medicine. The discovery of coffee influenced ideas about health and sickness, first in the treatises of such notables as Abu Bakr Muhammad ibn Zakariyya al-Razi, better known as Rhazes (854–925), and Abu Ali al-Husayn Ibn Abd Allan ibn Sina, also called Avicenna (980–1037), who extolled the value of coffee for treating certain illnesses. Centuries later, when early modern European physicians consulted the tracts of these predecessors, they also extolled coffee's curative powers.

Finally, it is possible to hear the first rumblings of Orientalism in the history of coffee. In descriptions of a compelling yet terrifying eastern Other, the narratives of those who traveled laid the foundation for what Edward Said would, centuries later, detail in his theory of Orientalism. While Said located his argument of the "Orient" as "almost a European invention," with a "special place in European Western experience," I argue that the foundation of these ideas was laid much earlier.[14]

Throughout this book, I will often turn attention back to the many histories previewed above as support for my assertion that while the coffeehouse has not been understood as a uniquely European invention, no clear link has been made to the role that contact with the Muslim world played in the history of the world's embrace of the beverage and of the public venue to which it gave birth. In this analysis, the coffeehouses of the world owe their existence to a number of forces, all of which originated in the East before they spread to regions where the public had a taste for new flavors. That these same people were also open to new forms of public social interaction proved fertile ground for what Elliot Horowitz argues was an "extended the range of possibilities for making use of the night (and daytime) hours for purposes pious or profane."[15]

This book makes coffee and coffeehouses central to the history of globalization while also making a space for understanding coffee's present. This final task would be difficult, if not impossible, without looking back, as coffee today remains inextricably tied to how people socialize and the debates that accompany those who rely on coffee production for their livelihood. As a result of the latter, coffee is now integral to an ongoing set of discourses about fair trade for farmers, questions of environmental sustainability, issues of national sovereignty, and the health effects of the daily cup. This book offers a tale of how the world has been indelibly changed by a peculiar drink and the singular institution to which it gave rise.

## Scope and Organization of the Book

Given the diverse histories to which coffee belongs, it is hardly surprising that articles and books about coffee and the social life to which it gave birth have engaged writers from a variety of dispositions. Both scholars and the popular press continue to attract readers on the topic, and thus approaches to the coffee phenomenon vary widely. In making my central argument, I approach coffee and the coffeehouse thematically and chronologically, reflecting the overlapping refrains common to all places with a coffee culture while also acknowledging that coffee has a historical trajectory across time.

For all that this book attempts to accomplish, it is worth noting here what my interpretation of coffee's history is not. At the start, this study was predicated on the idea that the history of coffee and the coffeehouse was essentially an early modern one that began in the waning decades of the fifteenth century and culminated sometime in the mid-eighteenth century. Research revealed this assumption to be misguided, for confining the investigation to such a relatively brief period of time rendered these two histories not merely incomplete but also erroneous. Limiting the study of coffee and the coffeehouse to early modernity made the study distinctly western-centric. Casting aside adherence to an approximately 300-year period in favor of a thematic approach that reached across time led me to some important revelations. Among these was the recognition that the history of coffee, as the catalyst for the flourishing of commercial globalization and as a sweeping change in human socialization, began in antiquity. While debates continue regarding the global turn, I posit that rigidly assigning an early modern European start date for this book would have required me to locate some anomaly that occurred in the West around the mid-fifteenth century, when human demand for luxury products from distant lands inspired merchants to set off to foreign ports in search of lucrative commodities. This entrepreneurial spirit would have, somewhere along the way, led to a chance encounter with one peculiar product that would subsequently alter their homelands forever. The research suggests that this was not the case. When I broadened the scope of this study, both historically and geographically, the evidence revealed that the coffeehouses of Europe and the Americas were appropriations of eastern culture. For just as the coffeehouse presented an enticing new opportunity for men in the Near East to socialize outside domestic space, it gave their counterparts in the West not just a similarly inviting possibility but also a means of gaining access to a world both fascinating and fearsome from the safety of home.[16] The chapters of this book are, therefore, arranged to take readers into a world long connected and whose interdependence and cross-cultural influences continue to expand as the centuries pass.

Chapter 1 examines several topics as background and context for the ones that follow, beginning with a look at foodways as an analytical lens through which to understand human history. As part of this discussion, the chapter takes a broad look at the science of taste. From here, the chapter moves backward in time for a broad look at the trading history in which coffee was but one commodity. With the assistance of works by Pliny the Elder and others, the chapter examines the natural and human worlds in which early commerce moved, including the empires of ancient Greece and Rome, the many islands of the Aegean, the Mediterranean Sea, the Levant, the deserts of Arabia, and that great trade route, the Silk Road. This chapter also includes a look at the contributions of such peoples as the seafaring Phoenicians, whose famous purple dye has led a decade of students to refer to them as the "purple dye people," the desert-dwelling Nabataeans and their administrative center at Petra in present-day Jordan, and the empires of Persia, from which came not just dyes but also perfumes, incense, spices, and new military strategies.

Little beyond myth is known of coffee's ancient history, so Chapter 2 begins with a few of those tales before turning to the emergence of the coffee bean in Ethiopia and to the dominance of Yemen, specifically the port of Mocha, in the coffee trade after Ethiopia invaded Yemen in the sixth century.[17] As part of this analysis, the chapter looks at early patterns of consumption in this region, including the role of coffee in Sufi religious rituals and its place in treatises on health by the physicians Ibn Sina and Rhazes. The chapter concludes with a brief reflection on sugar, which came to Jordan and the Levant around the eighth century from China with Silk Road merchants and took its place as part of the universe of products grown and enjoyed in the East and later demanded in the West.

Chapter 3 gives voice to travelers, whose narratives of adventure in the eastern Mediterranean first informed Europeans about coffee, producing curiosity about the beverage some time before it crossed the sea around 1528, just before the Ottomans occupied Yemen in 1536. Filled not just with descriptions of a sizzling hot and bitter brew but also with the unfamiliar sights and sounds of the coffeehouse, this chapter offers readers a window into the usefulness—and the pitfalls—of travel literature and the role they played in a nascent form of Orientalism. While less is available on how those in the East viewed their western visitors, this chapter considers the sources that are available, so as not to ignore the perspectives of the encountered, which are equally important.

The history of shopping, consumption, acquisitiveness, and the social nature of such activities open Chapter 4, placing the history of coffee alongside two other important edibles that arrived in Europe around the same time: chocolate and tea.[18] From there, the chapter moves to Venice, the first port of call for coffee outside of the Muslim world. Venice was also the city where it was likely that Italian merchants who did not travel had their first taste of the brew as they discussed matters of business at the house in the Rialto that was home to Ottoman merchants. This chapter demonstrates that the history of coffee is inseparably tied to the history of luxury goods and is therefore integral to the universe of early modern ideas about the acquisition and consumption of a variety of edible and inedible commodities.

Just as enjoyment of coffee spread around from East to West, attempts to regulate access to it followed a similar path. This is the subject of Chapter 5. In part because of its energizing chemical properties and in part because it encouraged the gathering of people (primarily men) in public places, coffee and coffeehouses met with considerable resistance in the Muslim eastern Mediterranean, throughout the Ottoman Empire, in Italy, in other parts of Europe, and in the urban centers of colonial America. Anxiety about coffee drinking, about whether the Qur'an permitted its consumption, and a general uneasiness with the deep color of coffee because it was similar to deep color of wine led Khair Bey, the governor of Mecca, to attempt to close the coffeehouses in his city in 1511.[19] Leaders from Cairo to Constantinople soon followed suit. Despite this opposition, in all instances coffee drinking not only continued but grew in popularity.[20] Such anxieties traveled with the bean, provoking objections from leaders of the Roman Catholic Church, who not only argued that coffee should be banned but also targeted early modern Venetian apothecaries. Because the inventories of apothecaries showed evidence of coffee, the Holy Office condemned their places of business as dens that were hospitable to the spread of heresy.[21] Warnings about the dangers of the coffeehouse and cries for regulation of the new institution also appear in social tracts, letters, and pamphlets from England to Philadelphia, demonstrating that the path to eventual acceptance of coffee was anything but smooth.

Chapter 6 brings together the elements from previous chapters to substantiate the argument that coffee and the rise of the coffeehouse led to new patterns of social interaction that began with the Arab coffeehouse and were then passed along to others through their exchanges with the Middle Eastern and Ottoman worlds. In this chapter, the coffeehouse becomes an important part of the social order of early modern Europe, in part as a result of what Brian Cowan calls "an intellectual culture of curiosity" that traveled to Britain from its place of origination in the Italy of the Renaissance.[22] As this chapter will demonstrate, however, the western coffeehouse owed its existence not to a new social order in Europe but rather to a history that long preceded that development. This chapter further discusses what happened after the opening of the first coffeehouses, taking into account a new generation of merchants whose trading companies sought to supply homes and coffeehouses. The chapter also describes that critical moment when coffee growing escaped the Yemeni monopoly. It discusses how coffee reached parts of India and its environs and South and Central America and how cultivation of the plants in these locations proved a useful tool for ambitious European colonizers.

Inspired by concerns that the ubiquity of coffee makes it easy to overlook the continuing challenges of people and nations that rely on coffee for some or most of their economic survival, the final chapter demonstrates that coffee has a present, not just a history. This chapter begins where the whole story began, in Ethiopia, a nation where coffee is still the defining national export and yet continues to face challenges related to both production and trade. The chapter also examines the state of coffee in other regions where it is grown, including Latin America, where, as in Ethiopia, trials relating to equitable pay and fair trade practices for small farmers and independent producers have captured the attention of the coffee-drinking public. In most places where coffee is grown, attempts to resist the threats large corporations pose are complicated by the need to institute sustainable agricultural practices. In this chapter, coffee is placed within a set of ongoing contemporary narratives that serve to remind readers that understanding the realities of coffee production is essential to an understanding of the modern world.

Throughout this book, every effort has been made to distinguish among the peoples of the East in the same way that Europeans are distinguished from one another: by where they live. To that end, the people of the Levant, derived from the Italian *levante*, are those who resided in the Eastern Mediterranean, including present-day Syria, Lebanon, Jordan, Israel, and the Palestinian Territories. Dwellers of the desert region further east are identified as Arab, just as the fifteenth-century Ottoman conquerors who came to dominate much of the region are acknowledged as Turks. When I know a person's or people's religious affiliation, I have noted it. Finally, I have sought to avoid such terms as "exotic," "marvelous," and even "Other," except when used by the writers of the past, whose descriptions tell us more about their perspectives of places and people that were foreign to them than they do about the people they encountered abroad. As Stephen Greenblatt explained in his 1991 book *Marvelous Possessions, the Wonder of the New World*, the "marvelous" was an important part of "the whole complex system of representation . . . through which people of the Middle Ages and Renaissance apprehended, and thence possessed or discarded, the unfamiliar."[23] Such words simply prove inappropriate outside of that context.

## Concluding Thoughts: A Look Ahead

Given all the work that has been done on coffee, it might seem as if there is nothing more to write. It is hoped that by the last sentence of the conclusion readers will have a new perspective. The story of a coffee-loving world, the origins of human devotion to an unlikely and bitter beverage, and the search for a better understanding of how coffee influenced the social landscape of cities and communities from Mecca to Massachusetts owes more to myth than to reliable historical evidence until sometime around the ninth century. Coffee drinking may well have begun in antiquity among people whose experiences have been lost to time. The first written, and therefore conclusive, evidence of coffee dates from the work of the scientist and philosopher Ibn Sina, who mentions it in his *Canon of Medicine*, completed in 1025. A bronze Egyptian container from the fourteenth century suggests that coffee was a private pleasure by the 1300s. The next documented consumers, the Sufi mystics of Yemen, appear 150 years later, around 1450, in reports of how religious men incorporated coffee into their religious ceremonies because of its stimulating properties.[24]

Coffee intake for more than medicinal and religious purposes seems to have become widespread in the Arab world by the end of the 1400s, as Muslim pilgrims introduced coffee to Persia, Egypt, the Levant, North Africa, and Turkey. By the mid-fifteenth century coffee was in relatively wide use throughout the region, evidence of its value as both a personal pleasure and a profitable item for trade.[25] It was not until the early sixteenth century, however, that coffee went from a beverage that cured illness, aided in religious ritual, or simply provided domestic pleasure to a commodity around which a new institution arose—the coffeehouse. According to Ralph Hattox, who wrote *Coffee and Coffeehouses; The Origins of a Social Beverage in the Medieval Near East*, coffee began to garner significant attention with the rise of these shops. "Letters, essays, books, and even . . . legal decisions" suggest that coffee's reputation often preceded its actual arrival into an area.[26]

The coffee consumed for centuries in the Middle East and Africa may have been first introduced in Europe by the Italian botanist Prospero Alpini, medical adviser to Giorgio Emo, the Venetian consul to Cairo from 1580 to 1583. (Alpini is also said to have acquainted his readers with bananas.)[27] Another account substantiates the arrival of news about coffee in Europe at this time, in 1582, although it makes no reference to Alpini as the source.[28] Although before the late sixteenth century, coffee may have been known to a small European elite through medical tracts, it was the increasing availability and popularity of travel narratives that widely disseminated information about coffee to a vast audience.[29] By 1615, traders from Venice had little difficulty spreading a new commodity throughout mainland Europe and beyond. Coffee reached London by 1650, around the same time that chocolate from the Americas and tea from India made their way into the markets of Europe.[30]

Coffee may not have had the revolutionary effect that the printing press had on the spread of religious fervor in the sixteenth century or the economic explosion that the factory initiated in the nineteenth century, yet it would be erroneous to dismiss its importance in the human story. Within the telling of coffee's past lies proof that a single commodity can bring together many histories and expand the social world of all those who put lips to cup in the company of others. Beginning, as so many good stories do, with some popular and well-worn myths and continuing through the seventeenth century, this book explores how one peculiar beverage wove together history. Although coffee remains even today an acquired taste, this book reminds us that a reckoning with food and drink have become essential elements of historical study, exemplifying how edible commodities offer a rich, and often delicious, window into shared pasts.

One final thought. The history of coffee and the coffeehouse present an opportunity to reconsider the contemporary animosities and misunderstandings that exist in and between the places visited in this book. More as subtext than explicit topic, the coffee and the coffeeshop that so many have embraced over the centuries invite new reflection on human history, a history that, like the present, has always been filled with times of cooperation and conflict, with the transmission of knowledge and technology for purposes both good and ill, and with a deep abiding interest in the people and the places that lie along the routes that have and continue to connect us to one another. Perhaps there is some new insight here that might move the conversation in the direction of beginnings, a moment to heed the words of the Arab poet Mahmoud Darwish, who in a poem set against the backdrop of the 1982 Israeli invasion of Lebanon, poignantly asked for "a five-minute truce for the sake of coffee."[31]

## CHAPTER 1

# Desert to Sea
## Coffee, History, and Place

*Coffee, for an addict like me, is the key to the day.*

—Mahmoud Darwish, 1982[1]

## The Mediterranean World: Geography, History, and Commentary

Geography may not conclusively determine a region's history or political structures, predict future wars or the potential for peace, or indelibly fix the cultures of the people who live in specific places. Yet without "a proper appreciation of the map," making sense of the world, both past and present, would be impossible.[2] This chapter begins by situating coffee and coffeehouses within the greater contexts of trade and exchange, for it is with the movement of peoples and cultures, particularly across the Mediterranean Sea, that coffee seduced much of the world.

Just the name Mediterranean Sea hints at its historic and contemporary importance. The Latin name, Mediterraneum Mare, derived from *mediterraneus*, a combination of *medius* (middle) plus *terra* (land/earth) and *mare* (sea). This sea in the middle of the land has been given many other names. Those who lived on the dry land surrounding it, those who sought to conquer and control its resources both human and natural, and those who plied its waters in pursuit of their fortunes assigned titles of their own to the Mediterranean Sea, selecting ones that reflected their relationship to the sea and/or its place in their imaginations. For the ancient Egyptians, the Mediterranean, like the desert, served primarily as protection against invaders, although there is no definitive information about what they called it. In the past, scholars have posited that the Egyptians called the sea along their northern coast the "Great Green," but this notion has since been largely rejected.[3] The Romans made Egypt a province of Rome in 30 BCE, following Mark Antony's defeat at the hands of Octavian (later known as Caesar Augustus) at the Battle of Actium and the deposal of the last Ptolemaic ruler, Cleopatra. As the Roman Empire expanded, rulers referred to the saltwater body not as Mediterraneum Mare but rather as Mare Nostrum, Our Sea, an attempt on the part of the empire to claim ownership of both the land and the water. The early Jewish community referred to the Mediterranean Sea in less proprietary terms, using the name Yam Gadol, the Great Sea, appropriating the name of the ancient Phoenician maritime god, Yamm, as their word for sea. For the Turks, the Mediterranean was called Akdeniz, or the White Sea.[4]

Reflecting on the historic importance of the Mediterranean Sea, Friedrich Hegel (1770–1831) proclaimed the Mediterranean as "the uniting element and the centre of World History."[5] In support of his assertion, Hegel looked back to the commercial prowess of the ancient Phoenicians, whose far-reaching ambitions drove them west around the Mediterranean carrying not just prized items for trade but also, according to Hegel, a "high degree of culture" wherever they went.[6] Hegel later substantiated his not-so-subtle claim that civilization flowed from west to east in his Lectures, where he wrote that it was with the Mediterranean-faring Phoenicians that another hallmark of civilization spread. According to Hegel, it was with this prosperous maritime trading empire that written language "received its first development."[7] Not all peoples had such a positive view of the Mediterranean. In particular, Arab geographers of Islam's Classical Age (~132 AH/750 CE–635 AH/1238 CE) described the Mediterranean as "poor, alien, and uninviting."[8] Far from celebratory, these men offered a vision of the Mediterranean that seems very different from the idyllic images of a coastal environment that fill history texts and continue to attract visitors who return home with photographs of blue waters, olive groves, and warm sunshine.

The Mediterranean's geological history helps explain why it has been viewed as a unifying force among the peoples and places it connects. The 36-mile-long Strait of Gibraltar, which runs between Spain and North Africa, connects the sea with the Atlantic Ocean, the source of its replenishment. It has been, equally, a territory of disunity and conflict. Just as the ethnic, linguistic, religious, and cultural diversity of this region has led to moments of cooperation and sharing, they have also caused people to rage against one another in social, political, and economic arenas, some-times to the point of bloody upheaval. These varying, even contradictory, visions caused uncertainty about how best to name the Mediterranean Sea. After considerable reading and contemplating, David Abulafia's title for the Mediterranean and the lands it touched as the "Liquid Continent" seems, for the purposes of this book, the most appropriate, as it succinctly describes a naturally created body of water that "embraces many peoples, cultures, and economies within a space with precise edges."[9] The natural world of the Mediterranean that has long been home to human societ-ies simultaneously affirms and defies the commonalties that their place around a shared body of water would seem to impose upon them. To understand the rich history of coffee and the coffeehouse is to appreci-ate the complexity of the Mediterranean, recognizing it as a geographic reality and as an idea, both of which have preoccupied the minds of scholars, scientists, and travelers since antiquity. In the story of coffee, the Mediterranean is a place that holds the stories of the populations who lived along its shores, at the same time that it bore witness to the histories of the outsiders from the European interior, the deserts of the Arab East, and from lands as far away as India and China who have for millennia penetrated the sea and its environs.

## A Little Geology and a Little Geography

The physical history of the Mediterranean Sea begins long before the first humans arrived on its shores. Experts date its geologic prehistory to a basin called the Neotethys, formed when the African and Eurasian tec-tonic plates converged in the late Triassic (251 to 199 million years ago) and the early Jurassic (199 to 145 million years ago). Always an almost completely landlocked body of water with a surrounding dry climate, the Mediterranean Sea experienced a period of severe evaporation that culminated in the Messinian salinity crisis about six million years ago, at which time it became, for a time, completely isolated from its source, the Atlantic Ocean, and essentially dried up.[10] The Mediterranean remained in this dry state, separated from its source, until approximately 5.33 mil-lion years ago, when a flood created so much force that the Atlantic Ocean once again broke through the Strait of Gibraltar and the waters of the Mediterranean were replenished.[11] Today, this fourteen-mile-wide strait between Morocco and Spain remains the lifeblood of the Mediterranean Sea.

Since its rebirth as a body of water, the extent of the Mediterranean Sea has grown to its present size of 970,000 square miles. At its deepest point, off the coast of Greece, the sea is approximately 16,800 feet, making it just under half as deep as the Pacific Ocean. With a depth of 35,797 feet at its deepest point, the Pacific is the deepest ocean on earth. The Mediterranean is also much shallower than the Atlantic Ocean, which is 28,232 feet at its deepest point.

The Mediterranean is also defined by its climate. Much of the Mediterranean climatic zone is relatively temperate: its cool wet winters and hot dry summers make for agricultural similarities that are relatively easy to spot. For example, olives are indigenous to a number of Mediterranean locales, including North Africa, the European Mediterranean, and the Levant, and thus have long been part of the diets of those who lived on the shores of both the eastern and western Mediterranean. Citrus orchards and vineyards have also thrived on both sides of the sea, demonstrating how similarities in climate and soil as well as access to the bounties of the sea have long bound together the cuisines and livelihoods of Mediterranean inhabitants. However, in their book *The Corrupting Sea: A Study of Mediterranean History*, Peregrine Horden and Nicholas Purcell warn against assuming that likenesses in climate, soil, and vegetation define the "relationship of man to environment" and note instead a "pronounced local irregularity" among Mediterranean populations.[12] Coffee drinking is one of these irregularities; those in the east were the only ones to consume it for all of its early history.

While Mediterranean soils and climate are not conducive to the nurturing of coffee plants, the proximity of the Levantine Mediterranean to Yemen and other parts of the Arabian desert meant that coffee drinking emerged in this part of the world soon after it gained popularity farther inland. Proximity to the source of coffee meant that a distinctive coffee culture arose in the Mediterranean East long before it became established in other parts of the Mediterranean world.

## The Human World of the Mediterranean

The Mediterranean is, of course, much more than just a physical entity, although without the ease of travel that the sea facilitated, the products hungry consumers craved would have had a much longer and more circuitous route to their final destinations. While there is little disagreement about the geological history of the Mediterranean basin, what the

Mediterranean means to the history of humanity has been the subject of much debate. Hegel's belief that the Mediterranean was essential to human history has since been expanded upon and redefined, beginning notably with Fernand Braudel's seminal two-volume work, *The Mediterranean and the Mediterranean World in the Age of Philip II*, which has offered an important reference point for many modern histories of the Mediterranean. Published in French in 1967 and first available in English in 1973, Braudel's work has influenced generations of scholars.[13] What makes Braudel's monumental work so compelling is the array of topics he tackles, which range from geography and the environment to economics and trade to events and politics. At the end of the second volume, Braudel concludes that in the study of history "the long run always wins in the end" and that if we are to understand "the very sources of life in its most concrete, every day, indestructible, and anonymously human expression," we would do well to look not only across vast expanses of time but also across a variety of disciplines, including history, anthropology, and geography.[14] As this book will demonstrate with more than a nod to Braudel, the travels and travails of coffee cannot be understood as a series of discrete events over a few short centuries. They are, rather, deeply embedded in the history of people's everyday existence.

Using the assertions of Fernand Braudel as a starting point for the sweep of Mediterranean history and drawing on David Abulafia's claim that "the human experience of crossing the Mediterranean or of living in the port towns and islands that depended for their existence on the sea" as central, this look at the human history of the Mediterranean begins with language, one of the most noticeable differences among people who claim a relationship to the sea.[15] The differences lie with the language families that have played their own important roles in this history of human relations. Those who settled in the Mediterranean West were descendants of people who spoke Indo-European languages and shared little linguistically with the people of the East who spoke Semitic languages. Over centuries of contact, the need for cooperation led to a number of adaptations within these linguistic families, imparted from one to another. As just one example, Muslim raids into Sicily from Tunisia during the seventh and eighth centuries resulted in a number of Arabic contributions to the Sicilian dialect, including the name of the precious spice, *zaffarana*, in Arabic *za'faran* (زعفران), or saffron.

Political ambitions, the desire for commercial advantage, and differences of faith have also caused strife. And yet it is the connections

Abulafia and others have stressed that are the most inspiring, as they seem to turn up in the least expected places. Such was the case in the West Bank city of Hebron on a warm morning some years ago. As I admired the skill of a glassblower in a city whose ancient past is imperiled by a volatile present, I was reminded of a visit to the island of Murano, Italy, on a chilly late December afternoon. With the aid of a Palestinian friend who helped me with my stumbling Arabic, I described the likenesses I noticed between his work and that of the Italians on Murano. With great patience, the glassblower explained that for generations, the artisans of both cities had shared the skills and knowledge that enable both to continue producing exquisite work on their respective sides of the Mediterranean.

It is this legacy of both goodwill and of ill feeling people on both sides of the Mediterranean feel toward one another that illustrates the importance of considering the long sweep of history as Braudel argues, the place of the environment in that history, as Horden and Purcell discuss, and the human experience that most occupies Abulafia. In the story of coffee, it is possible to see where these histories, and others, meet across the expanses of time. A key point of this book is the importance of the how people experienced the Mediterranean. Subsequent chapters explore how lives were changed and enriched; how ideas and identities were challenged, sometimes with tragic consequences; and how entire continents came to rethink their public interactions over the enjoyment of a bitter and stimulating beverage.

## The Mediterranean and the Silk Road in the History of Globalization

Modern scholars such as those briefly mentioned above are not the first to comment on the people, geography, and culture of the Mediterranean, nor are they first to report about these matters to an audience back home. Among the best known of the early observations comes from the Greek historian Herodotus (ca. 484–425 BCE). Herodotus's personal story remains somewhat elusive. From what is known, it seems that he was born in Halicarnassus, a Greek city in Asia Minor that was under Persian rule at the time of his birth, and that he died in Athens. He is best known today for his *Histories*, a lengthy text that focuses on the wars between Greece and Persia from 499 to 479 BCE. The book also recounts the author's vast wanderings. In his lifetime, Herodotus claimed to have ventured over much of the Persian Empire and farther afield to Egypt, Libya, Byzantium, Macedonia, and the northern reaches of the Black Sea. Herodotus does not mention the Mediterranean Sea by name in his *Histories*, but he does tell readers that "the entire sea outside the Pillars of Heracles, which is called the Atlantic, and the Red Sea are all one," suggesting that in Herodotus's time there was no differentiation of the Mediterranean from the Atlantic.[16] From his travels, Herodotus compiled information about the people who lived and traded with the seafaring Greeks along the shores of the sea. He also described the place that is "furthest to the south of all the world . . . Arabia," where "there is a most marvelous sweet smell."[17] Herodotus claimed that the Greeks were introduced to previously unknown products from the Arabian desert, including myrrh and cinnamon, through trade with merchants from the enterprising Phoenician Empire.[18] While these merchants were best known for the coveted purple dye they extracted from a sea snail called a murex, they also sold frankincense to their Greek counterparts. Herodotus seems to have been particularly fascinated with this aromatic; he devoted considerable time to describing how the plants were protected and how the resin was harvested. "Flying snakes" that, according to Herodotus, were as deadly to one another as they were to humans, guarded the frankincense. The creatures had to be lured from the bushes over which they held dominion with the "smoke of the storax," a gum that had also been brought into Greece by the Phoenicians.[19]

Herodotus and his contemporaries do not appear to have had any knowledge of coffee. The frankincense that so captured his attention and would continue to acquire devotees long after the Phoenicians disappeared and other suppliers took their place, however, provides a useful illustration of the role transfers of material culture played in creating an openness among consumers to the foreign and the unfamiliar. To illustrate the necessity of the commercial exchanges of antiquity, this book takes a short diversion to the history of high-quality frankincense.

Frankincense, the gummy resin of a rather stubby and finicky tree, is native to only one place in Arabia, the north slopes of the Qara Mountains of Dhofar in present-day Oman, near the border with Yemen. Dhofar could be the biblical region of Ophir from which King Solomon acquired much of his great wealth, including frankincense and gold.[20] Rising to an elevation of approximately 5,000 feet at their highest point, frankincense trees grow at the slightly lower elevations of the Qara Mountains, between

2,000 and 2,500 feet.[21] Frankincense was harvested in antiquity, as it is today, by cutting a long gash in the bark of the trees and then collecting the resin that oozes out.

The ancient peoples of Arabia exchanged frankincense across a wide swath of territory at considerable profit. Egyptian records beginning with the eleventh dynasty (2125–1985 BCE) list frankincense as one of the products imported into Egypt for the pharaohs, who burned it in their temples. Arabs also exported it by sea out of Egypt.[22] Archaeologists believe that frankincense was commonly used in rituals of purification such as those following the sack of a city.[23] Perhaps because of its contact with the Egyptians, frankincense appears in the religious rites of the monotheistic ancient Hebrews.[24] The Old Testament books Exodus and Leviticus both note the use of the incense in worship practices.[25] Phoenicians and Persians are also part of the story of frankincense, as were the Greeks, who used it in public festivals.[26] About 100 years after Herodotus described frankincense, the Greek writer Theophrastus (371–ca. 287 BCE), a philosopher who succeed Aristotle at his lyceum, discussed frankincense in his *Inquiry into Plants*, a ten-volume tome written sometime between 350 BCE and Theophrastus's death in 287. Theophrastus wrote that "among the plants that grow in Arabia, Syria, and India the aromatic plants are somewhat exceptional and distinct from the plants of other lands; for instance, frankincense."[27]

Evidence suggests that it was the Etruscans who first burned incense in the region of Italy.[28] After the founders of the Roman republic defeated the Etruscans, the aromatic was adopted as part of the religious ceremonies of ancient Rome, expanding throughout the Roman world, as the Roman dramatist Plautus (255–185 BCE) attested.[29] Plautus mentions "its importation from Arabia" for use as part of the worship of household gods."[30] As Rome became an empire, frankincense was incorporated into the deification ceremonies of worthy Roman emperors.[31] By the first century of the Common Era, Roman naturalist Pliny the Elder (23–79 CE) not only echoed the ancient Roman view of the Mediterranean as "our Mediterranean Sea" but also called attention to the "Arabians, most famous for their frankincense."[32]

Given the wide-ranging use of frankincense, it is not surprising that merchants sought a share in its profitable trade. For example, around the same time that Pliny was compiling his *Natural History*, an encyclopedic account of a vast range of topics, an anonymous Greek-speaking Egyptian merchant penned an account of his travels and commercial activities on the Erythraean Sea. *The Periplus of the Erythraean Sea* described a trade route that moved down the coast from Egypt to where the Red Sea met the Indian Ocean and then continued on all the way to contemporary Tanzania. From east to west, the route moved around the Arabian Peninsula and across the Persian Gulf to the western coast of India. Despite the brevity of the account, the author provided details about important centers such as Petra, a "market-town for the small vessels sent there from Arabia" that was the home of the Nabataeans.[33] He also commented on the character of the local inhabitants in the ports of call he mentioned. For example, he described the "Wild flesh-Eaters and Calf-Eaters" who lived beyond the region controlled by the inland Berbers.[34] Perhaps of greatest value to his contemporaries (and to those who came after), the anonymous chronicler of the *Periplus* described the imports and exports that might be found along the route, one of which was frankincense. He wrote of an ancient port city in Yemen called Cana (not to be confused with the Cana in Galilee mentioned in the New Testament Gospel of John), "where alone is produced the far-side frankincense, in great quantity and of the best grade."[35] He continued, "all the frankincense produced in the country is brought by camels . . . to be stored" and from there it was exported.[36] The merchant remarked that frankincense sometimes left from the Port of Moscha, or Mocha, also in Yemen, the same port that would later monopolize the export of coffee beans. The author of the *Periplus* described this harbor as follows: "the harbor called Moscha, and ships from Cana called there regularly; and ships returning from Damirica and Barygaza [ancient seaports in Kerala and Gujarat, India, respectively] exchanged their cloth and wheat and sesame oil for frankincense."[37] As this quote illustrates, foreign products traveled from all four cardinal directions to meet consumer demand. They were then displayed in ancient Arabian emporia, in outposts along the Silk Road, and in the seaports of the Mediterranean Sean and the Indian Ocean, beckoning to merchants who would gather them up for transport and sale to their clients. Galleys, part of the Greco-Roman fleet, were used in trade between Arabia and India. Sailing from Egypt, some of these ships specialized in the transport of incense, which is not surprising, since in 30 BCE, Egypt became a province of Rome.[38]

The *Periplus* describes Mocha as one of the busiest ports on the Red Sea.

> Immediately beyond Syagrus the bay of Omana cuts deep into the coast-line. . . . Beyond this there are mountains, high and rocky

Abraham Cresques, Catalan Atlas (1375), "Europe and the Mediterranean," from a nineteenth-century reproduction of the atlas.[39]

> and steep inhabited by cave dwellers[,] . . . and beyond this is a port established for receiving Sachalitic frankincense; the harbor is called Moscha.[40]

Ships from Damarica and Barygaza, both located along the coast of southern India along the Arabian Sea, would arrive in the port laden with wheat, cloth, and sesame oil to exchange for the superior-quality Sachalitic frankincense the Arabian merchants offered.[41]

In time, frankincense gained acceptance in the practices of Christianity, due in part to the fact that Christianity originated in places occupied by the Roman Empire and likely also because of its place among the triad of gifts the magi presented at the birth of the Christ child. Seven centuries later, frankincense appeared in a more limited role in the practices of Islam.[42] Buddhist rituals in ancient China also included Arabian incense.[43] Finally, frankincense was not confined to religious rites. In the Greco-Roman world it was heralded as effective for stopping bleeding and healing wounds.[44]

The primary frankincense producers of the Qara mountains were not the only ones to enjoy great wealth from its sale. An important source of this highly desired product, along with other spices and aromatics, were the Semitic Nabataeans, perhaps best known today for the ruins of their magnificent capital of Petra in Jordan. Records of the commercial prominence of the Nabataeans stretch from 300 BCE to 107 CE, although their trading activities began even earlier. They were brokers of luxury items that included spices such as cinnamon and pepper from India and nutmeg from the Spice Islands, silks procured from China, and aromatics and perfumes. The scope of their commercial reach illustrates the local trading relationships that existed among neighboring Arab regions and the long-distance trade that extended along the Silk Road. By 30 BCE, the Nabataeans had added a vigorous and lucrative trade with the Roman Empire to their commercial empire. Pliny once again comes to our assistance; he noted that the Nabataei were purveyors of a range of products that passed from their lands through the Arabian Desert to ports such as Gaza, where they were shipped across the Mediterranean.[45] For as long as six centuries, the Nabataeans fulfilled the desires of local and international consumers, although their great city at Petra and their role in global commerce would be history by the time coffee took the world stage.

Much of the success of the Nabataeans prior to the advent of shipping came from their intimate knowledge of where to find elusive desert water and how to tap into it. Petroglyphs of camel caravans in such places as Jordan's Wadi Rum, located approximately thirty-seven miles (around sixty kilometers) from the port of Aqaba on the Red Sea, and the remains of cisterns in the Negev regions north of Eilat, Israel, illustrate that the route Nabataean traders traveled followed the sources of water they had located using advanced techniques of hydrology and hydraulic engineering.[46]

Frankincense and the many goods that generated considerable profit were not, however, the only source of revenue for the merchants of Arabia. Because of the centrality of their location, the emporiums of ancient Arabia served as centers from which the spokes of trade extended in all directions. They were therefore home to a sedentary population of administrators who earned a living by providing services to those who passed through and by collecting the taxes and tariffs owed to the rulers. As Pliny explains, "All along the route [merchants] keep on paying, at one place for water, at another for fodder, or the charges for lodging at the halts, and the various *octrois* [local taxes]; so that expenses mount up to 688 denarii per camel before the Mediterranean coast is reached."[47] A total cost of almost 700 silver denarii was not insignificant. At a time when the daily wage for many workers, from camel drivers to teachers, was between 200 and 400 bronze sesterii per day, at the rate

Camel caravan, Wadi Rum, Jordan. *Photo by the author.*

of four sesterii per denarius, the cost to a merchant for a single load of goods could reach as high as 2,752 sesterii, or just over nine days' wages for ordinary men.[48]

The commercial role of the powerful resin from Arabia was analogous to that of coffee. Frankincense and coffee not only originated in approximately the same region, they also followed a similar trajectory of influence outward, specifically westward (coffee has never really enjoyed much favor in places to the east where the hot beverage of choice was tea). Coffee, like frankincense before it, also began as a product of local usage and then captured the attention of outsiders who adopted it for religious, medicinal, and pleasurable purposes.

The history of frankincense offers another similarity to the history of coffee, but one that is not quite as easy to document. Gary Paul Nabhan writes that the demand for frankincense "established an insatiable desire for 'the other,' the exotic or extra local."[49] Pliny foreshadowed Nabhan's assertion regarding the East as a place apart in his attempts to describe the riches of the world from Arabia to China. In his quest "to catalogue

DESERT TO SEA

the riches of Arabia and the reasons that have given it the names of Happy and Blessed,"[50] Pliny wrote,

> The riches of earth's bounty . . . inspires us with ever greater and greater wonder . . . to explore the depths of the Red Sea for the pearl and the bowels of the earth for the emerald . . . In Arabia there is also an olive endowed with a sort of tear out of which a medicine is made, called in Greek enhaemon, because of its remarkable effect in closing the scars of wounds. . . . These trees grow on the coast and are covered by the waves at high tide without this doing any harm to the berry, although accounts agree that salt is left on the leaves.[51]

If, as Nabhan argues, in antiquity, frankincense embodied the exotic, coffee and the coffeehouse had taken its place in people's imaginations and in their demand for items specifically because of their foreign provenance by the early to mid-sixteenth century.[52]

It is possible that Pliny was the first European to encounter the coffee bean. Although the description is too vague for a firm identification, Pliny writes in Book Twelve of his *Natural History* about a kind of nut that grows in Ethiopia and is used by both perfume producers and physicians in Petra:

> Ethiopian behen, which has a black oily nut and a slender kernel, but the liquid squeezed out of it has a stronger scent. . . . Perfumiers, however, only extract the juice from the shells, but medical men also crush the kernels, gradually pouring warm water on them while pounding them.[53]

Arguments can be made that confirm or refute the claim that Pliny's behen is the first written mention of coffee beans. Support for the notion that behen referred to coffee include his encounter with the bean in Ethiopia, his description of how a drink was prepared by pounding the nut and then pouring hot water over the grounds to make a drink, and his mention of its use by physicians, information that is confirmed in the sources that post-date Pliny. One important issue, however, complicates a firm claim that Pliny had indeed encountered coffee: there is no evidence to support the idea that the bean was ever used to make perfume. While it is interesting to envision that this Roman naturalist from the first century of the Common Era might have been the first person to write of the coffee bean, the information Pliny provides is not enough to make a determination.

## From Antiquity to Early Modernity:
## The Exchanges Continue

Looking east from the caravan stops that dotted the routes that terminated at the ports of Mediterranean Sea, it is possible to see in the distance those who made their living as merchants along another vital trade artery, the Silk Road. As early as 400 BCE, the emergence of cavalries in the Eurasian Steppe advanced the introduction of trade and facilitated the spread of communication in the region.[54] By 221 BCE, rulers of the Chinese Qin and Han dynasties used commerce in silk to promote diplomatic interactions with steppe nomads and to acquire horses from them.[55] Around 140 BCE, Emperor Wudi (156–187 BCE) of the Han Dynasty (206 BCE–24 CE) sought to push one of these groups, the nomadic Xiongnu, out of China, in part because they controlled the steppe lands that separated the emperor from India. Hoping for an alliance with enemies of the Xiongnu, the Yuezhi, also a nomadic steppe people, the emperor sent an envoy named Zhang Qian (164–116 BCE) on a westward mission that lasted an unexpected thirteen years because of the time Qian spent as a captive of the Xiongnu. The mission ultimately ended in failure because the Yuezhi had little interest in joining the leaders of imperial China in their campaign against the Xiongnu.[56] While Qian's mission may have been a diplomatic failure, all was not lost. Qian wrote an account of his journey that sheds some light on what he did accomplish. The original account of his adventures no longer exists. Fortunately, two other extant histories from this time contain significant portions of it, including references to places as far away as the Mediterranean—whose inhabitants would, in time, demand China's prized silk—and descriptions of the goods imported from India that Zhang Qian saw in the markets of Bactria, an area of Central Asia that today extends through parts of Afghanistan, Tajikistan, and Uzbekistan.[57] According to the surviving histories, Qian's report so impressed the Emperor Wudi that he became all the more determined to conquer the Xiongnu. He also extended China's Great Wall, a move that would ensure the safe passage of Chinese merchants.[58] As China, Central Asia, India, the regions of Arabia, and Europe became increasingly interconnected, new items that included perfumes, spices, grapes, walnuts, sesame seeds, garlic, and glass from as far away as Rome began appearing in China for the first time.[59] Contact with India during the reign of the Han Dynasty Emperor Wu (156–187, r. 141–87 BCE) also led to the introduction of Buddhism in China. Thus it was that the Silk Road evolved into a thoroughfare that connected people, products, religions, technologies, and tastes.

Many centuries later, the adventures of the Venetian merchant Marco Polo (1254–1324) attested to a world that was advancing relentlessly toward globalization. Beginning his journey at the "busy emporium" of Armenia, Polo related that there were "ample supplies of everything and commerce and industry flourish."[60] In his description of Ayas (present-day Ankara), a port in the region of what Polo termed "Lesser Armenia," he made special note of the "spices and cloths from the interior . . . and all other goods of high value" that might be found.[61] "Merchants of Venice and Genoa and everywhere else come [to] buy them, [and] merchants and others who wish to penetrate the interior all make this town the starting point of their journey."[62]

Marco Polo made no specific mention of coffee as one of the wares proffered by "Mosulin [merchants who] export vast quantities of spices and other precious wares," although he did remark on the use of incense in places such as India and China, where it was burned at a celebration of the birthday of the Great Khan (then Kublai Khan, 1260–1294, a grandson of Genghis Khan) that the Polo family attended.[63] Describing the festivities, Polo remarked that it was a time when "all the idolaters and all the Christians and all the Saracens and all the races of men offer solemn prayers . . . with singing of hymns and lighting of lamps and burning of incense."[64] This brief, easily overlooked slice of the *Travels* reinforces Pliny's *Histories*, the *Periplus*, and other narratives that described the vast reach of trade. Polo's text also demonstrates the role of the merchant not just as one who makes a living providing the goods that people want but also as a person who creates new demand for the previously unknown items they encountered. For example, Polo wrote of the province of Szechwan as a "great source of cloves" and other spices that "never come to our country" and were likely imported to China and India from the Moluccas or the Spice Islands.[65]

Polo's account serves as a bridge connecting the experiences of traders in the East and the West of the ancient world, the medieval era, and early modernity. For example, Polo notes of the Arabian port city of Aden that Pliny mentioned, "The city has a very good port; for I assure you that many merchant ships come here well-loaded with goods from India, and from here they export many goods to India."[66] Polo praises the city of Dhofar as a "very good port" that is "frequented by many merchant ships that import and export great quantities of merchandise." Polo even confirms the observations of Herodotus in his description of incense harvesting: small trees "are gashed with knives in various places, and out of these gashes oozes the incense."[67]

Polo's account does more than just reinforce the enduring nature of international commerce. Unwittingly, he also introduces another commodity that would captivate scores of Europeans during the Age of Exploration—travel narratives. Polo, who traveled east all the way to the court of the Mongol emperor Kublai Khan, wrote an example of the genre of travel literature, although his is not the first. As far as scholars know, the first travel narrative was written by the Greek geographer Pausanias (d. 180 CE), who chronicled his experiences in the regions of the Mediterranean, along the Nile River, and to the Dead Sea in his *Description of Greece,* completed around 150 CE.[68] Other predecessors of Polo include the Spanish Arab traveler Ibn Jubayr (ca. 539/1144–614/1217), who tells of his expeditions on the Mediterranean and Red Seas and to Mecca, Baghdad, and Damascus in the period 579/1183 to 581/1185.[69] Gerald of Wales (1146–1223), who lived during the same time as Ibn Jubayr, published his *Journey through Wales* in 1191 and his *Description of Wales* in 1193, both about his sojourns in 1181.[70]

Much like storytellers of all ages, Marco Polo may not have been precise in the retelling of his adventures at the far end of the Silk Road. He undertook his journey with his father, Niccolo, and his uncle, Maffeo, bin 1260, when the trio set sail from Constantinople.[71] The Polos did not return to their home in Venice until 1292, and Marco Polo did not dictate his version of the events that took place during the more than thirty years he was in the East until 1298. Polo, who was languishing in a Genoese prison after being captured during one of the four Venetian-Genoese trade wars that erupted between 1255 and 1381, told his story to a fellow prisoner named Rustichello.[72] The information Polo left behind reflects more about the person conveying the information than it does about the true natures of the people he met and the places he visited. This was of less consequence to the audiences who devoured Polo's travelogue even long after his death in the thirteenth century. For merchants, Polo's book detailed potentially lucrative trading prospects. For others, including the vast majority of people whose worldly knowledge was limited to "terminal points on the Mediterranean and Black Sea" and those who lived in fear of the horse-riding Central Asian nomads who posed a recurring threat to Europe, Polo's description resonated in different ways.[73] Later in this book, Polo's *Travels* will be joined by the details of other encounters, both real and fictional, including the monopods fabricated by John Mandeville in his search for the elusive (and fictional) Prester John and the markets of Aleppo, where Leonhard Rauwolf wrote of a hot dark brew extracted from a bean.

## International Exchanges or Globalization?

The evidence indicates that material and nonmaterial global encounters began long before the late Middle Ages, the Renaissance, and the exploits of Christopher Columbus, Vasco de Gama, Francisco Pizarro, and others during the Age of Exploration.[74] However, these connections across borders do not necessarily mean globalization as it might be recognized today. Not surprisingly, how to date the moment when the world became discernably global is a subject of some debate. Anne McCants argues that globalization is not necessarily an outcome of modernity. In a 2007 article titled "Exotic Goods, Popular Consumption, and the Standard of Living: Thinking about Globalization in the Early Modern World," McCants wrote that the "intercontinental luxury trades of the early modern period were in fact transformative of the European economy."[75] This assertion locates the beginning of the history of coffee in the West in the Renaissance and early modern periods, when modern ideas about acquisition, acquisitiveness, and consumption developed. However, as McCants notes later in her essay (and the discussion in this chapter illustrates), consumer goods from Arabia and farther east had been part of the markets of Europe long before this time. Thus, coffee moved into a space that had already been created, without which it may have taken coffee longer to gain acceptance and popularity. This reality of centuries—millennia even—of long-distance trade might support an argument for the "globalization of antiquity" at the earliest or at least by the Middle Ages, as silks, porcelain, and spices from the East and textiles from such cities as Bruges and Ghent appeared at markets and fairs on mainland Europe.[76] The expansion of Islam around the Mediterranean littoral and across the Indian Ocean long before the Renaissance further expanded the multidirectional reach of luxury goods, which suggests that we need to look father back in time for clues about the start of a global system of commercial and cultural exchange.[77] Not all scholars accept this proposition.

Of those who refute an early dating of globalization, Immanuel

Wallerstein, the author of *The Modern World System I: Capitalist Agriculture and the Origins of the European World Economy in the Sixteenth Century* (part of a three-volume work that looks at the development of world economic systems from the Middle Ages to the 1840s), accepts that while there was indeed commercial contact among various peoples prior to the fifteenth century, it was not of sufficient quantity to signal the start of globalization. Central to Wallerstein's argument is the premise that international trade was confined exclusively to luxury items, not necessities such as "grain, cattle, fish, sugar," and other foodstuffs.[78] Thus, according to Wallerstein, while luxury items were profitable, such commerce did not constitute a globalization of the economy.[79] In an 1988 article, Joel Mokyr supported Wallerstein's idea that international trade was confined to "small luxuries such as coffee and tea."[80] Several decades later, in 2002, Kevin O'Rourke and Jeffry Williamson noted that there is "no evidence supporting the view that the world economy was globally integrated prior to the 1490s."[81] Instead, O'Rourke and Williamson extend the date even farther forward, to the 1820s, when they suggest that "a very big globalisation bang took place."[82]

The argument of Wallerstein and others, while compelling, does not explain the cries of frustration across a wide "swath" of the European population when the collapse of Islamic trade in the Mediterranean restricted their long-standing and regular supply of pepper around 1400, an event that lends support to the notion that the world was tied together in significant ways before the end of the fifteenth century. In addition, a "trade boom" in Europe in the mid-sixteenth century made goods available to more people than those "located at the top of the income distribution," illustrating that more than just the wealthy could purchase a wide range of goods, as illustrated by the broad consumption of "colonial groceries: tea, coffee, sugar, and tobacco" and manufactured goods such as silk, chintz, and printed cottons. Among the poor, there was an "active trade" in used tea leaves and coffee grounds, indicating that people at the lowest end of socioeconomic order found ways to enjoy a much-diluted version of Europe's new favorite beverages.[83]

The research for this book supports an argument that globalization was an indispensable part of human history long before the cataclysmic events that began in the last decade of the fifteenth century or later in the early nineteenth century. This is not to say that this is the starting point for a global history of economic and ideological interactions. Nor is it reasonable to assert that globalization dates back to such places as the

Neolithic settlement Catalhuyuk (7500–5700 BCE) in southern Anatolia simply because archaeologists have uncovered evidence of efforts to establish communication routes across relatively short distances. And yet as the human population grew following the migration of our earliest human ancestors out of eastern Africa to other parts of the African continent and Eurasia at around one million years ago and as people organized themselves into settled communities and began the domestication of plants and animals, it does appear that the establishment of trade was one of their first activities. For example, the ruins of one of the oldest cities on earth, Jericho, have been found to contain products from places far away, evidence that contact with distant peoples began over 10,000 years ago. Wall paintings in a number of other early settlements in the Near East tell us that the inhabitants owned items manufactured in the region of the Red Sea and Taurus mountains, while farming techniques and Indo-European languages came to Greece in the seventh century BCE with explorers from Asia and continued to move into western and northern Europe. None of these examples are enough to support a dating of globalization to prehistory. What they do attest to is the idea that humans have had contact with others at relatively great distances from themselves for far longer than might be suspected and that these early contacts provide the foundation for the unfolding history of coffee.

In what ways is globalization different from early networks of communication or the presence of foreign trade goods among the luxury items found in ancient ruins? I argue that coffee represents simultaneously a continuity in millennia of commercial and cultural contacts and a disruption to these patterns. (I take up the latter point in subsequent chapters). The seafaring Phoenicians, the ancient Romans' imperial expansion, the travels of Zhang Qian along what would become the Silk Road, the ninth-century trade between Venice and Alexandria, the Crusades of the late tenth and eleventh centuries—all of the interactions of people throughout history are the contact points for the weaving together of the history of coffee and the coffeehouse with the history of globalization. A truly interconnected world may be a legacy of the Age of Exploration, but the story of people in search of novel products and diverse ideas goes back long before that time.

## Concluding Thoughts: Summing Up to Look Ahead

This chapter covered a large expanse of territory and more than a few historic eras. It introduced the themes that will recur throughout this book. From the idea that geography and the natural world played roles in the shaping of trade and the coming together of people and the assertion that economic and cultural globalization are processes that began thousands of years ago as recognizable phenomena emerges the evidence that supports the proposition that the history of coffee and the coffeehouse are the threads that link together seemingly disparate topics. Centering the history of coffee and the coffeehouse in their place of origin reveals coffee as both a continuity of trade with the East and a transformation because of its effect on human interactions. Indelibly a part of the regions to the east of the Mediterranean, coffee and the coffeehouse emerged in the West as appropriations of the habits of a foreign Other who had the solution to what men (and women) craved, an opportunity to leave domestic space behind for a few minutes or a few hours of conversation, debate, entertainment, and even the plotting of a revolution or two. The chapters that follow will return again and again to questions of globalization, what the ideas of East and West meant to the people of various ages, and the idea of the Mediterranean and the Silk Road as conduit for cargos, conflict, and cooperation. In this light, the history of coffee looks something like a commercial and cultural Janus, the two-headed Roman deity that looked both backward to the past and ahead to the future and thus adorned doorways and other passages, the keeper of enterings and departures. Just as the histories of the Mediterranean, the Silk Road, and the Arabian desert take us back to the source of coffee, so also coffee and coffeehouse take us into the future. As the last chapter will show, coffee has been a tool of colonization and imperialism in the past, a legacy that remains as elements of coffee's contemporary story in places where the cultivation and sale of coffee beans are entwined with questions about justice, fair trade for farmers and growers, and national sovereignty.

We can only linger so long with the caravans of Arabia, the harvesters of frankincense, and the travelers and merchants from the Mediterranean Sea and along the Silk Road and Mediterranean, although we will return to them. For us, the journey turns first to food history and the science of taste before looking backward to the truths (and the myths) of coffee and to its early history in the highlands of Ethiopia and Yemen.

CHAPTER 2

# Sociability, Chemistry, and Coffee's Eastern Origins

*One cannot think well, love well, sleep well, if one has not dined well.*

—Virginia Woolf, 1928[1]

*Where coffee is served there is grace and splendour and friendship and happiness.*

—Sheikh Ansari Djezeri Hanball Abd-al-Kadir, 1587[2]

## Of Caffeine and Coffee's Origins

For me, there is something immensely comforting in the ritual associated with preparing the first cup of the day, from grinding the beans to ensuring that the water is just the correct temperature to the slow plunge of the water through the grounds and finally the welcoming jolt that accompanies the first sip. For other coffee devotees I know, it is the beeping of the maker indicating that the coffee is ready that brings the assurance that all will be well. On my travels, I have found delight in a small cup of properly made Arabic coffee, and in moments of desperation, a packet of dried coffee crystals dissolved in boiling water has sufficed. This chapter opens with coffee's place in the expansive account of what people eat and drink, the meanings ascribed to culinary decisions, the rituals and rules of consumption, and the social patterns that accompany the ways humans meet a basic need of survival. The first part of this chapter also considers taste as something that is both chemical and constructed, both unique to each person's DNA and shared among people with similar cultural origins.

In the second part, the chapter shifts its focus to journey to the mystical, historical, and botanical origins of coffee. The chapter concludes with a few words on sugar, not only because it became a popular additive to coffee outside the Muslim world but also because around the eighth century, shortly before the first written sources mention coffee, sugar came to Jordan and the Levant with merchants traveling along the Silk Road. Coffee and sugar, therefore, occupied a similar geographic and social universe, although it does not appear that sugar was regularly added to coffee in the Levant; most sources mention the bitterness of the drink but make no mention of tempering the sharp taste by adding sweet sugar.

## Food: Culture, Socialization, and Civilization

According to one food historian, what we eat and drink is "perhaps the most distinctive expression of an ethnic group, a culture."[3] Several ideas are embedded in this broad assertion. These include what people believe to be healthy food, how food should be properly prepared so as to prevent illness, adherence to religious dietary laws, food as social status, food as hospitality, food as ritual, and public commentary on all things related to food and beverages. The ways people have devoured foods that are indigenous to their place of habitation, sought imported provisions as dietary supplements, and developed a liking for delicacies introduced through exploration, territorial expansion, and colonization remind us that food is sustenance and ritual, an impetus for exchange, and sometimes a justification for subjugating other cultures. Legends from the Ethiopian and Yemeni highlands claim that coffee is both beneficial to and detrimental to good health. They speak of its place in nocturnal religious rituals and its connection to other products. They illustrate how the cultural, political, religious, social, and economic lives of people intersect with coffee and why it is part of the history of what, how, and why humans eat and drink as they do.

John C. Super has asserted that food is not "simply planted, harvested, processed, transported, sold, and consumed." Rather, it performs "many and complex roles in human society," including connecting people's lived experiences to their history.[4] Immigrants perhaps understand Super's ideas about the connection of food to a shared past best. My ancestors from Italy's region of Liguria passed along to each subsequent generation the satisfaction of growing basil and then turning it into really good pesto. To the side of my family from the Italian region of Piedmont, no New Year's Day is complete without family and friends gathered around steaming bagna cauda, redolent with anchovies, garlic, olive oil, and butter, the centerpiece of a table laden with vegetables and bread. For my students of Irish extraction, potatoes are a food that is almost sacred.

In *Savoring Power, Consuming the Times: The Metaphors of Food in Medieval and Renaissance Literature*, Pina Palma elaborates on these ideas, noting that for historians, food is a "nontraditional mode of assessing the currents that characterize the times in which it is consumed."[5] When one grounds food "in philosophical, political, and theological beliefs" it becomes an indicator of the culture, daily habits, and desires of people and the times in which they live.[6] Take the olive, a crop whose shared importance unites people around the Mediterranean, as an example. It is believed to have originated in the Near East and that the earliest civilizations in the eastern Mediterranean first cultivated olive trees for the fruit and the oil they produced.[7] These were also the first exporters of the olive and its by-products. As Levantine peoples moved beyond the places of their birth, they took olives with them. Olives thus became one of the earliest items of exchange. The seeds within them became the progenitors of the trees that would take root in the hospitable climate of North Africa and the western Mediterranean.[8] Suited to the Mediterranean climate of the Levant, the North African regions of Morocco and Tunisia, and Greece, Italy, Spain, and southern France, olives and olive oil have long been ubiquitous as sources of food, of medicine, and as a beauty aid. Illustrative of Palma's point about the cultural significance of food, the olive and olive trees occupy prominent places in literature and religious writings. Sojourners to the Mount of Olives in Jerusalem or to the countryside surrounding it can find olive trees that date back 2,000 years or more.

As a religious symbol, the olive branch has long been a metaphor for peace. One of the earliest references is the dove in the Old Testament book of Genesis who returned to Noah's ark carrying an olive leaf as proof of dry land and of God's promise to never again flood the world (Gen. 8:10). In the New Testament, Luke wrote that Jesus "came out and went, as was his custom, to the Mount of Olives," (Luke 22:93) as he taught his disciples about love, mercy, and compassion. In the Qur'an, olives appear a number of times, including in Surah Six, The Cattle, which proclaims that ripe produce, including olives, is evidence of God's favor: "gardens of vines, olives, pomegranates, like each to each, and each unlike

Olive tree, West Bank, Palestinian territories. *Photo by the author.*

to each. Look upon their fruits when they fructify and ripen! Surely, in all this are signs for a people who do believe."[9] Literature from the third crusade contains a story of olive oil as a component of medicine:

> In Shayzar we had an artisan named Abu-al-Fath, who had a boy whose neck was afflicted with scrofula. Every time a part of it would close, another part would open. This man happened to go to Antioch on business of his, accompanied by his son. A Frank noticed the boy and asked his father about him. Abu-al-Fath replied, "This is my son." The Frank said to him, "Wilt thou swear by thy religion that if I prescribe to thee a medicine which will cure thy boy, thou wilt charge nobody fees for prescribing it thyself? In that case, I shall prescribe to thee a medicine which will cure the boy." The man took the oath and the Frank said:
> "Take uncrushed leaves of glasswort, burn them, then soak the ashes in olive oil and sharp vinegar. Treat the scrofula with them until the spot on which it is growing is eaten up. Then take burnt lead, soak it in ghee butter and treat him with it. That will cure him."
> The father treated the boy accordingly, and the boy was cured.

The sores closed, and the boy returned to his normal conditions of health.[10]

Olives are also extolled in poetry, as in this excerpt from "i love my country" (1939) by Nâzım Hikmet: "My country: / goats on the Ankara plain: / the sheen of blond, silky, long furs. / The fat plump hazelnuts of Giresun. / The fragrant red-cheeked apples of Amasya, / olive, / fig, / melon, / and of all colours."[11] The Italian botanist Prospero Alpini (1553–1617) noted that the people of Egypt had long used olive oil as a remedy for illness.[12] Olives illustrate the ways that specific foods have taken on a range of meanings over time. Over the centuries, the olive has become symbolic of a longing for home, of desires for peace, or of the abundance of God's bounty. They also had a part in creating a space for what coffee illustrates about human social interactions.

This historical understanding of how and with whom we sustain ourselves requires some assistance from the field of anthropology, in particular from Claude Lévi-Strauss (1908–2009), the French anthropologist and ethnologist. Lévi-Strauss drew inspiration from the Annales School, which Marc Bloch (1886–1944) and Lucien Febvre (1878–1956) founded in France in 1929 with the goal of emphasizing the interdisciplinarity of historical study. Members of the Annales School sought to integrate ideas from as wide a variety of sources and perspectives outside historical study as possible and incorporate them into the study of history.[13] Lévi-Strauss articulated his understanding of the connection between history and anthropology in his 1963 book *Structural Anthropology*, noting that "it would be inaccurate, therefore, to say that on the road toward the understanding of man . . . the historian and the anthropologist travel in opposite directions. On the contrary, they both go the same way," each contributing their own theories, discourses, and perspectives.[14] Lévi-Strauss contends that cooked food both socializes and civilizes.[15] For Lévi-Strauss, the consumption of raw food did not demand that people develop the skills necessary to create lasting relationships or lay the foundational structures necessary for people to organize themselves into living groups. Instead, he argues, humans became social when they began cooking for each other, for it is in the act of cooking, as opposed to eating a carrot right out of the ground or a fish just pulled from a stream, that brings people into community.[16] The transition from a nomadic to a settled life and the movement from hunting and gathering to growing crops and domesticating animals may be the more recognizable elements that contributed to the rise of civilizations, but for Lévi-Strauss, the task of cooking was an essential element in helping people develop the social traits that have made us quintessentially human.[17] Coffee, which is not cooked but is certainly altered by brewing, illustrates the socializing aspect of Lévi-Strauss's argument. Coffee did not add new possibilities for human interaction until it was ground, saturated with hot water to produce a bitter drink, and poured into cups, which could then be served to an assembled group, creating a hospitable environment for the transaction of business, the sharing of news, or the plotting of revolution.

Claude Lévi-Strauss's ideas about food meet the Mediterranean in the work of Fernand Braudel. Like Lévi-Strauss, Braudel argues that it is necessary to examine the rituals of "everyday life [which] consists of the little things one hardly notices in time and space," an approach that is particularly applicable to the study of food as both sustenance and ritual.[18] Over the last seven decades, other scholars, many also influenced by the Annales School, have begun using food as a means through which to reconsider human history. Among them are Jean-Louis Flandrin and Massimo Montanari, who delve into the ways food is part of our general cultural knowledge, those same "routines of daily life" Braudel described.[19] Reflecting Lévi-Strauss's assertion that cooked food brings people together, Jean-Louis Flandrin took a closer look at dining in the company of others, which he asserted had "a convivial social function."[20]

This discussion might suggest that it was not until the twentieth century that thinkers and writers became interested in people's culinary lives and by extension what it was about prepared food that encouraged sociability. However, this is not the case. Texts from ancient Sumer, Mesopotamia, and Syria reveal that people embraced the idea that "social eating and drinking" were foundational for creating and sustaining friendships and other personal connections.[21] Among these ancient cultures, a shared drink smoothed the path of commercial negotiations or the formalizing of plans for uniting two families through an advantageous marriage. Historians today have the advantage of access to sources generations of people have left behind as they reconsider millennia of human rituals and social discourses around food consumption, gaining insight into how these have (or have not) changed.

One place to look for an understanding of these human relations, both for men and for women, is in the baths of ancient Rome. While it seems that women gathered primarily for the purposes of bathing and likely a little gossip, for men, this opportunity had another component.

In many instances, the baths were places for men to enjoy food and drink after they had a good cleansing. The pleasures of the table and the accompanying etiquette reinforced the social order by cementing a variety of relationships and networks. Violating those rules risked incurring dire consequences. Who can forget the events that transpired after the Trojan prince Paris accepted the hospitality of King Menelaus of Sparta, including a great banquet, and then spirited Menelaus's wife, Helen, back with him to Troy?

Centuries later, during the Renaissance, the etiquette of eating and drinking assumed such importance that books on the subject began appearing. One of the most famous was Giovanni Della Casa's (1503–1556) treatise on courtesy that addresses a range of topics from dress to proper table manners. Della Casa's *Galateo: overo de' Costumi*, which was first published in Venice in 1558, two years after Della Casa died, was republished for an English audience in 1576 as *Renaissance Courtesy Book: Galateo of Manners and Behaviors*. This sixteenth-century discourse attests to the importance of cultivating good manners when dining with others. The author warns readers against wiping one's dirty fingers on the tablecloth, leaving the table with a toothpick in one's mouth, or wearing a toothpick around one's neck.[22] Renaissance texts like that of Della Casa were most concerned with proper behavior when dining with others at privately hosted banquets. They provide support for Lévi-Strauss's argument that it is in the company of people and cooked food that humans become socialized and therefore civilized.

Food and drink have always been necessary for survival. As survival became about more than just subsistence, an awareness evolved that some elements of eating and drinking required regulation. In antiquity, around 1750 BCE, the Babylonian king Hammurabi promulgated the first written legal code. The *Code of Hammurabi* laid out the punishments for a range of transgressions, including matters related to food. For example, "If a [female] tavern-keeper does not accept corn according to gross weight in payment of drink, but takes money, and the price of the drink is less than that of the corn, she shall be convicted and thrown into the water."[23] This is notable not only because it codifies the importance of fair dealing in matters of commerce, including the business of running an establishment that served drink, but also because owning a tavern in ancient Mesopotamia was a recognized profession for women. While the *Code of Hammurabi* gives no indication that respectable women joined, or did not join, men in their drinking activities, from passages in the *Code of*

*Hammurabi* it is clear that they were allowed to operate places where drinks were sold, and were therefore present in places of public socializing. It would be many centuries before women served (let alone drank) coffee in the company of men.

## Lessons about Taste from Chemistry

The work of historians, anthropologists, and others on the role of food as windows into the past of ordinary individuals and the ways food enriched and enlarged people's social universe leads to questions about food preferences, raising questions about why people vary in their responses to the taste and texture of different foods, finding them either pleasing or repugnant. In the discussion of coffee, the question of taste centers on bitterness, specifically how newcomers to coffee dealt with this attribute, which was an unfamiliar sensation to most consumers, particularly in Europe. A number of chemical and cultural factors influence an individual's perception of how things taste. Three colleagues in the chemistry department of my home institution, Carroll College, explained a little of the mystery of taste to me. What individuals taste is a rather "complex neural interaction between receptors on each person's tongue that respond to the five main kinds of stimulus—sweet, sour, salty, bitter, and umami."[24] When an individual's taste receptors interact with food, molecules gather information that is then sent to the brain. Since people have different numbers and types of taste receptors, sometimes several people eating the same food item will taste it quite differently.[25] For example, to some people, the colorless liquid benzaldehyde tastes and smells like almonds, but to others, it tastes and smells like cherries.[26] As one of my colleagues explained, fairly "complex taste molecules are recognized by specific receptors, and because there are a fair number of bitter receptors, several substances are perceived by the brain as bitter," a taste that is unpleasant to some but not necessarily to others.[27] It is possible that the bitter taste of coffee was either pleasing to it first consumers or at least was not perceived as unpleasantly bitter for two reasons. First, the bitter taste was not unfamiliar in a diet that included other such foods, including certain varieties of lettuce and chicory, two of the items that likely comprised the "bitter herbs" the ancient Israelites were commanded in the Old Testament book of Exodus 12:8 to eat with their Passover lamb. Thus, a bitter taste would have been familiar to the palates of early coffee drinkers. Had coffee's bitterness been unpleasant, honey or the sugar that had been grown in the region for centuries could have been added. However, even today the traditional preparation of Arabic coffee does not include sugar, even though sugar is available for those who want it. The second possibility is that because of the chemistry of the taste receptors of coffee's early consumers, it did not register as strikingly bitter. Strong, hot, unsweetened coffee was something of a shock for those in other parts of the world who first drank it, perhaps because their taste receptors registered it as harsh. For consumers whose repertoire of food choices generally lacked anything similar, the bitter taste was something that needed to be overcome. Some consumers added milk, sugar, or other flavorings. The same was true of chocolate. It was not until this New World treat entered Europe that sugar was added to mitigate its bitter taste.

From here, the story crosses a sea and then traverses a desert in search of the people who first encountered the coffee plant, discovered its energizing properties, experimented with its uses, and in time capitalized on its profitability. We first stop in the highlands of Ethiopia to hear a legend, one of the best ways to introduce any story.

## Coffee: Ethiopia, Yemen, and the Middle East

Despite William Harrison Ukers's claim that "[coffee] originated in Yemen and has spread, like tobacco, all over the world," just how it came to be enjoyed in the first place is something of a mystery.[28] It could be argued that this only adds to the allure of the story. The absence of hard facts leads to the temptation to indulge in a few moments of fanciful speculation about who first recognized its stimulating properties. More about that shortly.

What little is known outside the realm of myth and legend comes from archaeological discoveries. This work offers tangible evidence that the coffee plant is thousands of years old and existed in the wild long before intentional harvesting and, later, cultivation. The recovery of fossilized ancient plants suggests that coffee grew inconspicuously in the southern reaches of the Ethiopian highlands, an area of rugged mountains that reach almost 15,000 feet in the Horn of Africa, long before anyone realized it was suitable for drinking.[29] Coffee plants journeyed out of Ethiopia around 525 CE, when the armies of the Axumite kingdom, home to a people who spoke a Semitic language, invaded and conquered the Himyarite kingdom in the southwestern part of the Arabian desert (today it is part of Yemen).[30] The Axumites ruled Yemen for only fifty years. Although Ethiopian dominance over Yemen was short, it left an enduring legacy in the coffee plants that accompanied the occupiers. Soon after the Axumite army arrived, they introduced coffee cultivation in the highlands of Yemen, a region with geography similar to its counterpart in Ethiopia and a soil and climate that is suitable for coffee cultivation. Before long, coffee plantations had also been instituted, sowing the seeds of Yemen's future dominance of the coffee trade, a situation that would benefit Yemen for centuries.[31] In 575, Yemen was again invaded, this time by members of the Persian Sasanian Empire, who were followers of Zoroastrianism. The Persians retained control until the arrival of Islam in 7/628, after which the caliphs of Sunni Islam ruled the Arabian peninsula for the next 250 years. Throughout these political upheavals, coffee plants survived, the horticultural ancestors of the plants that are still harvested today.

However, there are more romantic stories about the origins of coffee that are worthy of the storytelling tradition of the coffeehouse. Perhaps the best-known tale is the legend of a goatherd named Kaldi who lived in Ethiopia. This story is told often and in virtually the same way each time. This version of the story of the discovery of coffee dates to around the year 800 CE. It likely developed after the years when the young man lived, given the archaeological evidence and the competing history that has coffee entering Yemen 300 years earlier when the Axumites invaded. According to the myth, Kaldi is said to have witnessed the stimulating effects a certain red berry had on his flock after they had chewed them. Once Kaldi himself tasted the beans, the story continues, "poetry and song spilled out of him."[32] Although the original myth does not take the story beyond Kaldi's discovery, had those he knew not been taken with coffee, the beans would have had a very short story.

Although the story of Kaldi is very popular, other legends exist. In one of these, the first person to consume coffee was a priest in Yemen. Banished to the mountains for improper conduct toward the daughter of the king and faced with starvation, the young priest survived by drinking a "decoction of [the] beans" he discovered on a plant with white flowers.[33] After his exile, the priest took the beans with him on a pilgrimage to Mecca, where he cured travelers experiencing "an epidemic of the itch."[34]

Yet another legend from Yemen goes as follows:

> The dervish Hadji Omar was driven by his enemies out of Mocha into the desert, where they expected he would die of starvation.

This undoubtedly would have occurred if he had not plucked up courage to taste some strange berries which he found growing on a shrub. While they seemed to be edible, they were very bitter; and he tried to improve the taste by roasting them. He found, however, that they had become very hard, so he attempted to soften them with water. The berries seemed to remain as hard as before, but the liquid turned brown, and Omar drank it on the chance that it contained some of the nourishment from the berries. He was amazed at how it refreshed him, enlivened his sluggishness, and raised his drooping spirits. Later, when he returned to Mocha, his salvation was considered a miracle. The beverage to which it was due sprang into high favor, and Omar himself was made a saint.[35]

A fourth rendering of coffee's origin story comes from the seventeenth-century writer Abu al-Tayyib al-Ghazzi, who claimed that when King Solomon came to a village stricken by plague, the angel Gabriel ordered him to "roast Yemeni coffee beans, from which is brewed a beverage that restored the sick to health."[36] Following this event, according to al-Ghazzi, coffee was forgotten until the tenth century.[37]

Al-Ghazzi is not the only person to make a connection between the origins of coffee consumption and religion. One such story suggests that the angel Gabriel presented the Prophet Muhammad not just with the revelations that became the Qur'an but also with coffee when the prophet was "supposedly stricken with narcolepsy."[38] Another tale has it that "coffee was brought to earth in order to revive Mohammad's flagging energies."[39] The authors of the New Testament, in contrast, were either not acquainted with coffee or, more likely, had little interest in what the people of the day were eating and drinking beyond bread, meat, fish, and wine, as stories of coffee are absent from the accounts of the life of Jesus Christ.

Katip Çelebi (1609–1657), a leading intellectual and social critic in seventeenth-century Constantinople, also attempted to explain the origins of coffee consumption. In perhaps his best-known work, a bibliography-encyclopedia entitled *The Balance of Truth* (*Mizan ül-hak fi ihtiyar ül-ehak*), completed sometime between the late 1640s and Çelebi's death in 1657, the author explains that

certain sheykhs, who lived with their dervishes in the mountains of Yemen, used to crush and eat the berries, which they called qalb wabun, of a certain tree. Some would roast them and drink their water. Coffee is a cold dry food, suited to the ascetic life and sedative of lust. The people of Yemen learned of it from one another, and sheykhs, Sufis, and others used it. It came to Asia Minor by sea, about 950/1543, and met with a hostile reception, fetwas being delivered against it.[40]

Edwin Arnold Lester, the English owner of several coffee plantations in India in the later nineteenth century, concurs that coffee originated in Ethiopia but asserts that it first traveled to Persia around 875 CE, reaching "Arabia from the latter country at the beginning of the fourteenth century."[41] Beyond the findings of archaeologists and the surviving mythology, coffee does not appear in any verifiable way until long after antiquity.

Wherever the truth lies, it bears recognizing that within the lore exists some element of truth. Archaeologists have found evidence that the coffee plant has an ancient botanical origin. From the legends, historians can piece together what might have happened when people discovered that the plant was edible. That version of the story may look something like this. Coffee first gained the attention of someone (or several people) who were watching over their livestock, noticed the erratic behavior of their animals, and went in search of the source, discovering that the animals had been eating raw coffee beans. Noting that the herds consumed the fruit of the coffee plants safely, the humans sampled the beans for themselves. Somewhere along the way, people decided that it was better to roast the berries and soak them in water to make a drink than it was to chew them raw.

Because Ethiopia invaded Yemen in the second decade of the sixth century, Kaldi's tale of the origins of coffee in Ethiopia needed revising to privilege Yemeni coffee. Enter al-Ghazzi and his claim that coffee was originally a product of Yemen that had been forgotten for a time. In light of a paucity of evidence, the stories lend support to various claims of ownership. For those who believe the story of Kaldi, Ethiopia becomes the birthplace of the coffee plant. This did not sit well with Yemeni producers, who may have objected to the idea that coffee was a commodity that a sixth-century invader had brought to their county. As a remedy, storytellers in Yemen created a new fictional account that relocated coffee's origins in Yemen, where it was rediscovered after a long hiatus in the first half of the 600s. This story not only reinforced Yemenis' claim that coffee is native to their country but also validated Yemen's monopoly on the export of coffee beans, which lasted into the sixteenth century.

The durability of the anecdotal evidence illustrates an important element of the history of foodways. People around the world cherish stories about their food traditions and pass them along to succeeding generations. In these stories, young goatherds, sheiks, and religious mystics all contribute to an understanding of the people who formed coffee's social milieu in Arabia. The stories that endure support the assertion that coffee was not just something people drank. It was just as importantly a part of their cultural identity, worth keeping alive in memory through the retelling of legends.[42] From this point, the journey of coffee is better documented.

## Before Sociability: Coffee, Medicine, and Faith

Al-Ghazzi's proposition that coffee was not discovered but rather reemerged in the tenth century has some textual support, for it was around that time that the Persian physician Abu Bakr Mohammad Ibn Zakariyya Razi (Rhazes) completed his notable work, *The Comprehensive Book on Medicine* (Kitab al-Hawi fi al-tibb), twenty-two volumes in which the physician carefully detailed his beliefs about health. Informed by the writings of Hippocrates (460–370 BCE) and other tracts from classical Greek medicine and by Rhazes' own practice as a physician, *The Comprehensive Book on Medicine* contains an entire volume on pharmacology, which provides one of the earliest written mentions of coffee.[43] Rhazes described coffee as a food that had both good and less desirable attributes. He wrote: "It is a drink that is good for those with hot nature, but it decreases the libido."[44] What is clear from Rhazes' writing is that by the second half of the ninth century of the Common Era, coffee was being consumed at least for medicinal purposes. Even though coffee was not part of the Greek medical tradition, Rhazes looked back to Hippocrates for the notion that the body was composed of four humors (blood, yellow bile, black bile, and phlegm), an imbalance of which was the cause if illness. In naming coffee as good for those with a "hot nature" (in humoral theory meaning those who enjoyed health and strength), it would seem that Rhazes recommended coffee for people who were not ill. For example, Rhazes' contention that coffee negatively affected the sex drive is curious. Coffee is a stimulant and would seem more likely to have the opposite effect on the libido. Since many types of illness can produce a decrease in sex drive, what was actually was causing the troubling decline in desire that people reported to the physician is not clear. Whatever the problem may have been, for Rhazes the solution could be found in forgoing coffee until the patient was once again healthy.

The next written evidence of coffee comes from another Persian physician, Abu 'Ali al-Husayn ibn Sina, better known as Avicenna (d. 429/1037), who lived in the ancient Silk Road city of Bukhara, then part of Persia (today it is located in Uzbekistan). Avicenna was not just interested in medicine; he was also attracted to the philosophy of Aristotle and wrote on a vast range of other topics including mathematics, psychology, geology, astronomy, logic, natural science, geometry, arithmetic, alchemy, and music. However, Ibn Sina's most notable works are related to medicine: the *Kitab al-Shifa* (Book of Healing) and *Qanoon fi Ṭibb* (*The Canon of Medicine*).[45] Ibn Sina specifically discusses coffee in *The Canon of Medicine* (416/1025), advising that "a cup of black coffee may be given" to stop vomiting.[46] In search of confirmation of coffee's positive uses and healthful benefits, the early modern Italian physician Prospero Alpini (1553–1617) referred to Ibn Sina in his own work, noting that "*caffea . . . cum Saccharo*" (with sugar) was still being used as a curative in early modern Egypt.[47]

It was not just physicians who offered their perspectives on coffee as medicine. In the first half of the sixteenth century, the words of the Turkish scholar Katip Çelebi (1609–1657) suggest that he was familiar with Rhazes' *Book of Medicine* and Ibn Sina's *Canon*. Here is how Çelebi described coffee:

> To those of dry temperament, especially to the man of melancholic temperament, large quantities are unsuitable, and may be repugnant. Taken in excess, it causes insomnia and melancholic anxiety. If drunk at all, it should be drunk with sugar.
>
> To those of moist temperament, and especially to women, it is highly suited. They should drink a great deal of strong coffee. Excess of it will do them no harm, so long as they are not melancholic.[48]

Similarly, twenty-eight years after the death of Çelebi, Philippe Sylvestre Dufour (1622–1687), a French apothecary and collector of oddities, asserted in his treatise *The Manner of Making Coffee, Tea, and Chocolate* (1685) that "Rhazes[,] a very famous Arabian Physician . . . did [assure] us that [coffee] is hot and dry, very good for the stomach."[49] Most likely this was an attempt to attract people to the new French practice of drinking coffee.

That the works of Rhazes and Avicenna were part of the coffee conversation when it arrived in Europe is not surprising, particularly in terms of questions about whether the brew benefited or harmed human health. The medical tracts of both men were important texts in European medical schools during the Renaissance and early modern eras, and physicians and other members of the literate public would likely have been quite familiar with their works. Europeans' familiarity with Eastern medicine is further evidenced by the fact that the treatises of Rhazes and Ibn Sina had been translated into Latin by the mid-sixteenth century, making their written texts accessible to those who did not read Arabic. In addition, given the fact that European doctors know of the writings of Rhazes and Ibn Sina, it is possible that the popularity of coffee consumption in Europe received a boost when it was prescribed as a treatment for illness.

Three hundred years later, in the early decades of the twentieth century, people were still contemplating the claims that coffee was medicinal. Most notable among these is the founder of *The Tea and Coffee Trade Journal*, William Harrison Ukers (1873–1945), who published his account of coffee's history in his book *All about Coffee*. When Ukers was in his late twenties, he served as the editor of a publication called *The Spice Mill*, the official publication of the Jabez Burns Coffee Company, a coffee roasting company founded in the early 1860s by English immigrant to the United States, Jabez Burns (the company is known today as Probat Burns). After Burns rejected Ukers's recommendation that he transform *The Spice Mill* magazine into a trade journal in order to reach a wider readership, Ukers supposedly quit his job and began *The Tea and Coffee Trade Journal*. He wrote *All about Coffee* in 1922 (after he published *All about Tea*). The journal Ukers founded is still published today and is available in both print and digital form under its original title.[50]

In *All about Coffee*, Ukers tells of Sheik Gemaleddin, a religious leader in Aden, Yemen, around the year 1454, whose story, according to Ukers, is illustrative of coffee's healing qualities.

> Sheik Gemaleddin Abou Muhammad Bensaid, mufti of Aden, surnamed Aldhabani, from Dhabhan, a small town where he was born, became acquainted with the virtues of coffee on a journey into Abyssinia. Upon his return to Aden, his health became impaired; and remembering the coffee he had seen his countrymen drinking in Abyssinia, he sent for some in the hope of finding relief. He not only recovered from his illness; but, because of its sleep-dispelling qualities, he sanctioned the use of the drink among the dervishes "that they might spend the night in prayers or other religious exercises with more attention and presence of mind.[51]

While Ukers concedes that it is likely that coffee drinking in Aden preceded the sheik's healing, in this selection he helps move the story of coffee another step forward, to its consumption in the late-night religious rituals of the Yemeni Sufis in Aden. Coffee most likely began its journey from use for healing to use as a beverage with the mystical sect of Islam.

## Beyond the Medicinal: Coffee and the Sufis

Sometime between the fourteenth and fifteenth centuries, coffee appears for the first time in the realm of religious practice, with the Sufi mystics of Islamic Arabia. Debates about the origins of Sufism persist. In one accepted version, the practice originated in Kufa (in present-day Iraq) in the second half of the eighth century, approximately 100 years after the death of the Prophet Muhammad in 11/632.[52] By the twelfth century, Sufi orders had become important social groups; they enjoyed great popularity that lasted into the fifteenth and sixteenth centuries.[53]

The practices of Islamic mysticism might be briefly described as including a continuous striving to "be aware of God's presence."[54] Transcending the divide between Sunni and Shi'i, the variations found in the legal schools of Islam, and even gender and social status, Sufis mysticism stresses contemplation, spiritual growth, and the development of the soul through practices such as praying, reading poems, reciting the Qur'an, playing music, and repeating divine names, or "Qur'anic formulas" (*dhikr*).[55] The dervishes of Sufism include a whirling dance into their practice in an effort achieve a closer relationship with the divine. This element of Sufism, which was not practiced by all adherents, began with the mystic and poet Jalal ad-Din Muhammad Rumi (1207–1273) in the mid-thirteenth century.

According to one account, it was a fourteenth-century Sufi hermit named Ali ibn Umar al-Shadhili, who lived near the Port of Mocha and regularly consumed both coffee and qat who first recognized the benefits of coffee.[56] Qat is an Arabian shrub whose leaves can either be chewed or soaked in water to produce a drink with stimulating effects similar to those of coffee. Katip Çelebi assigned a somewhat later date, 1454, to the time when Sufis began drinking coffee as part of their late-night ritual practices. Çelebi's date coincides with the date in other sources that describe the addition of coffee to Sufis' nighttime prayer rituals, as part of believers' *tariqahs* (devotional practices).[57]

By the late fifteenth century or the early sixteenth century, coffee had become a central part of the gatherings of Islamic mystics. It was praised for "its wakeful properties [that] incited them to mystical raptures during the performance of their lengthy and repetitive recitations."[58] The use of coffee among followers of Islam, which Sufi mystics began, in time gained acceptance among the worshippers of other faiths who sought to ensure wakefulness during prayer services that lasted long into the night hours. According to Elliot Horowitz, participants in Jewish rituals "involving nocturnal wakefulness" also benefited from the stimulating properties of coffee.[59] Even though Christians also sometimes engage in long nights of prayer, it does not seem that they embraced coffee or similar products as part of their worship.

In the fifteenth century, coffee consumption spread to other parts of the Muslim world.[60] Significant credit for the increasing use of coffee at this time belongs to three groups. First, as they traveled to fulfill their religious obligation of the hajj and to pay their respects at other holy sites, Muslim pilgrims introduced coffee throughout the Islamic world, bringing it to the attention of people from Persia, Egypt, the Levant, North Africa, and Turkey. The second group involved in the spread of coffee were Arab merchants. Quickly recognizing it as a profitable item for trade, these merchants encouraged widespread coffee consumption among those who were not yet acquainted with it.[61] Through traders, coffee entered the realm of everyday life as a private domestic pleasure.[62] Third, respected scholars and religious leaders helped coffee along its road to greater popularity. Among these men were Sheik Gemaleddin of Aden, whose "endorsement . . . was sufficient to start a vogue for the beverage that spread throughout Yemen, and thence to the far corners of the world."[63] Once people welcomed coffee as part of their daily lives, it did not take long for the brew to reach the final stop in its path to global influence, moving beyond the boundaries of cure, religious practice, and private consumption as it initiated a new institution—the coffeehouse. According to Ralph Hattox, after coffeehouses were established, coffee began to garner significant attention in letters, essays, books, and even in legal decisions and the reputation of coffee often preceded its arrival into an area.[64]

## The Dominance of Yemen and the Port of Mocha in the Coffee Trade

The increased use of coffee in the Near and Middle East meant a continuation of the prosperity that the Yemeni port of Mocha on the Red Sea had long been known for, a fame that began as early as 1000 BCE. At that time, a number of civilizations lived in the almost 900,000-square-mile desert of Arabia, including the Mineans, the Sabaeans, and the Himyarites, all of whom made their wealth by trading commodities such as aromatics, particularly frankincense and myrrh, and gold acquired from India. To reach affluent shoppers, goods began their journey as part of the great camel caravans that moved across the vast desert, an overland path that was both dangerous and climatologically inhospitable. Merchants were at constant risk of encountering raiding nomads and were punished by a scorching sun. Recognition that a safer and less arduous route was needed to reach consumers who lived in neighboring areas and in distant places led to the rise of maritime routes. Because of its position in the southern part of the Arabian desert on the Red Sea littoral, Yemen became the hinge in Mediterranean trade, linking markets as far away as Rome with commodities that were prized both because they were luxurious and because of the distance they had traveled. The detailed account of first-century trade along the Erythraean (Red) Sea already mentioned illustrates that Mocha was a lively port at that time, a locus for the export of goods such as cinnabar, a bright red mineral used in jewelry and dyes, pearls, and tortoiseshells. Mocha was also a point of entry for "rice and wheat and Indian cloth."[65]

Several centuries after an anonymous Egyptian merchant wrote *The Periplus of the Erythraean Sea*, Mocha's port was still the site of a lively traffic in traded goods, maintaining its reputation as the "busiest and richest port on the Red Sea."[66] Until the end of the seventeenth century, all coffee bound for Europe began its journey from this celebrated harbor. Mocha was able to control the flow of coffee to a waiting world was largely because virtually all of the coffee harvested for export was grown in Yemen, but political and military events also played a role. Beginning in the 1540s, Yemen fell under nominal control of the Ottoman Empire. Ottoman Turks had seized Constantinople in 1453 from the Byzantine Empire, which had ruled over eastern Christendom since 330 CE, the year Constantine (274–337) had made it his imperial city. The Ottoman rulers maintained both a military presence and an office of tax collection in Yemen on behalf of the Turkish empire but spared the city full occupation, a situation that facilitated trade.[67]

From Mocha, coffee was shipped up the Red Sea to Suez in northeastern Egypt, a distance of approximately 1,200 miles. As would be the case with all goods exported in the centuries before the Suez Canal linked the Red Sea with the Mediterranean, the beans were once again loaded onto the backs of camels for the 227-mile journey to warehouses in Alexandria, where they would be purchased by merchants from Italy, Portugal, the Netherlands, and England, and reloaded on ships for the 1,535-nautical-mile Mediterranean crossing (approximately 1,766 miles). By the time coffee reached its first consumers in the West, it had traveled approximately 3,193 miles over land and across two seas, an expedition that contributed to coffee's status as a luxury good.

In 1609, the British East India Company established a trading post in Mocha, hoping to defray the cost of trade. The Dutch East India Company followed suit in 1614.[68] Despite Yemen's willingness to accept a foreign presence in its well-positioned port, European traders quickly discovered that Yemenis jealously guarded their coffee plants, relying on Ottoman soldiers to ensure that foreign companies transferred only the beans. By the end of the seventeenth century, an estimated 10 million kilos of coffee beans had been exported from Mocha.[69] Another legend has it that a Portuguese merchant managed to smuggle a plant or two out of Yemen, an act that made possible the start of coffee cultivation in European colonies in other parts of the world, including East Africa, India, Latin America, and a variety of islands in the Pacific.

## Concluding Thoughts: Sugar

This chapter ends with a look at sugar, coffee's most common additive. As the popularity of coffee dramatically increased in Europe, along with that of chocolate and tea, in the latter half of the seventeenth century, the new consumers sought a remedy for the unfamiliar bitter taste of all three drinks. The story of the cultivation of sugar dates back as far as 10,000 years ago, to the southwestern Pacific island of New Guinea, where the inhabitants consumed it raw as a kind of elixir to cure ailments. At religious ceremonies, priests sipped sugar water from coconut shells. Sugar also featured prominently in ancient New Guinean myths, including their creation story, in which the first human male makes love to a stalk of cane and begins the human race.[70]

By 500 CE, sugar had journeyed far from New Guinea. Evidence from India suggests that sugar on the subcontinent was being processed into a fine powder and promoted as the cure for illnesses from headaches to impotence.[71] A century later, sugar appeared in the courts of Persia and was quickly adopted by Arab armies as they swept across the region.

As Sidney Mintz notes, "Sugar, we are told, followed the Koran."[72] Sugar reached Jordan and the Levant either just before the eighth century or in the early years of that epoch, carried by Silk Road merchants as they traveled west from China and India.[73]

By the medieval era, sugar is mentioned in Italian and Arabic written sources, a presence substantiated by archaeological records that indicate the presence of sugar in Europe in the Middle Ages.[74] The evidence suggests that sugar likely came to Europe with Venetian merchants involved in supplying everything from arms to comestibles to the crusaders who set out for the Holy Land in the period 1095 to 1204. In the course of provisioning military campaigns, these merchants began realizing considerable profits from importing eastern goods, including refined sugar, which they then introduced to people for whom honey had been the only sweetener since antiquity. Before long, the enterprising Venetians learned to refine sugar for themselves and began importing less expensive raw sugar.[75] This decision turned out to be fortuitous, particularly after the fall of Constantinople in 1453. Europeans of that time eschewed Levantine sugar, preferring a product manufactured closer to home, on plantations that had been established in Sicily and Spain. Thirty years later, the demand was met in part by cane grown on plantations on the Canary Islands, which the Portuguese had conquered in 1483.[76] After Columbus began his voyages in 1492, sugar from the so-called New World entered European markets, leading to the decline and ultimate demise of the sugar businesses in southern Europe.

And so the journey of coffee continues. In the next chapter, coffee becomes a link between East and West as European merchants, travelers, and others head east, returning home with tales of coffee, coffeehouses, and the enigmatic others who inhabited the Mediterranean region.

## CHAPTER 3

# Coffee Crosses the Mediterranean

*Coffee is the common man's gold, and like gold, it brings to
every person the feeling of luxury and nobility . . .*

—Abd-al-Kadir ibn Mohammad, 1587[1]

*They have another drinke not good at meat, called Cauphe
made of a berry, as bigge as a small Beane . . . beat to a powder . . . in taste a little Bitterish.*

—Sir Henry Blount, 1634[2]

*I will speak for the present of a certain Bean of Arabia . . .
whereof they make a Drink termed Coffee.*

—Philippe Sylvestre Dufour, 1685[3]

## The Journey Out of the East Begins

Sometime around 1520, Spanish traders brought chocolate to Europe
from the Americas. In 1610, Dutch traders, followed by the Portuguese
and the English, began importing tea from China. In the first ten to fifteen
years of the seventeenth century (available information suggests either
1610 or 1615), Venetian ships arrived with coffee.[4] This chapter follows the
journey of coffee, the coffeehouse, and ultimately the coffee plant out of
the Middle East, chronicling its reception by those living in Europe and
then by people around the globe. News of coffee's taste, its attributes as
a stimulant, and descriptions of the coffeehouse culture it engendered
preceded the arrival of the bean and the drink, topics that provide the

starting point for this chapter. The reports of merchants, the tales of travelers, and a scientific description of the plant indicate that coffee entered people's imaginations long before it reached their palates. By the time the first coffee beans were unloaded in the port of Venice, coffee was already emblematic of a region of the world that engendered both fascination and anxiety. As a result of first literary reports and then the movement of the bean, coffee, and the conviviality its consumption encouraged became indelible parts of a multifaceted global history. Coffee came to the West at a time when the demand for unfamiliar products had evolved beyond the novelty of presenting a new dish at a private dinner gathering. By sixteenth and early seventeenth centuries, new foodstuffs were contributing to permanent changes in people's tastes and appetites. It has been well documented that the appearance of chocolate, tea, and coffee in European markets expanded the tastes of those wealthy enough to afford them. What has been given less attention is how these same consumables caught the attention of those in the middle and lower social strata who sought to emulate the changes in lifestyle taking place among the wealthy and aristocratic. This was happening by the latter part of the seventeenth century. In *Worldly Consumers: The Demand for Maps in Renaissance Italy*, Genevieve Carlton has noted a similar phenomenon in the acquisition of maps. Carlton writes that by the sixteenth century, maps, as visual representations of "wonder and amazement," were relatively affordable for an increasing number of individuals who enjoyed increasing access to disposable income.[5]

The fact that food was becoming more interesting by the Renaissance presents a sharp contrast with the situation in the Middle Ages, a time when people's diets are often described in the most dismal of terms. Recurring bouts of famine brought on by poor weather and unsustainable farming practices and the devastation wrought by war and disease led to increases in mortality rates, migration to urban centers, and susceptibility to epidemics. Such events rendered food scarce, particularly the grain that was needed to make the dietary staple of bread. For most people, daily meals consisted largely of millet, maize, and other cereals; access to fresh vegetables and meat was rare.[6] So precarious was the matter of food security that in the sixth century, Procopius of Caesarea (ca. 490/507–ca. 560s), an advisor to Belisarius, the well-known Byzantine general during the reign of Justinian (483–565) and the author of a number of histories described the misery of starvation in Book Two of his *La Guerra Gotica*. In one example, Procopius notes that hunger caused people to become gaunt and pale, "*tutti divenivano emaciati e pallidi*" (all the people became emaciated and pale) and their skin took on a yellowish tinge.[7] This description of hunger would continue to be applicable for centuries.

The scarcity of food in general and the absence of food variety led Fernand Braudel to observe that before the fifteenth or sixteenth centuries, when social changes led to variations in people's food choices, the dining habits of Europeans lacked the "real luxury or sophistication" commensurate with that of places such as China and the Muslim East.[8] Braudel notes that in China, a "luxury" of cooking and dining was present as early as the fifth century and that such practices were in place in the Muslim East beginning in the eleventh and twelfth centuries.[9] Culinary diversity did not reach Europe until the fifteenth century, when people began having greater access to both quantities and varieties of food. As these changes in eating became increasingly extravagant, they were the source of worry for some. For example, in 1460 officials in Venice were so concerned about the habits of the wealthy that the Senate attempted, unsuccessfully, to ban the nobility from arranging costly feasts that included fish and shellfish, sausages brought in from Florence, cheese from the Marche, a region in the eastern part of Italy between the Apennine Mountains and the Adriatic Sea, and marzipan from Siena.[10]

## A Brief Diversion to the Pomegranate

Of all food tales, the journey of the pomegranate was the most analogous to that of coffee.[11] Today the pomegranate is heralded for its properties as a powerful antioxidant. The wild ancestor of the domestic pomegranate has an ancient history. There is evidence that the fruit originated in Central Asia and arrived in the Levant in the early Bronze Age (ca. 3200 BCE), where it was enthusiastically welcomed. Both Turks and Persians soon began carrying the fruit along their trade routes, and around 138/755 the pomegranate arrived in Spain, borne by refugees from the Umayyad Caliphate (41/661–133/750) as they fled the advancing forces of the Abbasid Caliphate (134/751–656/1258).[12] From their capital in Baghdad, the victorious Abbasids ushered in a period of advances in art, architecture, medicine, law, and economics and established a vast trading network that spread culture, religion, and novel business practices during what is often referred to as Islam's Golden Age. One story says that from his new home in Al-Andalus, or Islamic Spain, the defeated and exiled Umayyad prince, Abd al-Rahman, found a way to propagate his adored pomegranate.[13] When members of the prince's family left Damascus for Spain, a sister who remained behind sent several pomegranate plants and several young date palms with the departing relatives. From these first plants, Abd al-Rahman began cultivation of the fruit in 139/756 in his adopted city of Cordoba. With their novel sweet and tart taste, the bright red seeds and juice of the fruit proved so popular with Muslim, Jewish, and Christian communities that pomegranate cultivation soon spread throughout Islamic Iberia.[14] Evidence that religious and cultural communities soon began consuming pomegranates serves as a reminder that despite inequities in the distribution of political and economic power in Muslim-dominated Spain, which began with the capture of Granada in 93/711 and lasted until the *Reconquista* launched by Queen Isabella in 898/1492, the 800 years in between were also times of rich intellectual and cross-cultural sharing in language, learning, the arts, technology, and agricultural science and foodstuffs.[15]

## A Return to the Medieval World of Food and Culture

At the time when merchants from Italy's maritime republics were gaining concessions from Constantinople and crusaders were starting to make their way east, the western regions of the former Roman Empire began showing signs of recovery from the imperial corruption, invaders, territorial overreach, and economic turmoil that had marked the empire's collapse. By the tenth and eleventh centuries, signs that daily life was improving included the appearance at European markets and fairs of the luxury goods those who lived closer to the Mediterranean Sea enjoyed.[16] However, the fact that these products were accessible did not mean that most medieval Europeans had the means or the desire to transform their culinary practices. Most people in these regions were still subject to the ravages of weather and disease. Nevertheless, the fact that efforts were made to transport rare products thousands of miles suggest that a culinary inquisitiveness was emerging among Europeans. In stark contrast to the horrors of starvation Procopius and others described beginning in the eleventh century, by the thirteenth century the few families with disposable income had begun to incorporate a number of eastern spices and roots in their diets, both to improve the taste of food and because of the perceived health benefits of such items. For example, the rhubarb root from China was purported to make a good laxative, while galangal root (a member of the ginger family that has a citrus taste) from

China and India was valued as an early stimulant. By the twelfth century, nutmeg, cloves, ginger, pepper, and saffron from the Catalonia region of Spain were available in the markets of Europe. One of the best descriptions of the availability of imported products in Europe comes from Fra Bonvesino della Riva (ca. 1240–ca. 1313), a lay member of the Ordine degli Umiliati, or Order of the Humble Ones. In 1288, della Riva praised Milan's marketplace, both for the great number of merchants who were engaged in importing and selling goods and for the range of the products they sold. In his *Le meraviglie di Milano: De magnalibus mediolani* (On the marvels of Milan), della Riva called particular attention to cotton, wool, salt, silk, pepper, and other imported items.[17]

## Travelers and Their Adventures before Coffee Consumption

Chinese diplomat Zhang Qian, Roman naturalist Pliny the Elder, an anonymous first century CE Greek merchant, and the Italian Marco Polo are just a few whose words would inspire men, and sometimes women, to set out across the planet searching for wealth, spiritual enlightenment, knowledge, or just an adventure. This chapter focuses on a few of those whose words paint a picture of the visual, commercial, and cultural landscapes in which coffee and the coffeehouse arose. The words of these expeditioners also reveal much about the writers themselves, including the biases these sojourners carried with them and the sense of wonder new locales elicited in them.

Born twenty years before Marco Polo's death, Ibn Battutah (705/1304–771/1369) offered vivid descriptions of the places he visited during the nearly thirty years he traveled along the roads of the medieval eastern world. Battutah, who was culturally (but not ethnically) Arab-Muslim, described the impetus for his journey in this way: "My departure from Tangier, my birthplace, took place on Thursday of the second month of God, Rajab the Unique, in the year seven hundred twenty five [1324], with the object of making the Pilgrimage to the Holy House at Mecca and of visiting the tomb of the Prophet . . . at al-Madinah."[18] Following a circuitous route to Mecca that included Syria and Egypt, Battutah decided to continue on after his hajj, making his way to Constantinople and Central Asia. In Delhi in 736/1335, the city's sultan appointed him *qadi* (قاضي, Shari'a court judge).[19] Battutah remained in this position for ten years, after which he departed for China, eventually arriving back in Morocco in 750/1349. His roaming days ended in 755/1354, after one more trip that included parts of North Africa and Spain. Between 755/1354 and his death in 771/1369, Ibn Battutah gathered his detailed observations into a text he titled simply *Travels*, a text that includes an observation on the beauty of the port of Alexandria, Egypt, which he described as a hub for the transfer of goods that was alive with people of many cultures and religions.

> Among all the ports in the world I have seen none to equal it, except the ports of Kawlam [Quilon] and Qaliqut [Calicut] in India, the ports of the infidels [Genoese] at Sudaq in the land of the Turks, and the port of Zaitun in China all of which will be mentioned later.[20]

Just over 200 years later, Alexandria was still host to eager merchants from Italian maritime cities whose business took them along the eastern Mediterranean. Alexandria remained the point of departure for the west throughout the Middle Ages. It was from this port that coffee would begin the final leg of its journey to Europe. Venice was the common destination until English, Dutch, and Portuguese traders arrived in the fifteenth and sixteenth centuries.

Muslim travel narratives as complete as that of Ibn Battutah are rare, and although he cannot be assumed to speak for all those whose words have been lost over time, Battutah's work is an important example in light of the dearth of additional sources. The same might be said of the some of the earliest sources of information from a European perspective. European merchant manuals serve a purpose similar to that of Battutah's text: they relay observations and stories. One of the most complete and best-known examples is the handbook of Florentine merchant Francesco Balducci Pegolotti (1310–1347), whose *La pratica della mercatura* (Merchant's handbook) was produced during the same approximate time that Ibn Battutah was documenting his travels.

For the entirety of his career, Pegolotti worked as an agent for one of the wealthiest families in Florence, the Bardi, a powerful banking and mercantile family who rose to prominence in the early fourteenth century and played a key role in the city's economy until their bankruptcy in the mid-1340s.[21] For over thirty years, prior to the family's loss of fortune, Francesco Pegolotti carefully accumulated extensive information for his *Pratica* while conducting far-flung service for his employers in Spain, London, and other European locales.[22] Sometime around 1340, Pegolotti's service took him to the eastern Mediterranean, where he encountered an entirely new range of goods to entice his employers and the Florentine consumers they supplied.[23] These items, according to Pegolotti, included *mandorle* (almonds) and *oro e argento* (gold and silver) from Alexandria and *seta cruda da ogni ragione* (raw silk of every type), *cannella* (cinnamon), *cardamome* (cardamom), *zucchero* (sugar), *e polvere di zucchero* (fine or processed sugar), and *zafferano* (saffron) from Constantinople.[24] Pegolotti's handbook also notes the western goods available in the markets of cities such as Constantinople, including wine from Naples and clothing from Florence.[25] As interested as Pegolotti was in describing the array of items available, his *Pratica* also highlights the merchant's knowledge of pragmatic matters. For example, Pegolotti carefully recorded the conventions for buying and selling grain, the prices of products, the duties that had to be paid at the time of export, transportation costs between foreign markets and Florence, and even a table for the dates of Easter from 1340 to 1465.[26] Pegolotti's work portrays a vivid picture of how European businessmen navigated the universe of goods.

Unbeknown to Francesco Pegolotti, just as the fortunes of his Bardi employers were jeopardized, another upheaval was about to change the course of business from the eastern Mediterranean to the Silk Road: the Mongol invasions. The incursions of these originally nomadic peoples began in the thirteenth century, when they were united under the leadership of Genghis Khan (1162–1227), founder of the Mongol Empire. Conquering a wide swath of territory (approximately 12,741,371 square miles at its height), the empire of the Mongols lasted from 1208 to 1368.[27]

Mongols were often disparaged as little more than marauding, bloodthirsty barbarians, a title these expert horsemen sometimes earned in light of the destruction they visited upon those they conquered. Yet Mongol rule was not exclusively a time of despair for the populations that lived within the almost twenty-five million miles it spanned, from the steppes of Central Asia all the way to Central Europe. The empire Genghis Khan began in 1208 and his successors kept in place also bears the title Pax Mongolia for the military calm, political stability, and economic prosperity that characterized it. A direct result of this Mongol peace was over a century of active exchange in commodities, technologies, and ideas across Eurasia. For Pegolotti and his successors, the improved safety that existed along the trade routes throughout Mongol territory meant not only greater ease of access to profitable merchandise, it also meant a greater likelihood that the items merchants purchased in the East would safely reach markets back home. Safety and health were no small matters. Pirates on the seas, thieves waiting along land crossings, disease, dehydration, and wild animals all threatened every trade journey. The risk to men and goods was high and included loss of life for the merchant and his entourage or forfeiture of merchandise.

Despite the number of merchants who sought favored products, all hoping for the possibility of finding a new taste, coffee is nowhere to be found among the imported goods in writings such as Pegolotti's, even though the evidence suggests that it was known and consumed in the areas where he ventured. This may be because Arab merchants did not yet perceive coffee to be an exportable product. At the time coffee was consumed almost exclusively in homes or in private religious ceremonies. There is one other possibility, although it is purely speculative. Perhaps Pegolotti was aware of coffee but did not think it would have any appeal for Italians and overlooked its potential. All that was about to change.

## Travelers Write about a Curious New Beverage

Just over 200 years after Pegolotti completed his handbook, the Mongol Empire had been reduced to territory in Russia and the steppes. Its former lands were under the control of the Yuan Dynasty in China, the Ilkhanate in Persia, and the Chaghatai in Central Asia. Coffee and the coffeehouse were about to make their debut in European literature.[28] It was not, however, a merchant like Pegolotti but a German physician and botanist who offered the first European description of Near Eastern coffee culture. Leonhard Rauwolf (1535–1596), who spent 1573–1575 moving about Syria, Palestine, and Mesopotamia, wrote a memoir that included his experiences with coffee. Rauwolf's reason for traveling to the Levant and Mesopotamia was not financial; he went for academic and religious reasons. Rauwolf would have been familiar with the medical texts of antiquity and the work of the great physicians of the past, including Ibn Sina and Rhazes. He would also have been aware of the published works of his day such as that of Peter Schoeffer (1425–1503), who in 1485 printed a treatise on herbs, *Gart der Gesunheit*. In this text, the compiler(s), whose identity or possibly identities remain unclear, described a journey to the Near East that was in part a religious pilgrimage to the Holy Land that included explorations in Arabia and Egypt. In the course of their voyages, these anonymous author(s), "diligently sought after the herbs there, and had them depicted and drawn, with their true colour and form."[29] These words piqued Rauwolf's curiosity about the world on other side of the Mediterranean and prompted a desire to travel to the places he had read about. Rauwolf expressed his desire to see the natural environment of the medicinal plants these books described and to learn more about the daily lives of the people who lived in these regions. The Protestant Rauwolf also longed to see the lands of the sacred scripture he revered.

> I found also the fruitful places of the Eastern Countries described, which several authors, and above all the Holy Scriptures have mentioned; and from thence I was enflamed with a vehement desire to search out, and view such plants growing spontaneously in the Native places, and propounded also to myself to observe the Life, Conversation, Custom, Manners, and Religion of the Inhabitants of those Countries.[30]

Imbued with a spirit of adventure and a search for discoveries of his own, in May 1573, Leonhard Rauwolf set out with a friend on a journey to the places of his studies and his imaginings.[31] In mid-1574, after many months of travel, Rauwolf reached the ancient and famed city of Aleppo, Syria. Located in the northwestern part of the country, approximately sixty miles from the Mediterranean Sea in the west and the Euphrates River in the east, Aleppo was situated at the crossroads of several important overland trade routes, commanding a commercial and strategic importance that dated back to the second millennium BCE. The geography of the region had made it easy for waves of invaders to conquer the city over the centuries, including Hittites, Assyrians, Greeks, Romans, Umayyads, Ayyubids, and Ottomans. Through it all, the great *souq* (market) in Aleppo's old city welcomed caravans laden with silks and other textiles, spices, and precious metals. Rauwolf marveled at the diversity and provenance of goods in Aleppo's great emporium, remarking on the dangers merchants endured when they brought their wares to market, the habit of brokers of concealing precious stones to avoid paying an expensive tariff, and the first slave market.[32]

> From India they bring hither many delicate Spices, Cinnamon . . . long pepper . . . Cardamoms, Nutmegs, Mace, and China Roots, which the Arabians make more use of then . . . and delicate China Cups . . . and in very great quantity they bring that noble Root called Rhubarb. . . . And moreover, they sell several sorts of precious Stones, viz. Garnets, Rubies . . . Saphirs, Diamonds, and the best sincerest Musk in little Cods. These precious Stones are hid by the Merchants in the great Caravans that come from India, and they bring them secretly, because they dare not pay Custom for them, that they . . . may not rob them on the High-ways.[33]

Rauwolf also noticed the great diversity of the inhabitants. In addition to the Arabs whose ties to Aleppo dated to the time before the arrival of Islam, within the city there were communities of Turks, Europeans, Jews, and Christians. Between 1548 and 1675, Venetians dominated the silk trade from Aleppo; they maintained their own merchant colony in the city from 1548.[34] The colony remained in Aleppo until the seventeenth century, and from this outpost Venetians traded their own wool and silk cloth and the durable English woolen cloth known as kersey for raw silk.[35] In Aleppo, Rauwolf learned of an unusual beverage that was consumed "in the Morning early in open places before every body, without any fear or regard out of China Cups, as hot as they can, they put it often to their Lips but drink but a little at a time."[36]

Rauwolf wrote that the berries from which the drink is made were the "Buncho of Avicen, and the Bancha of Rafis and Almans exactly; therefore I take them to be the same."[37] Rauwolf noted how men enjoyed their morning coffee: "If you have a mind to eat something or drink . . . there is commonly an open Shop . . . where you sit down upon the Ground or Carpets and drink together."[38]

A hot bitter beverage that was the fundamental element of a custom of public eating and drinking for strictly social purposes would have been a novelty for Rauwolf in 1573, whose experience with establishments of public dining and drinking would have been confined to inns that housed travelers, monasteries that served the needs of pilgrims, and drinking establishments such as taverns that did not serve food and were generally associated with nighttime brawling and drunkenness. Rauwolf's host may well have been entertained by the way the physician marveled at coffee and its consumption, for by the time he arrived in Syria, the first coffeehouse had been established in Mecca, over 1,200 miles south of Aleppo, sometime before 917/1511.[39] From his experiences in the coffeehouses of Aleppo, Rauwolf also described the preparation of coffee, explaining that proprietors used berries "in size, shape and color almost like a bayberry, surrounded by two thin shells" and water to concoct the brew.[40] In his first encounter with coffee, Rauwolf confirmed for himself what he learned from Ibn Sina regarding the curative benefits of coffee, "chiefly [for ailments] of the stomach."[41]

As he left Aleppo, Rauwolf summed up his time in the city and his decision to move on:

> After I had stayed a good while in Halepo, and had seen and understood the Trade and Merchandises of the Inhabitants, together with

that of other nations, viz. Grecians, Armenians, Georgians, Arabians, Persians, and Indians, which come and go daily with their Caravans, and very well understood their Manners and Customs . . . and had also Collected a fine parcel of foreign and undescribed plants; I resolved to go farther eastward into Mesopotamia, Assyria, and Babylonia.[42]

Over the next months, Rauwolf's expedition took him to Baghdad, to Lebanon, and to a pilgrimage to the Christian holy sites in the "Glorious and Kingly city of Jerusalem."[43] Rauwolf noted all he saw in these cities and along the routes he took to reach each destination. However, he did not indicate any further encounters with coffee or the coffeehouse. This should not be read to mean that coffee consumption was not a practice of the inhabitants in other places, as indeed it was. A better interpretation might be that the longer Rauwolf remained in the countries of the Near East, the more ubiquitous coffee proved itself to be. Rauwolf devoted the remainder of his travel notes to the features that were unique to each of the places which he visited. For instance, he described the garden of the Franciscan monastery in Bethlehem as "rich of fine plants and good fruit."[44]

Rauwolf traveled to the Syrian cities of Tripoli and Aleppo, then to Baghdad and across the desert. His observations reveal important glimpses of the man himself, in particular how he came to understand the region. For Rauwolf, the entire Near East was a single location that, despite the diversity of landscape and inhabitants, was so alien that it defied all but one description, a place of the exotic. Rauwolf recalled that all wives "go very richly clothed with flower'd Silks artificially made and mix'd of several colors."[45] Rauwolf also described the sights and smells he encountered, noting orchards that were "filled with Oranges, Citrons, Lemons, Adams-Apples, Sébastien (a type of plum), Peaches, Morellos (a type of cherry), and Pomegranates, &c." and air that was "thick with incense."[46]

Despite the claims of Rauwolf (and others) that his goal was strictly observation and reporting, within the 300 pages he completed upon his return to Germany, Rauwolf reinforced the notion the East was the land of the mythical Shahrazad, who spun the tales in *Thousand and One Nights* to entertain her sultan husband in the hope that he would spare her life, an essentialized Middle East that had little in common with the complexities of the many cultures that shared a geographic area. This is important to note, for as the years wore on, Rauwolf did more than just contribute new medical knowledge that was useful for the physicians of his day. His descriptions of the East became part of the canon of letters, diaries, and oral transmissions Europeans created to capture the interest of a literate, curious elite, who at times found the words of these authors so captivating that they would set out for their own journeys to places that had previously existed only in their imaginations.

While Rauwolf deserves credit for being the first European to provide a written description of coffee and the coffeehouses of the Near East, in the years to come numerous others followed his example, including the Italian Prospero Alpini (1553–1616). As a fellow physician and botanist, Alpini was likely familiar with Rauwolf's description of his travels and may well have found in them inspiration for his own wanderings.

Born in the town of Marostica near Vicenza in the Veneto region of northeastern Italy, Alpini served a brief time in the army of Milan before entering the university in Padua in 1574 to study medicine. Alpini completed his medical degree in 1578 and began his career as a physician in the small town of Campo San Pietro, located in the Veneto region of Italy not far from Padua. As a Renaissance physician, Alpini would have been familiar with Ibn Sina's *Canon of Medicine* and possibly also Pliny's *Natural History*. These texts may have filled Alpini with a desire to see the natural world of these writings for himself, as they did his German predecessor. It seems that Alpini had yet another motivation for leaving his quiet small town and medical practice behind: a yearning for more excitement. Alpini fulfilled this wish in 1580, when he became the personal physician of the Venetian consul in Cairo, Giorgio Emo (d. 1605). Alpini remained at this post for three years, until 1584. Alpini then returned to his work as a small-town physician in the Veneto, this time in Bassano, where he remained until 1587. In that year, Alpini set out for Genoa, where he worked as the personal physician to Gian Andrea Doria (1509–1606), a nephew of the famed Genoese naval commander Andrea Doria (1466–1560) and a respected naval officer in his own right following his service in the Battle of Lepanto (1571). While in Genoa, Alpini also maintained a private clientele. In 1590, the Italian physician was on the move once more, this time to Venice, where he worked until 1594. He then served as a lecturer at the University of Padua. Alpini became the director of the university's botanical garden in 1603 and remained in Padua until his death in 1616.

In the midst of his travels and his medical practice, Alpini found time to publish two texts, *De medicina aegyptorium* (1591), one of the first studies of non-European medicine, and *De plantis Aegypti* (1592), on the flora of Egypt. In the latter text Alpini described how Egyptians boiled down *bon* or *ban* (beans) to create a drink called *caova* that they sipped instead of wine.[47] Interestingly, Alpini makes no reference to the coffeehouses of Cairo, even though they had appeared there early in the sixteenth century and were well established by the time he arrived at the start of the 1580s.[48]

In 1585, thirty years after the establishment of the first coffeehouse in the Ottoman capital of Constantinople, another Italian, Gianfrancesco Morosini (1537–1678), the Venetian *bailo* (diplomat) responsible for overseeing the affairs of Venetians working and living in the city, conveyed to the Venetian Senate that

> *Quasi di continuo stanno [i Turchi] a sedere e, per trattenimento, usano di bere pubblicamente, così nelle botteghe come anco per strade ... un'acqua negra, bollente quante possono sofferire, che si cava d'una semente che chiaman khavè, le quale dicono che ha la virtù di fare stare l'uomo svegliato.*

> Almost continually seated, [the Turks] for their enjoyment publicly drink, in the shops and also in the streets ... a black liquid, as scalding as they can tolerate it [and] extracted from a seed they call *khavè*, which they claim has the virtue of making men stay awake.[49]

Fifteen years later, another *bailo*, Piero Foscarini (d. 1648), confirmed the popularity of coffeehouses in his correspondence with the Venetian Senate, describing places where men could enjoy coffee, which he called *il vino dell'Islam* (the wine of Islam).[50] Ever watchful for new business profits, by 1676 the Senate had asked the Savi alla Mercanzia, the Venetian Trade Authority, to reap as much profit as possible from coffee sales.[51]

The travelogues of numerous other Europeans in the latter part of the sixteenth century and the early seventeenth century are replete with narratives of coffee. In 1601, the three English Sherley brothers, Thomas (1564–1630), Anthony (1565–1635), and Robert (ca. 1581–1628) traveled to Persia via the Levant. They likened the coffeehouses in Aleppo to the taverns back in their native England: "As in England we use to go to the tavern ... so they have their fair houses, where this coffee is sold; thither gentlemen and gallants resort daily."[52] It is not clear if the brothers understood that coffee did not have the intoxicating potential of the beer and wine served at taverns back in England. This may not have mattered to them, as their primary concern seems to have been presenting readers with a familiar image through which they could understand the sociability of the coffeehouses of the Near East.

In addition to travelogues and scientific works, some of the best sources of information on coffee comes from merchants and others employed by trading companies of this time, including the Levant Company (1581–1825) and the British East India Company (1600–1824), both based in England. These organizations were instituted to regulate English trade with Turkey and the Levant through headquarters in cities such as Aleppo, Constantinople, Alexandria, and Smyrna. As part of his job as a preacher to the Levant Company, William Biddulph (1601–1661) traveled to Aleppo in the first decade of the 1600s, where he recorded his encounter with coffee in his diary in 1609: "Their most common Drinke is Coffe, which is a blacke kind of drink made of a kind of Pulse . . . called Coaua, which being ground in a mill, and boiled in water they Drinke it as hot as they can suffer it; which they find to agree very well with them."[53] He also remarked on the social life of coffeehouses, which were locations for mingling and disseminating news: "Their Coffa houses are more common than Ale-houses in England, but they bee not so much sit in the houses as on benches on both sides of the streets neere unto a Coffa house, every man with his fin-ion ful. . . . If there be any news, it is talked of there."[54]

In his official capacity as part of the Levant Company's efforts to manage trade relations, Biddulph may have made a point of visiting coffee shops to learn more about the local culture. Additionally, as an employee of a trading company, Biddulph was likely invited to share the beverage with the local merchants who did business with his employers. He makes no specific reference to tasting coffee himself, concluding only that it "agrees very well with them against their crudities and feeding on hearbs and rawe meates."[55]

In 1607, the British East India Company merchant William Finch (d. 1613) wrote about the coffee-drinking habits of residents of Socotra, a small island in the Arabian Sea approximately 220 miles off the coast of Yemen. Finch's report suggests that coffee was not grown on the island but was a popular import: "The people of the island of Socotra have for their best entertainment a china dish of coho, a black bitterish drink made of a berry like a bay berry, brought from Mecca, supped off hot, and it is reckoned good for the head and stomach."[56] Despite its remote location, the presence of other sought-after products such as frankincense and the red sap of the dragon blood tree that were indigenous to the island had long made getting to Socotra worth the effort for the Egyptians, Greeks, and Romans of antiquity and in later centuries, the English. After this time, Socotra's importance declined, only to be revived in the early twentieth century when scientists discovered that the small island and the even smaller ones surrounding it are among the top five places on earth for the number of plant species that grow only there.[57]

In 1610, another English traveler, George Sandys (1577–1644), set out for the East from Venice following a route that took him to Constantinople, Egypt, the Holy Land, Naples, and Rome. That Sandys's reflections on coffee come from his time in Constantinople reminds us that coffee and cafes had been spreading beyond the Arab world for some time and that non-Arab Muslims who were forbidden to drink wine welcomed the beverage. From Constantinople, Sandys observed that the Turks believed coffee to have medicinal properties and that it might have been a substitute for the wine prohibited in Islam. In his *A Relation of a Journey Begun An. Dom. 1610*, first published in 1615, Sandys wrote that in the "'coffa-house'" there was the "kind of convivial social encounters . . . enjoyed in the taverns of London,"[58] where men met to discuss politics or to enjoy conversation. Sandys added a bit of new knowledge that was not reported by previous sojourners. He claims to have encountered a less savory reason that men gathered together over coffee, an "ulterior, sexual motive" by the "'coffa-men'" who kept "beautiful boyes, who serve as stales [male prostitutes] to procure them customers."[59] Sandys is not the only traveler to make this observation and yet there is little evidence of its merit, suggesting that western foreigners were so mystified by the ways of the East that they misread the social environment.

In 1615, another Italian Pietro della Valle (1586–1652), set out to find adventures of his own. From Constantinople, he commenced what would be almost twelve years of travel in the East. From 1615 to 1626, della Valle moved from Turkey to Egypt, the Levant, Persia, and the west coast of India. Throughout his expedition, he wrote detailed letters back home. His sons published these letters in three volumes in the 1650s. Another edition was published in French in 1663. From his time in Constantinople during the holy month of Ramadan, della Valle wrote to his friend Mario Schipano in Venice about a new beverage the Turks enjoyed called "*cahue*."[60]

Coffee continued to capture the attention of voyagers abroad, some of whom sought to add to the existing commentary. One such person was the Portuguese explorer Pedro Teixeira (ca. 1570–1641). In the book of his adventures in the East in the mid-seventeenth century, simply titled *The Travels of Pedro Teixeira*, the author demonstrated that there was still something to learn about coffee. According to Teixeira, within the coffee-house there was a leveling of the social hierarchy that had not yet reached Europe. He wrote, "Coffee is a vegetable of the size and appearance of little dry beans, brought from Arabia, prepared, and sold in public houses built to that end, wherein all men who desire to meet to drink it, be they mean or great."[61]

After visiting the coffeehouses of Aleppo, Teixeira relayed that "the coffeehouses are well-built and furnished, adorned with numerous lamps, for that their chief custom is at night, though they have enough by day also."[62] Teixeira's description of Aleppo includes the bustling market that had so impressed Rauwolf: "There are woven in Aleppo many good silks of all sorts." He also reported that in the first decades of the seventeenth century, eastern cities remained diverse locales, filled with Arabs, Turks, Venetians, English, French, and Flemings, all engaged in lucrative trade.[63]

While the accounts provided here are in no way exhaustive, they help illustrate the vast time span of European contact with the Mediterranean littoral and beyond, the influence of that contact on business and daily life, and the ongoing allure of coffee as a subject that Europeans felt was worthy of description as they moved from the Constantinople to the sacred city of Jerusalem, the great markets of Aleppo and Persia, India, and, in some instances, all the way to China. As travelers and merchants returned home, they brought with them knowledge of how to prepare coffee, the social patterns that accompanied its consumption, and descriptions of coffee as part of a great mural of life among an unfamiliar people. Retellings of the proper customs for preparing and drinking coffee so impressed early modern Venetians, Londoners, Parisians, and others that they eagerly adopted (and also adapted) both the beverage and the rituals.

It was not just coffee that received a hearty welcome; the written descriptions themselves found a warm reception among inquisitive early modern Europeans.[64] According to Karl H. Dannenfeldt, Leonhard Rauwolf's biographer, during the Renaissance, the accounts of merchants and the scientific texts of antiquity evidenced "attempts at classification and comparison" that "produced a new kind of scholar, the traveling scientist," whose accounts "far surpassed the usual pilgrim and merchant literature." These authors' descriptions of their adventures and their ordeals included tales of loss, hardship, and financial difficulties.[65]

The accounts of merchants and travelers resulted in the importation of unroasted coffee beans, in order to preserve them for sale for as long as the year or two the journey from Yemen to Europe took. By the end of the sixteenth century, coffee was becoming a thriving business, not just for Yemeni growers and exporters but also for European merchants. Although widespread knowledge of coffee reached Europe from the narratives of travelers and others, preceding its popularity with a European audience and raising its commercial value, coffee beans had likely been in Europe in small quantities for some time. Turkish merchants who carried it across the Mediterranean brought it to Venice around 1570 for their own personal use. Evidence of this comes from a number of sources related to the Ottoman community of Venice, including the inventory of an Ottoman textile merchant named Hussein Çelebi.[66] When he was murdered in Venice in 1575, the record of his meager possessions included a small coffee cup, or *fincan*.[67] Professional relationships and the demands of hospitality suggest that as early as the fourteenth and fifteenth centuries, Turkish merchants would likely have offered coffee to business associates and guests in Venice and Genoa.[68] Another support for the claim that coffee was known in Europe by the last decades of the sixteenth century comes from a piece of anecdotal evidence that tells of how an Italian traveler sent a few beans to a French-Dutch botanist and physician friend in 1596.[69] While coffee may have first traveled across the Mediterranean for personal consumption, it did not take long for it to become a luxury import that spread around Italy and other parts of Europe by the mid-seventeenth century.

## Concluding Thoughts: Trade, Coffee, and the "Other"

The noticeable upsurge in the quantity and quality of food by the latter half of the fifteenth century and the attendant changes in eating habits that accompanied the increasing availability of foreign merchandise is one of the continuities between antiquity and the medieval world. As early as 992 CE, just over 100 years before the Crusades set European Christianity on a collision course with the Muslim world, Venetian merchants emerged as the main sources for sugar for confections, silk for expensive brightly colored cloth, and incense for religious worship.[70] In the early eleventh century, Venetian merchants solidified the conduct of business through Constantinople, which at the time was ruled by Basil II (958–1025). Basil II's reign was marked by tense relations with the Fatimid Caliphate (297/909–567/1171), which by the first decades of the eleventh century ruled a region that stretched from its capital in Cairo to the borders of the Byzantine Empire just north of Aleppo, south to Jerusalem, and across large expanses of the North African and Levantine Mediterranean coastlines. Tensions between the Byzantine ruler and the Fatimid dynasty reached a boiling point in 1009 when Caliph al-Ḥakim bi Amr Allah

(387/996–412/1021) ordered the destruction of the Church of the Holy Sepulchre in Jerusalem, the site Christians venerate as the place where Jesus was crucified. While Basil II's contentious relations with his neighbors may have been troublesome for the Byzantine emperor, they proved valuable for Venice's merchant elite, whose primary concern was the stability of their supply lines with the East. Knowing that Basil II needed military support in his fight with the Fatimids, the Venetian doge Pietro II Orseolo (d. 1009) made an agreement with Basil II that included Venetian cooperation in transporting Basil II's troops in exchange for commercial privileges in Constantinople. This agreement launched nearly half a century of Venetian domination over trade with the eastern Mediterranean.[71]

Ninety years later, in 1082, Alexius Comnenus (1057–1118; r. 1081–1118) sat on the throne in Constantinople. The first-hand details of his rule come from a meticulous, if not always clear-sighted, chronicle written by his daughter Anna (1083–1153).[72] Comnenus is perhaps best known as the Byzantine emperor at the time of the First Crusade (1095–1099). By the late tenth century, Emperor Comnenus was having difficulties with the Muslim world, in this instance the Seljuk Turks, who had established an empire in Persia, from which they conquered Baghdad in 447/1055. The Seljuks had been threatening Byzantine territory since 390/1000. In 1095, fearful not only of the Turks but also of the Italian Normans invading from western Greece, Emperor Comnenus beseeched Pope Urban II (d. 1099) for assistance in protecting his dominion. The emperor, like his predecessor, looked to Venice for naval support, fully understanding that Constantinople continued to play an important part in Venice's commercial fortunes. The Venetians were not disappointed, as Comnenus rewarded them for their loyalty to his empire by granting them continued undisturbed access to trade across the entire eastern Mediterranean.[73] These concessions proved indispensable to the entrepreneurial ambitions of Venetian merchants, whose business practices received a further boost with the Crusades.

In 1095, Pope Urban II granted Comnenus's request for additional assistance against the Turks, in part because the request coincided with the pope's decision to initiate the first crusade. An effort meant to reclaim Jerusalem for Christianity, this was also an action through which the pope intended to reassert the power of the papacy, manage the behavior of unruly knights, and show support for Christians. Before the first official crusaders left Europe, however, Comnenus's territory was threatened by the People's Crusade (1096), a pillaging mob led by a popular

COFFEE CROSSES THE MEDITERRANEAN

preacher named Peter the Hermit. Terrified by what he saw, the emperor forced Peter's band across the Bosporus, where the Turks forced them to surrender; many were subsequently killed.[74] A more official force followed, led by such notable men as Hugh of Vermandois (1057–1102) and Godfrey of Bouillon (1060–1100). The warriors of the first crusade eventually reached Jerusalem in 1099, temporarily capturing the city. Conflict between Christian crusaders and Muslim armies continued until 1291, when the city of Acre fell to the Muslims.[75]

I relate the story of the crusades here because it is not exclusively a tale of violence and intolerance; it is also a story of profits for those who chose not to venture out against the enemy, both from outfitting crusaders for their journeys and from marketing the new goods that flowed from east to west during these wars of attempted conquest. So successful were some merchants that their descendants, including the Medicis, a merchant and banking family in Florence; the Sforzas of Milan; the Morosinis of Venice; and the Pallavicinis in Genoa became some of the great patrons of Italian Renaissance art and learning.

Besides the flood of precious metals and textiles that began appearing in greater abundance in the markets of Venice and elsewhere, the range of new foods that arrived—citrus fruit from the Levant, dates from North Africa, apricots from Syria, and eggplant from Persia—turned the city's markets into what Joanne Ferraro has called "an international food court" where adventurous Europeans could indulge their emerging taste for products that were not part of their traditional diet.[76] The international flair of Venetian markets such as the one at the Rialto does not mean that even daring eaters initially embraced all new foods; some took longer to be accepted than others. One of the best examples of a food that took a bit of getting used to is the eggplant. A native of Africa that spread to the Middle East and Asia, eggplant came to the tables of Venice in the twelfth century with Jewish immigrants, and was initially rejected because of reports that it caused insanity. The Italian name for eggplant, *melanzana*, comes from *malum insane*, an illness believed to render people insane.[77] The source of this accusation leveled at the humble eggplant may be its biology. Eggplant belongs to the nightshade, or Solanaceae, family of plants and seems originally to have been confused with its cousin, the deadly weed *Atropa belladonna*. Whatever the source of the claim, the eggplant quickly overcame its dubious reputation to take its place as a common ingredient in a number of European dishes.

The false accusation leveled against the eggplant also serves as a reminder that many new foods in past ages were initially rejected, much as certain new foods are today. In some instances, fear was justified, as was the case with the almond, which early farmers discovered had to be modified through domestication before it could be eaten, as the wild nut was poisonous.[78] Rejection of new foods from the East as potentially harmful to human health and unfamiliar in taste foreshadows later fears generated around the notably stimulating effects of coffee, a caution that was heightened by its unusual bitter taste.

The surge in goods and the written descriptions of the zoological diversity of the East laid the foundation for what would become an enduring fascination with the customs and cultures of an almost incomprehensible other. Readers contemplated with wonder Pliny's descriptions of "peacocks[,] . . . , the spotted skins of tigers and panthers[,] and the colourings of so many animals,"[79] including the camel, which Pliny described as having "an innate hatred for horses [and able to] endure thirst for as much as four days. They live for fifty years, some even for a hundred."[80]

Through the words of Pliny and in the travel narratives introduced in this chapter, the East has been rendered, in the words of Edward Said as a place that has been "since antiquity [one of] romance, exotic beings, haunting memories and landscapes, and remarkable experiences."[81] Said, the father of the theory of Orientalism. argued that the "Orient," or what is understood today as the Near and Middle East, was "almost a European invention," created "politically, sociologically, militarily, ideologically, scientifically, and imaginatively during the post-Enlightenment period."[82] This vision of the East gained prominence in the nineteenth and early twentieth century through descriptions of the entire region as exotic, sensualized, less civilized, and often dangerous, a perspective academics in disciplines such as history, anthropology, and philology advanced during a time that conveniently coincided, according to Said, with the competition among European nations for colonial supremacy in many parts of the world.[83]

Said's description of the East as a locus of romance and the marvelous, a placed fixed as the contrasting "image, idea, personality, experience" of Europe (and the West) does not, however, belong exclusively to modernity. As Said suggests, the roots of Orientalism were planted centuries ago.[84] Projecting Said's theory of Orientalism back to antiquity or even the Middle Ages is problematic, and yet, by listening to the words of the writers, travelers, and intellectuals who lived long before Europeans realized their imperial ambitions in the nineteenth and twentieth centuries, writers who described the "Orient" as a place both carnal and perilous, the notion that a nascent Orientalism is another thread that binds the ages of humanity becomes less of an intellectual stretch. In the next section, the voices of other travelers and adventurers support the notion of a burgeoning Orientalism that would read its apex with the work of Edward Said. The words of those who lived long before the modern era reveal that the foundation of Said's ideas date far back into history, to the incursions of Greeks and Romans in the ancient world and later to the commercial endeavors and written creations of premodern traders and travelers who fed the fantasies that swirled in the consciousness of the West for centuries, in time playing their own part in the coffee and coffeehouse craze.

This chapter comes to a close as coffee enters the Renaissance and early modern world, a time when coffee's popularity found its place among a sea of products imported from the Islamic world, bringing with it great profits and prodigious new ideas. Throughout the 1600s and early 1700s, some of this prosperity would be realized from the selling of mass quantities of coffee to a Europe brimming with new drinkers who sought out the world of the coffeehouse and a window into the lives of those on distant shores.[85] The new western demand for coffee was a welcome change for Muslim merchants, who had experienced the loss much of their income in the early 1500s, when European ships began sailing around the tip of Africa to do business at Asian ports. The coffee trade helped Arab merchants regain a little of their economic prowess, at least until the last quarter of the 1700s, when western nations started growing coffee in their own colonies in the Americas and Asia.

CHAPTER 4

# Coffee and the World
# of Commodities

*For Men and Christians to turn Turks, and think t'excuse the*
*Crime because 'tis in their drink, Is more than Magick, and*
*does plainly tell, Coffee's extraction has its heats from Hell.*

—Anon., 1663[1]

## Shopping, Consumption, and Acquisition

Profitable trade has always relied on the desire of men and women for items that they cannot grow or produce for themselves, a pattern that long predates written records. *Homo sapiens*, which first appeared 200,000 years ago, a distant relative of the first *Homo* species that appeared in Africa 2.5 million years ago and the only remaining human species, began spreading away from its home in East Africa around 70,000 years ago.[2] Archaeological evidence reveals that beginning approximately 30,000 years ago the successors of these *H. Sapiens* were the first human species to engage in trade. Beginning their trading activities in those areas that bordered the Mediterranean Sea and the Atlantic Ocean, our ancestors traded their seashells for the products of other groups of *H. sapiens* that they encountered. Around the same time, those *H. Sapiens* that had expanded into the South Pacific region and had access to obsidian were trading with neighbors up to two-hundred and fifty miles away who lacked the sturdy volcanic glass.[3] As time progressed, luxury goods constituted the majority of long distance trade, such that by the Renaissance savvy shoppers headed for local markets, or sent their domestic help, in search of treasures procured from far and wide.

What made Renaissance and early modern buyers different from those in ages past, if indeed they are worthy of special study at all? To the second part of the question, the assertion here is that there was indeed something particular about human acquisitiveness starting in the mid-fourteenth century, inaugurating a pattern that continued into the seventeenth century, a period when the details of personal inventories from all strata of society, even those that "experienced relative poverty," reveal that possessions increased with every generation.[4] It was during this same time that coffeehouses spread from Venice to London and coffee was making its way to parts of India and surrounding islands, as well as crossing the Atlantic to the Americas. Coffee was part of a Renaissance universe of things.[5] What made the demand for goods during the Renaissance so different from the thousands of years that preceded it?

Part of the answer lies in what people demanded. By the latter part of the Middle Ages, people wanted more than items that could be worn, displayed, or eaten; they also wanted less tangible things. Renaissance consumers coupled their desire for the latest luxury or curiosity with something more elusive, a desire for knowledge about far-off places and the people who grew the produce that graced their tables, harvested the aromatics that burned in their churches, crafted the items that filled their homes, produced the cloth that attired their bodies, and inhabited lands most would never see. The affluent stored and displayed everything from astrolabes to seashells to carved ivory in curiosity cabinets and filled their bookshelves with maps and the narratives of travelers. Even the less prosperous, while were more limited in what they could buy and in the ideas to which they might be exposed, could share in the joy of a story, fulfilled primarily in oral retellings of the adventures of merchants, soldiers, diplomats, scholars, pilgrims, and others who traveled simply to see new locations. All of this buying and storytelling also had a negative side: the aspersions Europeans cast on the people who dwelled in the East, the "many Arabs who are called Bedouins and Ascoparcz [and] lead a completely degraded life."[6] The chapter begins, however, with the adventures, some closely related to fact and others entirely fictional, of merchants, pirates, and pilgrims that would fill the Renaissance material world and become deeply embedded aspects of daily life.

## Out and About in the Early Modern Marketplace

Scholars have pondered when people became conscience consumers. Some argue that consumerism has no official (or at least no recognizable) start date.[7] This view is predicated on the reality that humans have always needed to acquire items their communities could not grow or produce on their own.[8] Despite the truth in this assertion, the trade in seashells and obsidian that early *H. Sapiens* engaged in would not seem to constitute a worldwide movement toward a global market. However, before we dismiss the idea of an ancient, if not prehistoric, start date for people as avid shoppers, we should consider that the maritime trading empire of the Phoenicians and the desert emporium that connected Greeks and Romans with China and India suggest that spending on goods both practical and peripheral is hardly a new phenomenon.

For other scholars, the start of consumerism does not begin until the Renaissance. The argument that demand for both luxurious and everyday goods reached new heights in the Renaissance is predicated on what Richard Goldthwaite describes as a "way of life . . . sustained by more and more possessions."[9] For those who subscribe to this position, the mid-fourteenth century, just after a wave of deadly plague temporarily left Europe, marked a departure from the medieval view that "it was simply better not to spend money."[10] In this age of rebirth, where the attainment of ever more merchandise was tempered only by a person's monetary situation, consumption generated a culture all its own based on both the luxuries and the necessities people from all strata of society, save for the very poor, demanded.[11] Preserved alligators, rich and colorful silk brocades, pungent spices, luscious fruits, tasty sugar, fine ceramics, and intricately adorned glass filled the markets of Europe, suggesting that the lives of the urban elite were caught up with the activities of acquisition and consumption that Goldthwaite described as an "empire of things."

Not all scholars agree with this previous assessment. They propose a later start for humans as enthusiastic buyers. Those who advance this position argue that consumerism did not start until the late nineteenth century, with the advent of department stores in London and Paris, the building of the Galleria Vittorio Emmanuele II in Milan, and other stores that provided one-stop access to a wide array of products. The proponents of this view also suggest that by the mid-nineteenth century the advances of the industrial revolution in producing less expensive goods made it possible for greater shares of the population, save for the urban and rural poor (on whose labor industrialization was built), to purchase both what they needed and what they wanted.[12] Changes in the way goods were produced during this time also came with societal changes that scholars have used as evidence to support their thesis that the onset of consumerism happened in modern times. The opportunity to purchase goods freed many from the constant demands of producing all of the necessities of daily life, which afforded greater time for leisure activities. The less affluent, who found work outside the home or off the farm, also became consumers of store-bought products that promised to make their lives after work easier, such as the canned goods that began appearing in the early 1800s.

Without entering too deeply into the consumerism debate, I argue that the sheer volume of goods available in early modern Italy and throughout Europe supports the argument that consumer society began long before the 1800s.[13] Pietro Casola (1427–1507), a clergyman who lived in the economically thriving city of Milan, provides an illustration of Venice's Renaissance marketplace. After visiting Venice, his starting point for a pilgrimage to Jerusalem in 1494, Casola remarked, "Who could count the many shops so well-furnished . . . with so many cloths of every make . . . and so many warehouses full of spices, groceries, and drugs?"[14] Many of these goods that Casola so admired had been imported by Venetian merchants from the Eastern Mediterranean.

The availability of products, the provenance of the goods for sale, and the access that people of at least moderate wealth had to the wares on display raises the issue of how people attained the goods that were the ingredients of daily life and what makes Renaissance shopping habits of particular note.[15] For those in Renaissance Europe with money to spend, from the wealthiest members of the nobility to middling merchants to the moderately poor who nevertheless had enough to purchase goods they could not produce for themselves, regular trips to busy urban marketplaces and country fairs were an important parts of social life. Evelyn Welch explores this topic in *Shopping in the Renaissance*, which shed light on the "experience of the Renaissance marketplace."[16] According to Welch, the act of shopping was not confined to any particular group. Female members of the Milanese nobility such as Beatrice d'Este, wife of the Ludovico Sforza (1452–1508), made occasional forays into the marketplace simply to find out what was available. High-ranking Venetian men appeared regularly at the Rialto, as did domestic servants on errands for their employers.[17] These centers of material fulfillment were also populated by the men and women whose prosperity depended on attracting the attention of potential customers with the quality of their wares.[18] In one example from outside of Italy, Christine A. Jones, in her work on artisans in early modern France, notes that an array of commodities, including such luxuries as full-length mirrors and items made of porcelain, could be found in the markets of France.[19]

At the foundation of the vibrant early modern social and cultural milieu were merchants who brought the world of the marvelous to the imaginations of men and women through the goods they supplied.[20] As mediators between East and West, these businessmen created new tastes among their patrons, both for novel food items and for the unusual artifacts that filled early modern curiosity cabinets. These merchants were also among the first to introduce new ideas and new technologies, such as information about the lateen, or triangular sails Arab navigators used in the southern Mediterranean. The Portuguese prince Henry the Navigator used such sails in the caravels he dispatched in 1441 and 1442 to chart the western part of Africa between the Sahara Desert and Gulf of Guinea.[21]

Communication was integral to the business dealings that brought goods to market. As Pegolotti's *Pratica* illustrates, matters such as prices, quality, and weights and measures were of great concern for merchants on both sides of any transaction. Equally important, those involved in trade needed an understanding of something more elusive: the cultural norms of those they interacted with. This included proper techniques for bartering, appropriate behavior in social and business settings, and the nuances of language.[22] The breakdown of any of these could mean the difference between success and failure and the loss of future partnerships.

From the earliest encounters of the two groups, Muslims in the Near East used the term "Franks" to describe the Europeans they did business with. Prior to the start of the Crusades in 1095, the Franks in question were primarily Byzantine Christians who had fled Roman persecutions and a collapsing empire for a new life in cities along the eastern Mediterranean beginning in the fourth century CE. One such place was Acre, located along the northern coast of present-day Israel. Acre's natural harbor had served for centuries as a place of connection for both maritime and overland trade routes and was therefore a pivotal point for commerce throughout the Levant. In 1185, Abu al-Husayn Muhammad bin Ahmad ibn Jubayr (540/1145–614/1217), secretary to the governor of Granada in Andalusian Spain, traveled through Acre as part of caravan of pilgrims destined for Mecca and Medina to make the hajj.[23] While Ibn Jubayr was in Acre, he commented on "the custom house, which is a caravanserai . . . in Acre . . . the capital of the Frankish cities in Syria." There, "the Christian scribes of the Customs sit with ebony inkstands ornamented with gold, writing in Arabic, which they speak."[24] Non-Arab Christians speaking Arabic must have struck Ibn Jubayr as an anomaly, or he likely would not have made specific mention of it in the book of his *rhila*, or spiritual journey, to Islam's two holiest cities.[25] This is one example of European merchants' long-standing knowledge and use of Arabic, which continued into the Renaissance and early modern eras.

Commerce in the premodern world demanded an acuity with languages. Ibn Jubayr called attention to the fact that for European merchants, fluency or at least competence in Arabic paid generous dividends. Thus, in addition to the European language of their home countries, and in some instances Latin as well, merchants engaged in trade with the East realized that their fortunes depended in part on their ability to overcome a significant language barrier. It was not uncommon for traders to have their sons instructed in the Arabic language. Even though Venetian merchants had access to and made use of interpreters, scholarly study of Arabic appears as early as the twelfth century in parts of Europe.[26] In southern Italy and Sicily and in trade centers on the Mediterranean such as Venice and Pisa, both scientific works such as the astronomical texts that influenced Copernicus (and his successors) and nonscientific works were being translated from Arabic original sources, mirroring the recovery of other writings from antiquity in their original Greek or Latin during the Renaissance.[27]

However, directly connecting specific merchants with what they knew and how they transmitted their knowledge remains a challenge, as very few left written records of their encounters, as Francesco Balducci Pegolotti did. As men of commerce whose livelihood depended on their success in meeting the demands of consumers while remaining constantly on the lookout for new products to entice their patrons, most entrepreneurs had little time to pen tracts about daily life on foreign shores. This is not to say they did not share what they saw and experienced with family and friends during their visits home. Indeed, it is quite likely that the interpersonal interactions that occurred between those who had business in coffee and their family, friends, and business acquaintances played a crucial role in coffee's place in the Renaissance world of consumers.[28]

## Travel Literature and Consumption

As Europe entered the last decade of the 1400s, the desire of many to travel beyond their boundaries ushered in what is often referred to today as the Age of Exploration. The voyages of Christopher Columbus set off a wave of expeditions across the Mediterranean and two oceans, the Atlantic and the Pacific. Wayfarers, fortune seekers, and agents in the service of monarchs, ruling elites, and prosperous merchant houses took to the seas and embarked on overland treks. By early modernity, missionaries had joined the ranks of those moving around the globe as new religious orders such as the Jesuits took the message of Catholicism east to India, China, and Japan and west to the New World in the decades after the Council of Trent (1545–1563). This section examines the reception of coffee, beginning with those who described their journeys long before the pivotal year of 1492 and who inspired those who came after them. The first purveyors of a new type of literature, these authors engaged their readers with descriptions of lands with unknown wild beasts, men with a single large foot known as monopods, and claims to have entered the land of an elusive Christian king named Prester John. By the fifteenth and sixteenth centuries, these stories were demanded and consumed like the movables that accompanied their authors back home. From texts that resemble the travel guidebooks of today to the pragmatic accounts of goods and trade practices to descriptions of far off people and places, pilgrim literature provides a beginning for this discussion, as these are among the earliest examples of the genre.

Sometime between 326 and 328 CE, Helena (ca. 250–ca. 330), mother of the Roman Emperor Constantine (272–337) and a convert to Christianity long before her son made his deathbed profession of faith, embarked on a pilgrimage to the Holy Land intent on reclaiming the true cross, the cross upon which Jesus was crucified. Her travels around Jerusalem and its environs did not yield the sacred relic, but they did lead to the approximate demarcation of such important sites as those of Christ's birth in Bethlehem and his crucifixion in Jerusalem, the Church of the Nativity in Manger Square and the Church of the Holy Sepulchre, respectively. Helena's voyage also resulted in the establishment of churches and shrines throughout what is today Israel and the Palestinian territories. The growth of Christianity prompted others to follow her example, and before long the details of her quest became a guide for future travelers to the sacred sites she named. It was not just Christians that wrote and made of use of pilgrim literature. Jewish and Muslim travelers, also left texts designed to guide pilgrims. By the Middle Ages, these writings had become part a larger genre Bernhard Bischoff refers to as the "literature of itineraries."[29] Originally intended as practical guides for travelers, sometimes even including accurate maps and accounts of the languages spoken, this literature was also popular as a source of entertainment, particularly for those without the means to travel.[30]

Among the best known of the Jewish writers of the Middle Ages was Benjamin of Tudela (1130–1173), originally from the city of Tudela along the Ebro River in Spain. Benjamin's *Sefer ha-Massa'ot* (Book of travels) was compiled from his rather extensive wanderings sometime around the year 1173 and includes both what Benjamin of Tudela saw for himself and what he learned from secondary sources.[31] Even though, as Martin Jacobs notes in *Reorienting the East Jewish Travelers to the Medieval Muslim World*, there are "geographical inconsistencies" in part of the *Massa'ot*, it does seem that Benjamin himself ventured from Spain to Syria and Palestine, with various stops along the way.[32] Even though Benjamin's commentary includes information gleaned from others, his writing falls in the category of itinerary literature because it fulfills one of the most important purposes of the genre: it describes the places he claims to have visited and uses a "system for organizing diverse stores of information—both empirical and imaginary—about foreign lands."[33] For example, Benjamin's simple notation of "Arab merchants" who sold food to both Muslims and Jews as they walked the same pilgrimage route to venerate the tomb of the prophet Ezekiel in present day al-Kifl in southeastern Iraq would have informed travelers about the availability of food in the area and confirmed that it met the religious standards of adherents to both faiths.[34]

Ibn Battutah took his effort to accurately represent the local people he met in his travels a bit further. Battutah related that when he stopped in the village of Karsakhu, situated along the Nile in contemporary Mali, he

> went down to the Nile to satisfy a need and one of the Blacks came and stood in the space between me and the river; I was amazed at his appalling manners and lack of decency. I mentioned it to someone, who said "He did that only to protect you from the crocodile by putting himself between you and it."[35]

There are two important messages for today's readers in the quote above. First, Ibn Battutah forthrightly indicated his opinion of the people of sub-Saharan Africa, the "Blacks," as he called them. In his view, they lacked both the manners and the decorum of the people from his native Morocco, 1,000 miles to the north. Despite what Battutah initially concluded was a serious violation of his privacy on the part of his hosts in Karsakhu, the quote also suggests Battutah's recognition that they knew something about the importance of hospitality. Indeed, either for future personal reflection or for the benefit of readers, Battutah acknowledged that he had misperceived the Malian people by relating that in fact the local villagers extended to him an act of both hospitality and courage by protecting him from crocodiles, a danger that was unfamiliar to him.

Not all writers demonstrated Benjamin's or Battutah's attempts to be impartial in their descriptions of foreign places, as evidenced by the disparaging comparisons that fill much of the literature. For example, a Jewish travel writer of a later age, Meshullam of Volterra (d. ca. 1507), who reached Jerusalem in 1481, warned those that followed him that "the Ishmaelites [Muslims] are to be likened to camels, and are similar to beasts. . . . They crouch and eat on the ground without a [table] cloth but only a red leather [mat]."[36] Meshullam's words are joined by William Biddulph's similarly uncomplimentary observations about the Arab Muslims. Writing from Aleppo, Syria, in 1603, Biddulph referred to the "crudities" of the Muslim diet, which he claimed was composed of "hearbs and rawe meates."[37] Biddulph noted that some men also used opium, "which maketh them forget themselves."[38]

Despite the biases of the authors who contributed to this genre, they did make the movement of people determined to leave home a bit easier for a number of reasons. For instance, many of the authors were relatively precise about a number of helpful details, including how many days it took to journey between cities or resting places, what travelers might expect in terms of a welcome from the local people, the diversity of people who lived in urban centers such as Damascus and Jerusalem, the accommodations available, and the availability of food and drink.

Travelers such as merchants also benefited from accurate information. This was especially true of those conducting business from the port of Venice with counterparts in the eastern Mediterranean and Arabia. Indeed, while business dealings constituted the largest share of profitable contact Venetians had with the Ottoman Empire, they were not the only source of revenue. The sultans at Constantinople, who exercised power over the trade routes of the eastern Mediterranean, also administered the cities and sites sacred to Christianity. This meant that travel for commerce was also often travel for religious reasons. As the number of Christians destined for Jesus's birthplace in Bethlehem, the site of his crucifixion and resurrection in Jerusalem, and all points in between grew, a combination of reasons for travel emerged. Pilgrims from Italy and throughout Europe who were destined for the Holy Land often traveled on Venetian merchant vessels that were already making the crossing to convey them across the Mediterranean Sea.[39]

By the mid-twelfth century, the desire to visit holy sites had expanded to include a quest for holy people. Most notable among such individuals was the fictive Christian king of Africa Prester John, who was apparently still very much alive almost 350 years later 1497–1499, the time of Vasco da Gama's (1469–1524) first voyage, as evidenced by an entry in da Gama's journal. After landing on the Island of Mozambique, located off the north coast of the southern African country of the same name, da Gama wrote that "we were told, moreover, that Prester John resided not far from this place; that he held many cities along the coast, and that the inhabitants of those cities were great merchants and owned big ships."[40]

By the Renaissance and early modern periods, the journeys of both entrepreneurs and religious devotees had become ever more popular as sources of practical information, as entertainment, and as important sources of knowledge about distant lands and societies.[41] Personal narratives riveted larger and larger audiences, particularly as the printing press, also an eastern import, changed the literary landscape of Europe. Woodblock printing on cloth was developed in China as early as the third century of the Common Era, and by the eleventh century the Chinese had developed the first wooden moveable type. This technology did not gain a foothold in Europe until 1450, when Johannes Gutenberg revolutionized the landscape of human communication with the development of his printing press. Fifty years later, there were as many as 27,000 printed books, the majority of which were in Latin, although texts in the vernacular were also becoming available.[42]

The momentous events of the sixteenth and seventeenth centuries —two Reformations, one Protestant and the Catholic response, the subsequent redrawing of territorial maps, and the ensuing peasant revolts, to mention just a few—owe much to Gutenberg's press. Equally important, increased access to the printed word turned the deeds of travelers into commodities that brought stories and illustrations to an interested European audience. For the literate, this meant greater opportunities to read the tales for themselves. For the larger share of the population, literacy rates were slow to follow.[43] Nevertheless, the spread of printed books meant an increased demand for travel chronicles. It should also be noted that the handwritten texts that served as the original sources for printed books and were available in Europe long before 1450 joined a substantial body of handwritten Ottoman, Arab, and Chinese annals that contributed to Europeans' knowledge, or misconceptions, of far-off places.

The sheer availability of travel texts and the public demand that fueled their production should not be conflated with the authenticity of the accounts. The claims about coffee and other observations of Leonhard Rauwolf, William Biddulph, and other agents for the British and Dutch East India Companies and those penned by men employed in the service of a merchant house or bank or with a maritime trading business of their own have one advantage in terms of general reliability: there is good evidence that these men actually made the journeys of which they wrote. Such is not the case for all accounts. One example is *The Book of John Mandeville*. The name John Mandeville may or may not have been this fourteenth century author's real identity, and if John Mandeville was not his name, this is merely the first of many dubious claims he made throughout his *Book*. Although he regaled readers with descriptions of his escapades in cities such as Beirut, "where Saint George killed the dragon," which he described as "a good city [with] a good and strong castle," Mandeville could have gleaned this information from any number of texts.[44] Criticism of Mandeville came swiftly, indeed almost immediately, after he published in the mid-fourteenth century. As one early modern reader decried, "Mandeville's longest journey was to the nearest library" where, according to Iain Higgins, he most likely consulted two contemporary texts.[45] In the first, Dominican friar William of Boldensele wrote of a journey he made to the Holy Land in 1332 in a treatise entitled *Book of Certain Regions beyond the Mediterranean*. The second was written by Odoric of Pordenone, a Franciscan who visited India and China as a missionary in the 1320s and left behind an account in *The Travels of Friar Odoric: 14th Century Journal of the Blessed Odoric of Pordenone*, which he dictated while living in Padua in 1330.[46] Even though it seems likely that the mysterious Mandeville never ventured far from his home in England, his account was nevertheless quite popular. It seemed to speak with authority on any number of topics, including "the right way to go straight to the holy city of Jerusalem"[47] and the role of Genoa and Venice as two of the embarkation points for "Tartary, Persia, Chaldea, and India."[48]

From a contemporary perspective, texts such as *The Book of John Mandeville* might easily be dismissed as useless because of its inaccuracies, prejudices, and sensationalism, such as the story of a half-man, half-goat Egyptian monster Mandeville supposedly encountered.[49] This would be a mistake for a number of reasons. First, it would limit our understanding of what stories like this meant to the public from the Middle Ages onward. While accuracy mattered to those planning a voyage, it may have had less value for those primarily interested in a fireside adventure on a dark, wintry night. Indeed, such prominent figures as Leonardo da Vinci and Christopher Columbus owned copies of *The Book of John Mandeville*, although we cannot know how much of the narrative they accepted as fact.[50] Both Da Vinci and Columbus were likely also familiar with the narratives that influenced Mandeville, and they were probably no different than others of their day who enjoyed a good story.

The second danger in consigning Mandeville's account and other similar works to the trash bin of history lies in their value as windows into how Europeans developed their ideas about others. Many travel narratives are valuable because of what they reveal centuries later about the authors themselves. Early accounts generally regarded non-Europeans as barbarians and savages with fantastical physical appearances who lived across oceans that were filled with sea monsters, and in some instances led impossibly rarified daily lives. One such examples come from yet another dubious claim from John Mandeville, who alleged that in his palace in Susa in the Zagros mountains of present-day Iran, Prester John ate at dining tables made from "emeralds . . . amethyst[s] and gold."[51]

By the start of the seventeenth century, authors increasingly attempted to write objectively, albeit with varying degrees of success. As Stephen Greenblatt notes in *Marvelous Possessions*, "Europeans felt powerfully superior to virtually all peoples they encountered."[52] Greenblatt also cautions readers to let the travelers speak for themselves from across the expanse of time instead of assigning the values and attitudes of the contemporary world to them. In particular, Greenblatt encourages readers of travel narratives to listen for the "sense of wonder," both positive and pejorative, that the authors expressed in their "instinctive recognition of difference."[53] One example is John Mandeville's description of Chaldea, located in present-day southern Iraq:

> [The] land of Job borders on the kingdom of Chaldea. In the kingdom of Chaldea the men are handsome and they go about very

nobly dressed with golden scarves, and their clothes too are very nobly adorned with gold embroidery and large pearls and precious stones. The women are all very ugly and badly dressed, and they all walk barefoot and wearing a miserable, baggy garment, cut off at the knees.... The women are quite dark, ugly, and hideous, and they are certainly not at all beautiful, but they lack graciousness.[54]

The striking difference between Mandeville's description of the men and that of the women may not simply suggest that the author was a misogynist. Instead, the short passage illustrates Stephen Greenblatt's admonition to look beyond the words. In doing this, it is possible to see a Europe grappling with its encounters with the world, with people whose looks and manners were indescribably foreign but also strangely captivating. The narratives that are part of this chapter, therefore, illustrate not simply premodern attempts to describe the world far from them; they also reveal some of the marvel the vast majority of people who would never venture far from home experienced.

It cannot be ignored that the books that were prized for the wonders they revealed could at times lead to serious trouble for those who possessed them. Such was particularly true of peasants who were generally believed to be not only illiterate, which some were not, but also unsophisticated, superstitious, and easily led astray. Such was the case for the Friulian miller Domenico Scandella, called Menocchio, whose story Carlo Ginzburg told in *The Cheese and the Worms*. Menocchio was ultimately executed by the Inquisition in 1601 after two trials by the Holy Office, fifteen years apart, for ideas he formulated at least in part from the books the inquisitors found in his possession, including what one witness concluded was a copy of the Qur'an and a copy of John Mandeville's *Book*.[55]

What does any of this have to do with coffee? Knowledge of the literary tradition that reveled in the telling, or at least the imagining, of human exploits in far-off lands is the social world that surrounded the early modern Europeans who first learned about coffee. From the reflections of Rauwolf, Sandys, Biddulph, and others, future coffee drinkers learned both how to prepare a cup of coffee and about the personal interactions in coffeehouses that would later fuel the imaginations of readers who sought to emulate them. It did not take long for coffee to become the beverage of choice for men who gathered not just to hear the tales of Prester John or Pietro della Valle's early seventeenth-century account of his travels in Egypt but also for conversation over a hot cup of coffee and sometimes tobacco smoking.[56] Coffee was thus consumed in two ways: in the literature of the day and as a product that later moved out of tales and into the urban marketplace.

Europeans' awareness of foreign peoples and ways through books and oral retellings was augmented by the presence of merchants and dignitaries who hailed from Constantinople and throughout the eastern Mediterranean and lived in their cities. Unfortunately, less is known about how visitors and temporary residents such as the merchants in Venice who lived and worked from their warehouse on the city's Grand Canal viewed those who lived in the West. We know that Muslims did not view Europeans favorably during the Crusades. One example comes from Usamah Ibn Munqidh (1095–1188), who lived in the city of Shayzar in northern Syria. After crusaders attacked the Syrian city of Antioch in 1098, Munqidh wrote that the Franj were "beasts superior in courage and fighting ardour but in nothing else, just as animals are superior in strength and aggression."[57] Unfortunately, due to a lack of sources from later eras, we can only speculate about how these ideas changed, for good or ill.

## More about the World of Things

The travel narratives that were so popular in early modern Europe were not the only way those in the West sought to materialize the East. Elite westerners were also very interested in collecting and displaying novel and unusual objects. This hobby dates to the ancient past. The booty that resulted from Roman empire building in the East filled the markets of the ancient world, as archaeologists who excavated in the city of Milan in 1991 found when they uncovered a Roman burial tomb that dated from the mid to late imperial era. A sarcophagus at the site contained the skeleton of a young woman dressed in "rich attire" who had been laid to rest with objects that could only have been attained via the emporia of Arabia, including lumps of frankincense, gold, amber beads, and an ivory fan.[58]

By the Renaissance and later, it was not tombs but private museums, known as *Wunderkammer*, or curiosity cabinets, that testified to the desire of Europeans to prove their worldliness, or at least demonstrate that they had the means to purchase rare objects from faraway places. These often-magnificent cabinets were strategically placed to enable visitors to admire the goods the cabinets' owners had accumulated, either from their own travels or from the wayfaring of others. The cabinet in the late fifteenth-century *studiolo* of the ducal palace in Gubbio (ca.

1479–1482) housed an astrolabe, an armillary sphere (a model of celestial objects), and numerous books. One hundred and seventy years later, the frontispiece of the *Musei wormiani historia* (1655), the catalog of the curiosities amassed by the seventeenth-century Danish polymath Olaus Worm, illustrates the collector's interest in stuffed animals.[59]

Adventures, artifacts, and edibles were not the only ways early modern Europeans satisfied their desire for the unusual. In her beautifully illustrated text *Bazaar to Piazza, Islamic Trade and Italian Art, 1300–1600*, the art historian Rosamund Mack details the impact of international trade in luxury goods on the artistic tastes of Italians.[60] In the early 1300s, Islamic-inspired motifs and designs on such landmarks as Saint Mark's Basilica and the Doge's Palace in Venice began to appear.[61] The façade of the latter, which was begun around 1340 and finally completed during the first half of the fifteenth century, faces the city's Grand Canal and the Piazza San Marco, celebrates Venice's long history as a "gateway to the Orient."[62] Similarly, Saint Mark's Basilica, the façade of Santa Maria Novella in Florence, and the façade of Cattedrale di San Lorenzo in Genoa all reflect Italy's interaction with the Islamic world and the skill of the Italian architects who rendered structures that combined both eastern and western styles.

Around the same time that architecture began reflecting an eastern gaze, Arabic calligraphy started appearing on textiles and frescoes and in paintings and even the frames for Christian images. Almost entirely without meaning, this Kufic, or "pseudo-Arabic," script celebrates Europeans' appreciation of the beauty and grace of Islamic calligraphy, a trend that continued into the early sixteenth century, when such ornamentation declined.[63] One of the most striking examples of pseudo-Arabic in an artwork is in the halos of Gentile da Fabriano's (1370–1427) holy family, part of the artist's *Adoration of the Magi*, completed in 1423.

One hundred years after Fabriano's death, artists were still captivated by this artistic device. An example is Gentile Bellini's (1429–1507) *The Virgin and Child Enthroned* (ca. 1478). Bellini's use of the lettering can be seen on the carpet that Mary's feet rest upon and on her robe. It is not surprising that we find eastern influences in Bellini's work. In 1479, the doge of Venice sent Bellini to Constantinople as a visiting painter to Sultan Mehmed II (835/1432–886/1481). One of his tasks was to paint a portrait of the sultan.[64]

The evidence suggests that by the fifteenth century, the volume of imports of eastern and Islamic luxury goods was matched by the volume

Frontispiece, *Musei wormiani historia. Courtesy of the Smithsonian Libraries, Washington, D.C.*

Doge's Palace, Venice, Italy. *Photo by the author.*

of exports of Italian products to those regions, demonstrating that trade and influence moved in both directions across the land and sea routes that connected East and West. Textiles, ceramics, and glass poured into Europe from China, North Africa, the Levant, and Persia at the same time that such items as the famed glassware of Murano was receiving a warm reception in the regions to the east. According to Venice's ambassador to Constantinople in 1560, both glass and textiles from Venice were valued imports to the Ottoman capital. In this way, merchants from different birthplaces emerged as vital in the creation of "a community of taste" that connected people on opposite sides of the Mediterranean littoral. It was in this vibrant world that coffee found a new home.[65]

## The Multidirectionality of Influence: Coffee in Early Modern Europe

Bustling markets filled to overflowing with glass vases, gold thread, freshly caught fish, and colorful fruits and vegetables all meant to tempt shoppers to part with their coins provide a vision of a space that was new and exciting, a cosmopolitan environment that welcomed coffee as one of three "exotic edibles," the other two being chocolate and tea. These were the "hot beverages [that were] the most unusual and recent new-comers to the sphere of artisanal knowledge."[66] While the busy market of late 1500s Venice was coffee's first port of call, introduced either by the Italian botanist Prospero Alpini in the mid-1580s or a bit earlier in 1582, it had expanded its sphere of influence by the first part of the seventeenth century.[67]

In 1615, traders from Venice found wealth by exporting coffee beans throughout mainland Europe and beyond, including England and France, around the same time as chocolate from the Americas and tea from China began to enter European markets.[68] In the case of France, as hot drinks developed into sensational commodities, coffee became more than just a desired new taste; those who roasted, brewed, and served it were seen to have acquired a valuable skill.[69] In one example, the "great seventeenth-century 'intelligencer' and man of science," Samuel Hartlib (ca. 1600–1672) included coffee as part of his efforts "to record all human knowledge and make it universally available for the education of all mankind."[70] Hartlib left over 25,000 folios, including two letters to the Anglo-Irish philosopher and chemist Sir Robert Boyle (1627–1691). In one of those letters, undated, but possibly written in 1657, Hartlib specifically mentioned coffee:

A gentlewoman who came to visit me, assured me, upon her own knowledge, that two persons, visited with this late sickness, and by sweats likewise brought into a consumption, have within a fortnight, or little more time recovered, and are now also grown fatter and healthier than formerly, by the only use of the Turkish drink coffee. The one of these persons thus cured was a young gentlewoman, and the other an ancient gentleman; and of the truth of this I doubt nothing, the authors being all persons of quality and credit. Upon this, I was earnestly pressed to send for a bottle; and so I has one last week; and though I have taken it but three mornings, yet I find my stomach more clean and stronger to digest, my brain clearer, and my sweats somewhat abated. And I am the rather convinced of the efficacy of it, because, as my lord Verulam commends it, it is the Turks wine; and they, as I understand, are generally healthy, strong, fat, and big men. And as their chief feeding is rice (which also I find a great nourisher, and amongst the variety of meats provided for me, I am weary of them all but this) so their chief drink is coffee, at which they tipple, with a fool, to make them sport. Now, Sir, the intent of this relation is not to inform you, either of the drink, or berry it is made of (of which I have tasted, and find the drink to have its only taste without other ingredient) or the virtues of it; to all which I believe you are no stranger; but only give you in this testimony, that you may spread its benefit towards this new disease, which I hear is with you; and not only in these parts, but elsewhere, in Oxfordshire, Norfolk, in Hampshire, &c. wheresoever an epidemical disease useth to rage in the inlands and sea-coasts by us, Rochester, Dover, Rye, &c. Another purpose of this paper is, to beg of you some of the freshest berries, which may be had of some Turkish merchant, with his directions to make it drink; which, if it may be had, I know you may command; and this for my own recovery. I have sent now for another bottle, and it will last me a week more; but, to save this trouble, I beg yours, and hope they will spare of their store, and discover the use of it to one, who intends no gain by it.[71]

Within his discussion of coffee, Hartlib conveyed its curative powers and his view that the Turks were healthy and robust because the consumed it. Indeed, although he professed that he has no intent to herald coffee's merits, Hartlib appears to have been a fan of it. This letter provides important clues into the belief among some members of the British elite that coffee was one of a number of pharmaceuticals of eastern origin. Coffee, Hartlib claimed, had cured two people ill with what he described as a "consumption." Hartlib also found that his own health had improved through his experimentations with coffee. Asserting that coffee procured from the Turks and Arabia was an effective medicinal, Hartlib put it in the same category as an herbal compound that English apothecaries referred to as Venice treacle, a term that encompassed a number of blends, some of which contained fifty-five different herbs. Such "treacles" were thought to be "universal panaceas" into the late eighteenth century.[72] The earliest of these compounds, mithridatium, is attributed to Mithridates VI, who became the king of Pontus in 120 BCE. In 900 CE, the compound theriac appears in the *Leechbook of Bald* as a medicine King Alfred (849–899) of Elias, who at the time was Patriarch of Jerusalem, had requested. As the centuries passed, these compounds made their way west, possibly with the arrival of Muslims to Spain. They were manufactured in Venice beginning in the twelfth century.[73]

Treacle was also produced in Genoa. English landowner Sir John Paston (1442–1479) attests to having acquired some containers of it from a Genoese apothecary in 1466, even though treacle had been produced in London since 1423. In this year, the "Commonality of Physicians and Surgeons of London" commissioned apothecaries to monitor the quality of the compound produced in shops throughout the city. This is important because until these treatments were deemed ineffective in the mid-1700s, the conventional wisdom was that when they failed to cure, the fault lay with the apothecary, who purportedly had measured the various components improperly.[74]

Samuel Hartlib was still praising coffee in 1659. In a letter dated April 20 of that year, Hartlib wrote to English scholar John Worthington (1618–1671) about a certain Mr. Pococke, likely the English biblical scholar Edward Pococke (1604–1691), who had "lately translated out of Arabick something of an Arabian physician concerning coffee, of which papers, because he will suffer very few to printed, I enclose you one."[75] The letter does not name the physician, although Hartlib may have been referring to Ibn Sina's *Canon*. This quote suggests that Hartlib, who recognized that Sina's *Canon* was still widely consulted throughout seventeenth century Europe, did not know that the ninth-century physician was not an Arab. It is likely Hartlib assumed that because Sina hailed from the Islamic world and the *Canon* had originally been written in Arabic that Sina must have been an Arab, when he was in fact Persian. Pococke likely did recognize the religious and ethnic diversity of Sina's time, as he had translated other tracts from the medieval Arab world, including an Arabic commentary on the *Mishnah* by the Jewish philosopher Moses Maimonides (1135–1204). What Hartlib did rightly note in his letter to Worthington was Sina's claim about the medicinal benefits of coffee. Hartlib does not mention coffee as a social beverage among the Turks, perhaps because he never traveled east and therefore had to depend on the descriptors of others for his knowledge.

The influence of Hartlib's association of coffee with the Arabs and Turks of the eastern world would come to play a part in shaping English ideas about both. Writer and scholar John Evelyn (1620–1706), asserted that wherever coffee went it would prove to be the source of both delight and dismay: "there were 30 or 40 young men in Orders in his parish . . . who [were] reproved by him on occasion for frequenting taverns or coffee-houses."[76] These references, however brief, illustrate the prevailing idea in the England of the mid to late seventeenth century that coffee was closely connected to the habits of people living in the East.

## Concluding Thoughts:
## Conflict, Cooperation, and Coffee

Before we leave markets alive with people and products, wealthy homes inhabited by collectors who displayed treasures from abroad, and the pleasures of fireside travel, the story of coffee and the early modern social world it was instrumental in creating invites a reexamination of the relationships that existed among the three faiths that trace their religious descent to a man from the ancient Sumerian city of Ur. The story of coffee and the goods that preceded it clamor for a fresh investigation into the nature of the ties that both bind and divide Jews, Christians, and Muslims. While the discussion of this chapter centers on the cooperative relationships that existed between Europe and the world on the eastern side of the Mediterranean Sea, it is best not to idealize ostensibly more peaceful times. Conflict, often bloody, has also been very much a part of this multidirectional history, made even more opaque by an othering of the eastern world.

Little interested in colonizing their neighbors, the Semitic Phoenicians established centers throughout the Mediterranean world and in time forged a great commercial empire. The Romans, who sought the eastern aromatics and silks the Phoenicians purveyed, used their powerful army to conquer much of the territory with which Rome had trading relations. Beginning in the eighth century, the armies of Islam spread a new faith that would ultimately reach as far west as France, only to be halted by the military commander Charles Martel (686–741) at the Battle of Tours in 732. As armed efforts so often do, Muslim advances aimed at bringing people into Dar al-Islam (the House of Islam) had the side effect of opening possibilities for trade and commerce that had not previously existed. Over 350 years later, the Catholic Church—with the support of knights and the nobility—began the first of what would be nine Crusades that were waged between 1095 and 1271 for control of a land sacred to all three Abrahamic faiths. Although they did not succeed with their official goal, the Crusades proved profitable indeed for the enterprising merchants who earned wealth both from outfitting the crusaders and, more important, from the traffic in luxury goods made available to them as a result of this contact. Members of the three main monotheistic faiths also lived together and interacted harmoniously for centuries, if not always extending to one another political and social equality, as the case of Spain illustrates.

From the eighth century to 1492, the mingling of peoples in Spain resulted in exchanges and advances in science, technology, literature, food, and food production. Particularly relevant to coffee were the exchanges in agricultural science inaugurated when the Andalusian region of Spain became home to literate farmers of all three faiths. From the eighth century onward, such farmers relied on a first-century work, *De re rustica* (On agriculture), for information about farm management as the Phoenicians conducted it and on an eighth-century text, *Agricultura nabatea*, which contained even older farming methods from the Negev.[77] Later, when the first coffee plants were smuggled out of Yemen, it is reasonable to suggest that those who intended to grow their own plants had acquired at least rudimentary knowledge of the techniques necessary for successful cultivation.

Once people began sharing knowledge of farming, the acceptance of new tastes was not far behind. Food, notes Massimo Montanari, has always been a "fertile area of exchange," that culminates in a "taste for diversity."[78] This taste was not simply about food; it was about all of the ways early modern Europeans consumed the East in new forms of art and architecture, in the pages of travel narratives, with the collection of artifacts, with the acquisition of new languages, and in luxurious adornments for the body. A space for coffee and its attendant social value could be realized only in a world that was open to changing tastes, in which people sought to fulfill desires for the material, the literary, the sensory, and the wonderful. This consumption also had a more sinister side, for it led to ideas of a treacherous eastern other. In the views of Europeans, this other might be gracious in a coffeehouse that also played host to those who looked to indulge in stronger drugs or satisfy sexual desires that, while not unknown, horrified their European guests, all of which was reported to family and neighbors back home. It comes as little surprise, then, that the East evolved into a fearsome yet compelling locale where the air carried both the Muslim call to prayer and the aroma of spices, coffee, and perfume; the daily rhythms of life moved at a different pace; and all the women became Shahrazad.

That world would likely have been something of a revelation, in both cultural and material terms, to those whose families had lived in the Near and Middle East for millennia. The world of goods did not just belong to early moderns in Europe. As George Clunas rightly reminds us, "The luxuries being traded were at the same time objects of consumption in the places where they were produced."[79] Silks imported from China were also worn there, and the sugar Europeans enjoyed also sweetened the diets of people in the Middle East. Aromatics, perfume, and coffee were all part of the daily lives of the people who produced and exported them. In some instances, they were luxury goods even in their places of origin —not everyone in China could afford to dress in luxurious fabrics. In other instances, however, average people had access to the same goods those of higher social and economic strata enjoyed. In the case of coffee, it was not the luxury beverage in the Near and Middle East that it would start as in Europe.

Finally, for Europeans to properly enjoy coffee, they needed knowledge that originated in the East. Proper knowledge of how to roast the beans and then submerge the grounds in hot water to make a cup of coffee could be gained only from a small number of sources: from those who had traveled to the East to satisfy some personal or religious longing, from those who had business that took them to the East, or through direct contact with merchants and others from the coffee-drinking world who traveled to Europe.

The historic connections between the eastern and western Mediterranean that fill this chapter can still be seen in so many ways today. I am always struck by the comforting familiarity of the geography of food. The landscapes of Israel, the Palestinian territories, and the coastal regions of Morocco, Italy, Spain, and France are constant reminders of a shared

Mediterranean culinary history. Terraces of grapes and olives on both sides of the Mediterranean yield harvests that grace the tables of my Italian family and my Levantine and North African friends, as does the coffee without which no meal is complete.

Coffee's acceptance in Europe, despite its pungent smell, initially disagreeable bitter taste, and unfamiliar physical effects was so far reaching that by the 1640s imports had reached the status of pepper, the leading spice import during the fifteenth and sixteenth centuries. As many as seventeen million pounds moved through the Ottoman Empire on its way to Venice and then to France, England, and elsewhere.[80] The challenge of uncovering the history of coffee and the coffeehouse to illuminate its pivotal role in changing patterns of socialization in Italy and Europe comes in part from the complex history in which this book situates it. From the previous chapters that located it in ancient texts to the travel narratives of this chapter, which place coffee as one of many items within the universe of early modern acquisition and consumption, it would seem that coffee made an easy transition to life in the West. In the next chapter, the story moves away from coffee as a curative, as an example of the otherness of the East, as the reason for the establishment of the coffeehouse, and as an edible that excited the palates of curious and acquisitive Europeans. This part of the tale focuses on the anxieties that the look and physical effects of coffee excited among both religious and secular elements of society from Mecca to Venice to London to colonies in North America and all points in between.

## CHAPTER 5

# Anxieties about Coffee

*For they said, apart from its being roasted, the fact that it is drunk in gatherings, passed from hand to hand, is suggestive of loose living.*

—Katip Çelebi[1]

*Retailing of coffee might be an innocent trade, but as it was used to nourish sedition, spread lies, and scandalise great men, it might also be a common nuisance."*

—Judicial Pronouncement, London 1675[2]

## The First Cries of Opposition

As the quotes above suggest, the joys of coffee and the amiable pursuits of the coffeehouse did not inspire the goodwill of all. Indeed, within the context of coffee's place in the history of globalization, the controversies that surrounded the institution and led to the attempts of religious and lay authorities to regulate the coffeehouse serve as reminders that no history is entirely positive. That a well-loved local coffeehouse would today be the target of outside efforts at control might well strike us as surprising. In today's social environment, such places seldom arouse the suspicions of local law enforcement, government officials, or religious leaders. Indeed, men and women who lead congregations have long encouraged their members to remain after mass or services for coffee and community. The situation was quite different in the early centuries of coffee consumption, when it was not immediately accepted in public venues in the East or in the West. Rather, vociferous objections to the behaviors that coffeehouse patronage might inspire were voiced across time and cultures. This chapter offers a comparative look at efforts to regulate coffee and the coffeehouse and examines the reasons why they were the source of concern so widely, from members of the religious establishment in the holy city of Mecca to commentators writing about the boisterous cafes of Europe and colonial America.

Questions about whether coffee drinking should be permissible began long before the first shops dedicated to offering the beverage appeared. At the root of the apprehension was coffee's noticeably stimulating effects on the body and the mind. Temporary physical alterations were particularly disconcerting before the early decades of the nineteenth century, for until this time the chemical property that gave coffee its stimulating qualities had not yet been identified. While everyone recognized distinct responses once they had sipped for the first time, possibly a faster heartbeat, jittery fingers, or greater clarity of thought, what caused the increase in mental alertness and the accompanying physical jolt was as alarming for some as it was thrilling for others. An understanding of the science behind coffee's effects on humans and animals began with the work of the German chemist Friedlieb Ferdinand Runge (1795–1867). In 1819, Runge first identified a "pure compound" that he named *kaffein*.[3] In 1895, another German chemist, Emil Fischer, built on Runge's work, completing the "first total synthesis of caffeine."[4] Fischer went on to win the 1902 Nobel Prize in Chemistry for his research on the chemistry of sugar. It is likely that the lack of a scientific understanding of coffee's biology was what led to the first vociferous debates in the Middle and Near East. Although adherents of all three Abrahamic faiths enjoyed coffee, the alarm was first sounded in the sixteenth century by the religious leaders and scholars of Islam who lived in Mecca.

## Antagonism and Failure in the Islamic World

Among the Islamic prescriptions that govern daily life are two that speak directly to food and drink, specifically the prohibitions against drinking alcohol and eating pork. Kosher laws in Judaism also forbid the eating of certain foods, including pork, but do not forbid alcohol. These restrictions are generally absent in Christianity, save for the denominations that abstain from meat on Fridays during Lent and the Protestant churches that discourage the use of alcoholic beverages and/or hot drinks such as coffee and tea. Given that coffee and the coffeehouse originated in a place where Muslims have long been in the majority, this chapter begins with the work of the distinguished scholar of Islam, John L. Esposito. Offering a trajectory of coffee's influence in the Middle East, Esposito explains that in the fifteenth century, demand for coffee had increased enough to make it a lucrative crop for Yemeni growers and merchants. One century later, Yemeni merchants facilitated its spread into Egypt, Syria, Turkey, and Persia. By the end of the sixteenth century, coffee could be found all over the Islamic world.[5] As a trade commodity, the beans initially raised few, if any, concerns among local leaders or members of the *ulama* (the community of religious scholars).

The consumption of coffee was quite another matter. Unsure if coffee should be forbidden to the devout, religious intellectuals looked to Islamic teachings regarding food for answers. This effort began with the revelations of the Qur'an, given to the Prophet Muhammad between 610 and his death in 11/632 and later elaborated on by the various schools of jurisprudence that arose after Muhammad's death, four Sunni and three Shi'a.[6] Since all schools of Islamic jurisprudence regard the Qur'an as their foundational text, supplemented with the Hadith, the reports that pertain to the sayings and actions of the Prophet Muhammad I present here examples from the Qur'an to which religious experts turned as they reached their decisions about whether to affirm or condemn any new food or drink. For example, Surah 36, entitled Ya-Sin (a title derived from the two letters with which the surah begins, يس) contains two of the verses that are often consulted in discussions of proper diet:

> In the lifeless earth we make alive, and out of which we bring forth grain, whereof they may eat and [how] we make gardens of date-palms and vines [grow] thereon, and cause springs to gush [forth] within it so that they may eat of the fruit thereof.[7]

This passage has been interpreted as a directive regarding the produce from the earth that may be eaten, particularly grain. Other verses speak more directly about what is forbidden, such as Surah 6, Al-An am (The Cattle), verse 118, which says "eat, then of that over which God's name has been pronounced," an element of the proper slaughter of animals that render them allowed (*halal*).[8] Verse 145 of the same surah advises more specifically: "I do not find anything forbidden to eat . . . unless it be carrion, or blood poured forth, or the flesh of swine—for that, behold, is loathsome."[9] Leaders later looked to these sources as they sought legitimacy for their efforts to regulate coffeehouses in the Islamic world, although the absence of a direct mention of coffee made the task a bit more challenging for them.

The first problem was the appearance of coffee, which some scholars likened to the look of wine. Closely related to how coffee looked were the invigorating effects it had on the body that, while not inebriating, did cause physiological alterations. Wine commonly appears in pre-Islamic Arabian poetry, and during the time of Muhammad inhabitants of Mecca and Medina drank wine, most commonly one made from fermented dates, as grapes were scarce and difficult to grow in the desert climes of Arabia. Indeed, the extract from Surah 36 might allude to the acceptability of wine, as it urges the faithful to grow palms and vines so they can eat the fruit they produce. Another interpretation rejects this reading and instead sees these verses as giving Muslims permission to eat grapes in their whole and unfermented state but not in any other form. Further complicating the matter, a prohibition on wine consumption was not part of the Prophet Muhammad's early teachings; that came later in his prophetic life, after he observed occasions of public drunkenness and the resulting scandals. In the wake of these events, Muhammad received new revelations that abrogated the early ones and resulted in the prohibition of wine and other intoxicants. One of these later revelations goes as follows, also from Surah Al-An'am (The Cattle): "They will ask thee about intoxicants and games of chance. Say: 'In both there is great evil as well as some benefit for man: but the evil which they cause is greater than the benefit which they bring.'"[10] A clearer prohibition appears in Surah 5, Al-Maa Idah (Spoils of War), verse 90: "O You who have attained to faith! Intoxicants, and games of chance, and idolatrous practices, and the divining of the future are but a loathsome evil of Satan's doing."[11] From these passages comes *nabidh*, a term that refers to a ban on all fermented drinks because they result in inebriation.[12]

With the Qur'an and the Hadith as starting points, deciding how to classify coffee and later determining the legality of coffeehouses were among the "great legal, intellectual, and literary obsessions of the age" throughout the Islamic world.[13] Much of the problem for scholars who sought to rule on the permissibility of coffee in light of both revelation and tradition was the fact that the diet of the people of Arabia during the time of Muhammad did not include coffee. This meant that nothing in the Qur'an or any examples from the Prophet's life could be used as reference points. This put coffee, at least initially, in rather ambiguous beverage territory as leaders struggled with both its physical manifestations and its wine-resembling opaque appearance.

The lack of clear direction from religious texts, the reported words and actions of the Prophet, and the rulings of the first four caliphs, often referred to as the Rightly Guided, meant that legal scholars took the matter of coffee drinking seriously, weighing a number of considerations against one another. As just one example, while experts acknowledged that the taste of coffee bore little resemblance to that of wine, it did have the capacity to alter human behavior. Therefore, members of the ulama had to ask themselves important questions such as whether coffee was a devilish and evil intoxicant akin to those warned of in the Qur'an and therefore deserving of a place with wine and other available inebriants such as hashish, opium, and qat.[14] Or was coffee generally harmless, as drinking it did not appear to lead people to commit acts of impropriety?[15] In search of support of their position that coffee was not permissible, the more conservative religious scholars of the fifteenth and sixteenth centuries looked to one particular Hadith that they claimed proved that any food or beverage that altered human physiology was illicit: "Every intoxicant is *khamr*, and every *khamr* is unlawful."[16] Others dismissed the idea that coffee was *khamr*, arguing that it was never explicitly barred in the Qur'an or the Hadith. Among the adherents to this second position were the Sufi of Yemen, who continued to use coffee during their night-time prayers. While it cannot be asserted with certainty, it is possible that the Sufi sought to demonstrate that coffee might not be the sinful drink its critics said it was by continuing to use it.[17]

In time, it was determined that coffee as a beverage was allowed in Islam. This was not the end of its travails, however. The establishment of the first coffeehouses revived past debates. If we accept Esposito's dating of coffee as a desired commodity to the mid-fifteenth century, then it is likely that coffeehouses began to appear sometime between then and 1511. The first documented coffeehouse was in existence by 917/1511 in Mecca. It is this location that helps explain the unwanted attention of religious leaders and the scholarly community that these first coffeehouses garnered.[18] Not the backwater it has been described as before the rise of Islam gave it a new religious significance, Mecca had in fact long been an important stop on the trade routes that joined the southern Arabian Desert to the Mediterranean. In this city, merchants traveling east from Europe met to exchange goods and greetings with their counterparts who had made the journey westward along the Silk Road. During the Roman conquest and into the Byzantine era, Mecca grew in importance as not just a commercial hub, but also as a pre-Islamic religious center, visited by pilgrims who traveled great distances to pay their respects to the gods and goddesses housed in a cube-shaped structure called the Ka'aba (الكعبة).[19] With rise of Islam, Mecca and the Ka'aba gained new religious significance, and the black stone was appropriated by the new faith. According to Islamic tradition, it was Adam who first built a structure around the stone. This original edifice was destroyed in the flood of Noah, which left behind only the foundation. The site continued to grow in importance with Abraham who, it was revealed to Muhammad, rebuilt the shrine, or Ka'aba, over the black stone with the assistance of his son, Ismail. In Islamic tradition, it was this son, not Isaac, that Abraham was later ordered to sacrifice before God stayed his hand. It remains today the site of the hajj, the pilgrimage that is one of the Five Pillars of Islam. All believers must make this journey, if their health and finances allow, at least once in a lifetime.

By the start of the sixteenth century, the Ottoman Turks had gained control of the holy sites in Mecca and Medina. From their capital in Constantinople, the new rulers established their control over both cities and over the annual pilgrimages that yielded great prosperity for the Ottoman royal house but fueled discontent among those who were now dominated by a foreign power. In 917/1511, just as the Ottomans were attempting to gain control over the moral and social lives of the inhabitants of Mecca, a new debate erupted over the city's coffeehouses, resulting in their temporary closure. Much of the information about the resulting prohibition that ultimately failed comes from the writings of several jurists who were opposed to coffee consumption.[20] These men were joined in by the city's *muhtasib* (محتسيب), an official charged with regulating commercial activity and safeguarding the public interest in the marketplace. One version of the story has it that the governor of Mecca, Khair Bey (d. 1522), was returning from his prayers when he encountered men in the midst of a celebration that included the wildly popular drink *qahwa* (قهوة). Disturbed to learn that coffee was being enjoyed in establishments that ostensibly served up other illicit delights, the bey reportedly scolded the revelers and disbanded the gathering. Apparently still troubled the next morning, the bey convened a meeting of the ulama to discuss the question of coffee. The outcome was a failed attempt to rid his city of the coffeehouses.[21] Another report expands on the supposed activities in Mecca's coffeehouses, suggesting that the bey's concerns were more likely fueled by rumors that uncomplimentary references to the governor were originating in these establishments. Yet another version of the story does not directly name Khair Bey as the original instigator of the ban on coffee. In this iteration, two physicians were at the center, having convinced Khair Bey to seek a prohibition on coffee on the grounds of its questionable properties.[22]

Wherever the truth of source of the prohibition lies, all three renderings agree that a hearing was held to debate the matter at which the two physicians decried coffee as "harmful to the well-balanced temperament" and presented medical evidence to support their assertions.[23] This testimony, perhaps along with Khair Bey's desire to prevent people from gathering to defame him, ultimately led the jurists to conclude that Islam forbids coffee drinking and by extension gatherings in public establishments dedicated to the purpose of drinking coffee. Taking advantage of a ruling in his favor, the bey promptly announced the official closure of all coffeehouses.[24] Controversial from the beginning, the prohibition proved impossible to enforce. Some responsibility for this failure belongs to religious scholars who had attended the hearing but did not concur that coffeehouses should be illegal. In addition, it is possible, even probable, that while the official coffeehouses were closed, people continued to come together for coffee and socializing activities in other locations. Because there was no firm religious support for the ban and because it was impossible to regulate all social gatherings in the city, the coffeehouses of Mecca reopened, and well-known patterns of socializing resumed. For a time, it seemed that the question was resolved in favor of the general public, at least until 932/1525–933/1526, when another controversy developed. This time, a jurist who was visiting Mecca heard allegations that unwholesome activities were taking place in the city's coffeehouses and urged a reconsideration of the ban. A representative of the Ottoman government once again attempted to close the city's coffeehouses, but city officials upheld the legality of drinking coffee in private. This closure proved no more successful than the first effort and within a year the coffeehouses in Mecca had once again opened. No future attempts were made to close them.[25]

News of the two unsuccessful closures in Mecca did not deter other places from attempting actions of their own against coffeehouses. In the 1500s, 906–1008 AH, several cities launched efforts to stop the consumption of coffee entirely. In part, these decisions were rendered after complaints by local imams, who based their decision on the ambiguous legal status of coffee in the Qur'an and their own observations that more men gathered in coffeehouses than went to the mosques for prayers.[26]

In 922/1516, the Ottoman Empire under Selim I (875/1470–926/1520) added Egypt and the Levant to the territory under its dominion, a move that brought administrative efforts to regulate the coffeehouses of their new holdings. This preoccupation with coffeehouses continued into the latter half of the 1600s, as evidenced by the "Mühimme Defteri," or "Register of Important (i.e. Public) Affairs," for Palestine between the years 960/1552 and 1024/1615.[27] While few of the original reports and petitions to the government in Constantinople for this period have survived the test of time, 150,000–200,000 copies of the "Mühimme Defteri" remain, including two firmans, or decrees, regarding coffeehouses in what was then referred to as Palestine, a territory that encompassed present-day Lebanon, Syria, Israel, the Palestinian territories, and south beyond the Tigris and Euphrates Rivers.[28] The earliest of the two decrees was issued from Jerusalem, on December 3, 943/1565, the final year of the reign of Selim I's son, Suleiman the Magnificent (r. 926/1520–974/1566). The Ottomans had been ruling Palestine for almost fifty years by the time of this "Order to the Cadi of Jerusalem," suggesting that Ottoman officials had long been observing the culture of the coffeehouse throughout their vast empire.[29] This order provides support for the notion that objections to coffee and coffeehouses were almost always framed within a religious context and were meant to apply only to Muslims. The order decried the calamitous deterioration in piety as men abandoned worship in favor of congenial discourse with friends. It would appear from these orders that in the centuries before coffeehouses were established, attentiveness to prayers was paramount, while after the institutions were established men cast aside their religious obligations and the coffeehouse became a space for the worst sort of behavior. Such piety may or may not have actually been the norm. Nevertheless, volume V, number 612 of the "Mühimme" states in part,

> Whereas from olden times there was no coffee-house in Jerusalem and the local inhabitants were assiduous in [their] divine worship and pious devotion at the five times [of daily prayer], coffee-houses have [now] been newly established at five places. They are the meeting places of rascals and ungodly people [who] day and night do not cease to act wickedly and mischievously, perniciously and refractorily, [thus] keeping the Muslims from pious devotion and divine worship. [In your opinion] it is [therefore] necessary to remove, eradicate, and extirpate the coffee-houses from these venerable places.[30]

The decree continues, "I have commanded that you [the qadi] shall personally attend to the matter with diligence and eliminate such coffee-houses."[31] There are no reports of just how the qadi attempted to deal with the situation. As coffeehouses remained, however, it is likely that the Jerusalem ban of 1565 was no more successful than previous prohibitions had been.

In an apparent acknowledgment that coffeehouses were impossible to close completely, on July 22, 963/1584, the Ottoman authorities in Palestine made a change in policy in Gaza, a twenty-five-mile strip of land along the Mediterranean Sea approximately sixty miles from Jerusalem.[32] Inhabited since the fourth millennium BCE, the great harbor at Gaza City was once one of the most important ports on the eastern side of the Mediterranean. The following "Order to the Cadi and the Bey of Gaza" illustrates the new attitude toward the coffeehouse,

> The bearer [of this], a person named Badr b. ar-Rajabi (?), has come [to Istanbul] and has stated that he lives in the town of Gaza, [where] he has opened a coffee-house and [in this way] is working to make his living. Though he is not doing harm to anyone and though two other coffee-houses are doing business in the small town mentioned, a fief-holder named Ahmed has now stopped [him], telling [him] not to do [such] business. A firman has therefore been written to the effect that, if no harm is done by him to anyone's property or waqf or to the imperial domains, he shall not be interfered with.[33]

This change in position raises questions about what may have caused a softening of Ottoman policy. One explanation for the more moderate stance is the passage of time. By July 1584, Murad III (r. 982/1574–1004/1595) was the head of a sultanate that was still enjoying temporary control of the Mediterranean despite the defeat of his predecessor, Selim II (r. 974/1566–982/1574), at the Battle of Lepanto in 979/1571, when the Ottomans were defeated by the forces of the Holy League.[34] It seems that with the benefit of hindsight and aware of the failures of his predecessors to prohibit coffeehouses, Murad III was willing to accept a more measured approach, at least in the territories outside Turkey that were under Ottoman domination. Another plausible reason for the decision is that it was easier for the officials of Murad III in Gaza to allow proprietors the freedom to operate their coffee businesses provided no religious or imperial properties were damaged.

The problem with this interpretation is that Ottoman attempts to regulate coffeehouses elsewhere continued into the next century. This leads to the possibility that the Gaza decree does not represent a move toward greater tolerance of coffeehouses in Ottoman domains but was rather a method of dealing with one specific owner. Allowing the Badr named in the firman to continue as the owner of a coffeehouse would make him an easy target for prosecution in the event of misbehavior and serve as evidence of a lenient Ottoman stance toward well-managed coffeehouses. Additionally, since the owner in question was working and providing for himself, and likely for a family, Ottoman officials may have seen no advantage to closing his business, thus making him dependent on the government or members of the local community for survival. The ease of identifying and prosecuting a specific person in the event of misdeeds, instead of punishing all coffeehouse owners, demonstrated that the Ottoman occupiers were munificent. This avoided the embarrassment of another failed coffeehouse ban and allowed the owner to keep his livelihood provided he followed the prescriptions of the decree.

Just short of 100 years later, Murad IV (r. 1033/1623–1050/1640) claimed the Ottoman throne and inaugurated a new round of attacks on what he believed were the corrupting vices in his empire. Murad IV not only ordered that all coffeehouses be torn down but also forbade the use of tobacco and opium.[35] The intellectual Katib Çelebi, reiterating Murad IV's concerns, noted that while the sultan's will prevailed inside the capital, his wishes were generally ignored in remote villages.[36] In his commentary on coffee, Çelebi wrote:

> For they said, apart from its being roasted, the fact that it is drunk in gatherings, passed from hand to hand, is suggestive of loose living. One coffee-house was opened after another, and men would gather together, with great eagerness and enthusiasm, to drink. Drug-addicts in particular, finding it a life-giving thing, which increased their pleasure, were willing to die for a cup.
>
> Story-tellers and musicians diverted their people from their employments, and working for one's living fell into disfavour. Moreover the people, from prince to Beygar, amused themselves with knifing one another. Towards the end of 1042/1633, the late Ghazi Sultan Murad, becoming aware of the situation, promulgated an edict, out of regard and compassion for the people, to this effect: Coffee-houses throughout the Guarded Domains shall be dismantled and not opened hereafter. Since then, the coffee-houses of the capital have been as desolate as the heart of the ignorant. In

ANXIETIES ABOUT COFFEE

the hope that they might be reopened, their proprietors did not dismantle them for a while, but merely closed them. Later the majority, if not all of them, were dismantled and turned into other kinds of shops. But in cities and towns outside Istanbul, they are opened just as before. As has been said above, such things do not admit of a perpetual ban.[37]

As Çelebi explains, despite disapproval from Constantinople, bans on coffeehouses in all territories of the empire finally ended in the late 1600s, in part because the task of policing them proved too onerous but also because coffeehouse proprietors gave generous charitable donations to their local mosques.[38]

The language of discontent that began with Khair Bey in Mecca in 917/1511 and was echoed over and over again by religious and secular leaders for over 150 years, illustrates the ambiguous status of coffee. It also says something about the place of religion in the early modern eastern Mediterranean as belief came into direct conflict with the marked changes in the social patterns of daily life that appeared with the emergence and popularity of coffeehouses, which were patronized by men of all ages and social strata. The rapid growth in popularity of a place that served a dubious, even potentially illicit, beverage would have raised more than an eyebrow among the leaders of the Islamic faithful. Consumers would, at least at first, have listened to the prohibitions of scholars and the mosque would also have feared punishment for wrongdoing at the hands of the government. As the evidence reveals, however, religious proclamations were not enough to keep men from gathering over coffee to catch up on the latest news, play games such as chess and backgammon, listen to book readings and recitations of the Qur'an, and enjoy entertainments such as puppet theater, despite vociferous denunciations that coffeehouses were direct threats to the moral fiber and stability of cities and towns from Aden to Constantinople.[39]

Secular authorities also relied on the discourse of Islam, although this would have had less resonance with the Christians and Jews who made their home throughout the empire and who likely also sought out the diversions of the city's coffeehouses. Successful closing of the troublesome coffeehouse, even if it had been a real possibility, would have required more decisive intervention from the Ottoman Porte, whose burden it was to convince patrons during the mid-sixteenth century that coffeehouses were truly the havens of vice and immorality they were purported to be.

It was not enough to complain that coffee lured Muslim men away from their prayers. Those in opposition had to prove their conviction that the coffeehouse tempted men of all three faiths into a debauchery that threatened their salvation.

It was masculine public space in Arabia, the Ottoman Empire, and the eastern Mediterranean that was at the center of coffeehouse controversies, enticing "rascals and ungodly people" to enjoy its pleasures.[40] Had coffee remained a beverage that enhanced Sufi worship or continued simply within the confines of private life, it is unlikely that rulers, scholars, and social commentators would have given it much thought once it was declared acceptable in Islam. In short, coffee as a beverage for personal enjoyment was never really the problem. What ignited the passions of both coffeehouse patrons and those who opposed them was what took place in the public locations dedicated to coffee consumption.

The resilience of the coffeehouse may perhaps best be illustrated not by premodern efforts to close them forever but by the reality that they remained as important centers for the dissemination of information into the 1900s. At the turn of the twentieth century, when literacy rates in the Middle East were low, men could go to coffeehouses for a cup and to hear a reading of the newspaper. In later decades, men who could not afford a television sometimes shared the cost of installing one in their favorite coffeehouse. Even today, coffee remains a significant part of societies from the Arabian Peninsula to Turkey. And they are not all just places for male socialization. For example, in Morocco it is possible to find coffeehouses that cater to women and to mixed groups of men and women who wish to gather in coffeehouses for social interaction

The matter of the coffeehouse in the realms of the east had been mostly settled by the latter part of the 1600s. Even if the outcome was not entirely satisfactory for all, the failure of successive coffeehouse prohibitions seems to have convinced leaders and religious authorities that such efforts were futile. That was not the case across the Mediterranean Sea. The hulls of ships arriving from the East bearing coffee also brought the anxieties that coffee and the life of the coffeehouse had unleashed across the sea. Similar fears were to find a new voice, revealing themselves to be almost as problematic in Europe and the Americas as they had been thousands of miles to the east.

## Coffee, Coffeehouses, and Unease Travel West

While the evidence that suggests that multilayered networks of exchange and the tales of merchants and travelers carried knowledge of coffee's stimulating attributes and the rituals of the coffeehouse to curious Europeans some time before the beverage itself arrived, it does not provide clues about why once coffee reached Europe it sparked similar attempts to regulate its public consumption. It is unlikely that details of the coffeehouse bans came to the attention of travelers and merchants during their visits, as most European chroniclers did not possess knowledge of Arabic or Turkish and would thus not have been aware of the debates raging around them. Further, had Europeans known of disputes within religious and municipal circles they most likely would have included such information in their narratives. And yet the condemnations of coffee discussed in this section bear interesting resemblances to those of the bey of Mecca and the officials of the Ottoman Empire. There are several reasons why this might have been the case. Regardless of the location where it was consumed, coffee had the same physical effects on the body. For those who were unfamiliar with the properties of coffee, bursts of caffeine-induced physical and mental energy would likely have raised concerns and invited denunciation. In addition, social gatherings in public spaces attracted the attention of authorities, irrespective of where the gatherings were occurring. And as it had in the Islamic world, coffee raised alarm among religious leaders in some parts of the Christian West. This section attempts to sort out the issue of apprehensions about coffee and its public enjoyment as both moved west into Europe.

Just as there are some entertaining stories about the origins of coffee, the reception of coffee in Europe has a legend of its own. At a time when the Catholic Church was coming to terms with the aftershocks of the Protestant Reformation, which was both a religious and a political movement, Venetian merchants are said to have offered Pope Clement VIII (r. 1592–1605) a distraction from his official duties. Clement VIII began his religious career as a canon lawyer and would therefore have been well educated about the prescriptions of the faith. By the late 1500s, as the coffee trade gained momentum it aroused the suspicions of members of the Catholic clergy who pressed for coffee to be banned and labeled as Satanic. The pope allegedly spared coffee a dire fate when a Venetian trader offered him a cup in 1600.

Lore has it that after taking a sip the pope was persuaded to declare the brew acceptable for two reasons. First, according to the story, Clement VIII declared coffee delicious and suitable for Christian consumption. Second, the leader of the Roman church shared similar concerns with Muslim clerics about the need for sobriety among those they shepherded. In Clement's case, members of his flock generally preferred drinks that were fermented. Recognizing that coffee did not induce drunkenness, the pope gave it his official blessing, and thus another legend in the story of coffee was born.[41]

Not all secular and religious authorities agreed with the pope, particularly as coffeehouses grew in number. Many may have had the same apprehensions as Khair Bey and others, that the coffeehouses of their cities would become centers of dissent, lawful gathering places for troublemakers who met under the guise of socializing. The earliest evidence of such anxieties comes from coffee's first port of call in the West, Venice. The upheavals that ensued throughout Europe over the eighty or so years after Martin Luther nailed his *Ninety-Five Theses* to the door of a church in Wittenberg in 1517 prompted rulers and city residents from to Aachen in western Germany to Venice to seek a redefinition of their relationships with the Church. In response to Protestant challenges from Wittenberg, the hierarchy in Rome convened the nineteenth ecumenical council, commonly known as the Council of Trent, which met three times during the period 1545 to 1563 in the northern Italian town of Trent. While the council condemned the actions of those in revolt against the Church in Rome, it also sought to solidify the teachings of the faith, combat heresy, eradicate superstition, and prosecute witchcraft.[42] The latter two tasks began three years before the council first met at Trent with the establishment of the Roman Inquisition in 1542. Venice, with its thriving port, busy markets, and diverse international community, attracted considerable attention from the Inquisition, and in time a thriving branch of this body operated in the city.

The Inquisition had a direct influence on the rise of the coffeehouse, and a look at this body's other efforts at moral regulation in Venice provides valuable context. The inquisitors, who consisted of six members, three clerical and three lay, met every Tuesday, Thursday, and Saturday. Much of their energy was directed at potential threats to religious practice among Venetian residents, most notably those related to claims of magic and witchcraft. The members of the Venetian Inquisition were so worried about these two matters that in the period 1580 to 1650, they tried over 700 people for offenses related to them.[43] It fell to the three clerical members to determine sentences, while the three lay members were charged with ensuring that the penalties, one of which was execution, were enforced.[44] Venice's lucrative book industry was at the center of fears about the potential for moral decay, and Venice's literary sector illustrates the social environment into which coffee later entered.[45] During the time of Pope Paul IV (1476–1559), attempts to regulate what people read prompted members of the Holy Office to promulgate the first edition of the *Index librorum prohibitorum* (List of prohibited books).

In a city awash in books, policing Venice's booksellers and publishers, not to mention readers, some of whom had amassed great personal libraries, was no easy feat.[46] In the second half of the sixteenth century, approximately 500 Venetian publishers who were active in Venice produced over eight million books.[47] Alarm over what people might read was not new to Venice, as the Church and the Venetian state had historically censored texts for doctrinal and political reasons and for a professed desire to "[protect] public morality."[48] Among the texts deemed most threatening to religious virtue in the seventeenth century, and therefore of greatest interest to the Inquisition, were Jewish texts, the works of the pagan authors of antiquity, and the Qur'an.[49] For example, as early as 1537/1538, the printer Paganino Paganini and his son Alessandro Paganino, also a printer, produced the first printed edition of the Qur'an in Arabic, of which only one copy has survived.

According to Italian scholar Angela Nuovo, this Qur'an belonged for a time to Teseo Ambrogio degli Albonesi of Pavia (d. 1540). Sometime in the latter half of the sixteenth century, inquisitor Arcangelo Mancasula, vicar of the Holy Office of Cremona, possessed it, although how it ended up in with him is unclear.[50] Throughout the latter half of the sixteenth century, the attention directed at regulating readership and printing led to the large-scale destruction of banned titles. However, instead of eradicating Venetian society of them, such policies only drove commerce in these texts underground.[51] By the end of that century, the Venetian government, determined to exercise greater control over the ethical, religious, and social lives of its citizens and decrease the influence of Rome, had enacted regulations of its own that effectively limited the interference of the papacy in Venice, although by this time much damage had been done to the city's literary culture.[52]

Books were not the only objects of the inquisitors' attention. By the first decades of the 1600s, the apothecary shops that abounded in the city had attracted their share of unwanted notice because inquisitors suspected they were sources of more than just remedies. After coffee beans came to Venice, evidence of the product appears among the inventories of apothecaries, acquired from Venetian merchants or possibly from the Ottoman merchants doing business in the city.[53] When the first coffee beans arrived in Venice around 1570, there was already a significant community of Turkish merchants who lived and worked from a house designated by the *signoria*. This community was located in the area of the Rialto, not for convenience of the merchants but so Venetian officials could control their activities. These Turkish residents are most likely the earliest source of the beans made available to local apothecaries.[54] On one level, jars of coffee beans for sale on apothecary shelves would have attracted little notice. Physicians and other purveyors of medicines would have known of coffee's medicinal uses, and the presence of coffee among the other remedies dispensed in such shops would not, upon first consideration, have seemed a threat to urban stability.

The problem, at least for the inquisitors of Venice, was what took place inside at least some of the city's apothecary shops, which had long been noted as places to acquire a number of eastern products. For example, inquisition records from the year 1571 demonstrate that incense, which was acceptable for use in Catholic churches, had also been used in one instance to drive the devil out of a woman named Lucretia and in another instance to heal a woman who was reported to the Holy Office after expressing her belief that she had been possessed by the spirit of a dragon.[55] Coffee was also found among the inventories of apothecaries, garnering new attention for the shop owners in a city where public venues for socializing did not exist until the mid-seventeenth century. As men commonly gathered at the shops of their local druggists, these locales emerged as increasingly popular venues for assembling and eventually became places to also enjoy drinking coffee. As Filippo de Vivo explains, apothecary shops were venues for "sociability and leisure, comfortable places for gathering, conversing, and exchanging news," a fact that was not lost on proprietors, who may well have begun serving coffee up as an enhancement to the pleasures of lively conversation.[56]

Determined to control the spread of heresy and political instability and to police the dissemination of information and regulate what people were reading, Venetian inquisitors often scrutinized apothecaries for evidence that proprietors had intentionally turned their shops into centers for discussion of subversive and unorthodox ideas. Acutely aware of the potential for apothecary shops to become so much more than places where people could procure the medicines they needed, the Holy Office at times sent spies to apothecary shops it had determined were particularly worrisome, targeting proprietors.[57] Those who sold coffee beans also knew how to prepare a proper cup, opening up the possibility that these shops were the precursors of European coffeehouses, intermediaries between coffee consumption in private homes and public coffeehouses.

It might be said that in Italy, as in the Muslim world, religion was a primary force in the conflicts that arose between those for whom the coffeehouse became an integral part of daily life and those who would have preferred its demise.[58] Despite literary and other treatises that suggest that as early as the 1570s there was growing interest among Europeans about coffeehouses as places for gathering, fear of unwanted attention from the Inquisition likely contributed significantly to the rather belated opening of the first public coffeehouse in Venice, which, according to some sources, happened in 1645, just a few years after the inquisitors departed from Venice.[59] Other writers say that the first coffeehouse opened significantly later, in 1682.[60] Regardless of the exact date, although the office of the Inquisition had closed its doors when coffeehouses finally reached Venice, that does not mean that they had a clear path. Far from warmly welcoming the new institution, members of the Venetian government attempted to use their powers to restrict all unregulated social outlets that they believed threatened their civic goals in much the same way as they endeavored to police access to books. As one commentator urged, even though Venetian authorities were unwilling to close all coffeehouses, they should at least " not allow of any Coffee-houses in the City, that are able to contain great numbers of People."[61] In other words, Venetian officials, for the sake of peace and harmony in their city, would do well to limit the number of people who could gather simultaneously in a coffeehouse. Over 100 years later little had changed, as is illustrated by a report from July 1779, in which a coffee maker, or *caffettiere*, reported that the French ambassador had stopped for a quarter of an hour in his *bottega*, or shop, and had inquired about how the Venetian government regulated such shops.[62]

Not surprisingly, despite the efforts of religious and secular authorities, attempts to regulate coffeehouses were no more successful in Venice than they had been in the Ottoman and Arab worlds, and they became embedded in the daily lives of Venetians.

It was not just Venetians who were embracing the coffee habit. An article in the *Journal of the Society of Arts* claims that the drink first came to England with a Mr. Daniel Edwards, who "returned from Greek city of Smyrna in 1652, and brought with him to London a Ragusian Greek named Pasqua Rossée." According to the article, Rossée made coffee for Edwards, his employer, each morning, a service that attracted the curiosity of Edwards's neighbors and friends, who wanted to try the drink and to know "the nature and origin of the beverage supplied." Edwards, who soon grew weary of so many guests in his home, remedied the problem by opening "public rooms" in St. Michael's Alley, Cornhill, in central London, where Rossée "would make and sell coffee to the public." It was not long before the coffee habit spread, bringing with it attention from English authorities who found the new establishments "distasteful." By 1663, all coffeehouses had to be licensed by the "General Quarter Sessions for the county in which they were kept." Twelve years later, coffeehouses as places for "social meetings, and eventually for political ones" concerned King Charles II (1630–1685). Suspicious that the real purpose men gathered was to organize his overthrow, in 1675 Charles II ordered the "close of the coffee-houses altogether."[63] The proclamation states:

> Whereas it is most apparent that the Multitude of Coffee-houses of late years set up and kept within this kingdom . . . have produced very evil and dangerous effects; as well as for that many Tradesmen and others do herein mis-spend much of their time . . . the Chief Magistrates in all cities and towns . . . [shall] recall and make void all Licenses at any time granted, for selling or Retailing of any Coffee Chocolet, Sherbett, or Tea."[64]

Not surprisingly, Charles II's ban on coffeehouses met the same fate as those that preceded it elsewhere. The proclamation noted that the ban was to take effect on January 10, 1676, but it was withdrawn two days before that, on January 8.

## Concluding Thoughts: The Acceptance of Coffee

Although King Charles II was likely unaware of it, his proclamation illustrates that apprehensions regarding coffee drinking transcended religion and culture. Whether coffee was served in Constantinople, Jerusalem, London, or Venice, its reputation as an instigator that lured men to engage in dangerous talk that might result in even more treacherous actions followed coffee wherever it went. Leaders feared the plotting of violence that would mean the upending of the political and religious status quo. The subtext of the bans suggests a certain perplexity among those in positions of authority. They seem almost mystified by the power of coffee to draw men out of their homes and into public shops, where they might, or might not, engage in all manner of mischief. Leaders appear to wonder what made coffee drinking a social event, and as the answer was not apparent, they saw no recourse but to issue sweeping pronouncements that called for the monitoring and often the closure of coffeeshops.

The next chapter examines the devotion that coffee garnered among the populace, an affection that made prohibitions against it impossible to sustain. As dedication to coffee drinking in commercial establishments grew, new patterns of socialization also arose. In England, these new patterns were evident shortly after the first coffeehouse opened in 1650.[65] The effects of coffee on patterns of socialization had been observed elsewhere, particularly in Venice, some years earlier, as men, and later women, discovered that eating and drinking outside the home presented opportunities to escape their regular responsibilities from time to time.

## CHAPTER 6

# Coffee and New Patterns of Socialization

*They have in Turkey a Drink called Coffee, made of a Berry of the same name as black as Soot, and of a strong scent, but not aromatical, which they take, beaten into powder, in Water as hot as they can drink it. And they take it, and sit at it in their Coffeehouses, which are like our Taverns. This Drink comforteth the Brain and Heart, and helpeth Digestion.*

—Sir Francis Bacon, 1627[1]

*Wherever it has been introduced it has spelled revolution. It has been the world's most radical drink in that its function has always been to make people think.*

—William Harrison Ukers, 1922[2]

## Coffee Embraced

In 1669, the Turkish ambassador Suleiman Aga captured the notice of the people of Paris when he brought coffee with him on a mission to the court of Louis XIV (1638–1715). It was not long before the beverage had enchanted the people of the city. Throughout the seventeenth century, more and more people embraced coffee. Europeans began imitating their Italian and Eurasian neighbors, congregating in cafés and coffeehouses with family, friends, neighbors, and business associates, a cup of the strong brew in hand. This chapter demonstrates that the sociability of the coffeehouse is a borrowed or more accurately an appropriated form of interaction that was bound up in new habits of consumption and expressed in the adoption of the material and the intellectual production of distant places. During this century, coffee also contributed in distinct ways to evolving European notions about peoples they could conceive of as exotic others because they lived at great cultural and geographic distances from Europe. The chapter emphasizes that the coffeehouse, an "essentially Muslim establishment," was an import from the East, creatively reimagined in the West to suit the desires of consumers for new modes of social engagement in the public sphere.[3] Beginning in the seventeenth century, the coffeehouse became part of European efforts to craft a perceived chaotic eastern exoticism into something less unruly, something more "civilized." Issue will be taken in this chapter with the notion that the coffeehouses of the West were essentially divorced from those of the East. Rather, I argue that, first, coffeehouses from London to Venice did not spring up primarily in response to the cultural changes that were taking place in Europe, and second, that the coffeehouses of the western world were much more than chances for Europeans to experiment in the ways of the East. For reasons explored in this chapter, the coffeehouses of Ottoman Turkey, the Levant, and Arabia proved to be useful imports as people in other parts of the world developed innovative ways of thinking about the role and function of social space. At the same time, the thoughts of those who wrote about coffeehouses provided the language that future intellectuals would use to develop the ideas that would ultimately become what Edward Said identified as Orientalism. First, however, the chapter explores some history of the consumption of food and beverages outside the home.

## Dining Out in the Premodern World

An ethos of dining out, meeting for a coffee, or gathering with friends for a drink did not exist on either side of the Mediterranean until the first coffeehouses of Arabia in the early sixteenth century. This was not the case in China, Japan, and India. As it turns out, the history of dining out in eastern and southern Asia has a place in the story of coffee.

In the eight century of the Common Era, the Buddhist monk Lu Yü (733–804) wrote the *Classic of Tea*, in which he explored topics ranging from how to brew a proper cup to literary and poetic references to the beverage. Invoking Chinese myth, Lu explained that tea was "discovered by an emperor of the third millennium B.C.E, Shen Nung, also known as the Divine Husbandman."[4] Shen's encounter with tea took place when he came across a burning camellia bush, "to which tea is very closely related botanically, when he began to marvel at the aroma which assailed him. Understanding its source, he then introduced tea and its cultivation to his people."[5]

Indian and Japanese Buddhists tell a different story of how humans discovered tea, one in which the protagonist was an "early patriarch who fell asleep against his intent."[6] Their legend continues:

> When he awoke, he cut off his eyelids to thwart his enemy sleep. However, when the eyelids struck the ground, tea plants sprang up in their place. Thus was born an antidote to sleep with which one could [find] solace[in] the midnight hours without resort to the rigorous measures of Bodhi Dharma.[7]

From at least the sixth century of the Common Era onward, tea replaced both yogurt and water drinks at monasteries and in villages throughout China as both a pleasure and a cure.[8] As Lu explained, "Tea is of a cold nature and may be used in the blockage or stoppage of the bowels," or if one is "suffering from aching of the brain." It was also a "common beverage" for the healthy.[9]

Lu devoted the entire second part of his work to how to prepare tea, including the shape of the brazier on which the water is boiled; the "netting or gauze . . . meant to serve as a strainer," which should "be made of fine silk"; the type of trees used to make the water dispenser, "the pagoda tree, the catalpa, and the *tzu*."[10] The section ends with the best material for the tea bowl, "Yüeh Chou," a vessel made of jade and "having a greenish hue, [which] enhances the true color of the tea."[11] Lu then turned to how to brew and drink a proper cup, noting that the "first cup should have a haunting flavor, strange and lasting" and concluding that "moderation is the very essence of tea. Tea does not lend itself to extravagance."[12] Also in this section, Lu described the "nine ways by which man must tax himself with tea":

> He must manufacture it.
> He must develop a sense of selectivity and discrimination about it.
> He must provide the proper implements.
> He must prepare the right kind of fire.
> He must select suitable water.
> He must roast the tea to a turn.

He must grind it well.

He must brew it to its ultimate perfection.

He must, finally, drink it.[13]

Explaining the cultural importance of tea throughout China, Lu wrote that tea "has been traditionally taken so extensively that it is immersed in our customs and flourishes in the present Dynasty both North and South. From Ching to Yü, it is the common drink of every household."[14] By the mid-sixth century, tea had traveled out of China with Buddhist monks who took their religion, food, plants, and intellectual pursuits to such places as Japan and Korea.[15] However, according to Rachel Laudan, tea was not embraced in Japan until the fourteenth century, 200 years after a second migration of Buddhist monks had arrived, bringing with them not just tea but also noodles and chopsticks.[16]

By the late thirteenth century, the growth of cities such as Hangchow and Shanghai had led people to adopt new patterns of social activity that centered on tea, including visits to a local teahouse.[17] Almost 300 years before the first coffeehouse appeared in Mecca, government officials, military officers, and wealthy merchants throughout China were making their way to teahouses, where they enjoyed a cup of tea and perhaps a meal of local delicacies as they transacted business or simply enjoyed performances of song, storytelling, and poetry. For the less affluent, small shops provided tea and light fare.[18]

Europe lagged behind in the joys of dining out, although at times necessity demanded it. Travelers, pilgrims, merchants, soldiers, diplomats, and teachers had long had occasion to seek out meals in inns and monasteries.[19] Apprentices at times chose to eat out in public houses, hoping for a short respite from the watchful eyes of their masters, despite the fact that some employers provided food as part of a worker's pay, and members of the lower strata of society craving a hot meal sought out prepared food because many lacked the kitchen facilities, utensils, and even the firewood they needed to prepare their own meals.[20] Drinking establishments, specifically taverns, also have a place as precursors to both the coffeehouse and the restaurant, as do the lavish banquets that took place in private homes and public spaces.[21]

By the Renaissance and into the sixteenth century, there arose a "literary fondness for outdoor meals,"[22] as we learn from Francesco Colonna's *Hypnerotomachia Poliphili* (The dream of Poliphilus; 1499).[23] Rural picnics most likely appealed to city dwellers because they had an idealized and romantic vision of the pastoral life shepherds and other country dwellers led, although few would have left their cities to live full time in the country.[24] Celebrations of weddings or the visits of prominent people were also occasions for public dining; the rules for which were the same as those for other types of banquets.[25]

It was not until the late eighteenth century, however, that restaurants as we know them today began appearing, and at first they were a distinctly urban phenomenon. Credit for the earliest eateries has historically been given to France, where a Mr. Boulanger of Paris first supposedly welcomed guests to his establishment.[26] However, Rebecca Spang has challenged this attribution. Spang's research failed to uncover reliable mention of either Boulanger or his establishment, and as a result, we do not know who opened the first restaurant.[27] Wherever the first restaurant appeared, these eateries proved popular and profitable and they soon spread to Venice, Vienna, London, and as far away as St. Petersburg.[28]

During this transition to dining out as a part of the fabric of society, coffee blurred the boundaries between private and public life, changing behavioral norms and altering long-held notions of which activities belonged to the private sphere and which were acceptable in public. Before a convincing argument can be made that the coffeehouse was the primary catalyst for pleasurable experiences enjoyed with family and friends around sustenance, a number of questions require answers. These include, why and how did coffee become the vehicle that drove this change? What led people out of their homes to enjoy this particular beverage and not something else? It might be argued that the first part of the answer lies with the teahouse.

It is difficult to ignore the similarities between the teahouse and the coffeehouse in their respective cultures of origin. Hot tea was touted as a curative, as an enjoyable beverage, and as useful for Buddhist monks who drank it to remain wakeful during their meditations.[29] In his *Treatise on Food*, the emperor Shen Nung wrote that tea "gives one vigor of body, contentment of mind, and determination of purpose, when taken over a long period of time."[30] Lu also cited a "mixture of onion beards and bitter tea" as a useful concoction for calming children who were "preternaturally excitable and given to sudden starts."[31] Tea preparation, as Lu explained, demanded careful attention to detail. Over time, the ritual became deeply embedded in the lives of nobles and peasants not just in China but throughout Asia, wherever monks and merchants ventured, eventually giving birth to the institution of the teahouse.

Consider the possibility that the origins of coffeehouse culture may be the teahouses established in towns, cities, nearby shrines, and at picturesque spots in the countryside all along the Silk Road.[32] This is distinctly possible, given the argument of some historians that contact between southwest China and Arabia dates as far back as the Tang Dynasty (618–907). Arab traders brought gifts from China that included tea, which we know they knew of as early as 900.[33] As tea leaves and knowledge of teahouses accompanied merchants and monks westward, they might have planted the first seeds for the coffeehouses of the future. One bit of evidence that teahouses and coffeehouse may have had a parallel journey comes from a 1664 pamphlet that extols the "Vertues and Excellencies of this Leaf and Drink."[34] The anonymous author of this leaflet provides an explanation for how knowledge about how to prepare and drink tea traveled with merchants. The author asserts that "about the yeer 1657, Thomas Garway of London Merchant, living in Sweeting's Rents neer the Royal Exchange, did purchase a quantity thereof, and there first publiquely sold he said Tay in Leaf and Drink made according to the Directions of the most knowing Merchants and Travellers into those Eastern Countries."[35]

According to Beat Kümin, in the later fifteenth century, "drinking houses" in Italy, France and England began serving cold foods such as bread, cheese, fruit, and sausages along with the usual wine, beer, and cider.[36] Takeout food was available from stalls, peddlers, and stores with streetside counters, a tradition that began in antiquity, particularly in Asia.[37] Mobile kitchens continue to fill the cravings of people today in a contemporary equivalent, the food truck. Around the same time that coffeehouses were dominating London's social scene, taverns began augmenting the libations they offered with "a dazzling spectrum of delicacies."[38]

## Public Life in the Early Modern Near East

Tea, and even knowledge of the teahouse, may well have reached Arabia by the tenth century, when the beverage may have been consumed in homes. However, there is no evidence that teahouses were established beyond China, other parts of Southeast Asia, and along the Central Asian parts of the Silk Road. Even if tea drinking became part of private life in Arabia, it was coffee Near Eastern men developed a preference for. By the early sixteenth century, this had led to a noticeable change in their patterns of interaction—and to the establishment of the coffeehouse. This preference for coffee nevertheless owes a debt to tea and the teahouse, as it is possible that when the two drinks met, men were inspired to blend their much-loved coffee with a new way to enjoy it.[39]

The wide availability of coffee beans meant that not only was the drink readily available to virtually all strata of society but most people had the knowledge and equipment necessary to brew it for themselves because it had long been a domestic pleasure. This meant that there was little need for the skill some coffeehouse proprietors touted.[40] Rather, the suggestion has been made that the coffeehouse was not embraced because its preparation required the skills of a professional but rather because it gave men "something that [they] obviously had a desperate urge to do—get out of the house."[41] In societies where men and women did not socialize together and the presence of unrelated males in the home meant that wives and daughters were often expected to remain out of sight, the coffeehouse became a place for men to congregate without interfering with domestic tranquility.

In addition to the rather pragmatic idea that men just wanted a place to go, in both Arabia and the Levant public spaces were already alive with people going about their daily affairs, from shopping and praying to celebrating milestones such as births and marriages. Two hundred years before the first coffeehouse, Ibn Battutah praised this aspect of the city of Aleppo, calling particular attention to its public square as home to a vibrant market, claiming that it "cannot be paralleled for beauty or size."[42] Battutah described the area around the city in effusive terms: "The spirit feels in the environs of the city of Aleppo an exhilaration, gladness, and sprightliness."[43] Markets and squares outside Arabia and the Levant were similarly admired. For example, Ogier Ghiselin de Busbecq (1522–1592), Holy Roman Emperor Ferdinand I's (1503–1564) ambassador to Constantinople from 1554 to 1562, lavished praise on the Turkish capital in his *Turkish Letters* (1595), declaring that "no place could be more beautiful or more conveniently situated."[44] Abu al-Hasan Ali al-Tamgruti, the Moroccan ambassador to Constantinople from 1589 to 1591, wrote that "almost no port in the entire world [is] as grand, as deep, as well sheltered against all winds, as Constantinople."[45] It makes sense that a population accustomed to public squares abuzz with all manner of activity, including men meeting informally at the businesses of friends, would greet coffeehouses with enthusiasm as places dedicated to the pleasures of coffee and conversation.

These firsthand accounts of the beauty and vivacity of eastern cities before the sixteenth century are crucial to supporting the assertion that the establishment of coffeehouses gave rise to a nascent public sphere in the sixteenth century. It is true that the presence of people outside their homes making purchases in the marketplace, exchanging greetings with friends, and congregating in the streets outside of stalls and shops does not necessarily constitute a public domain, particularly if that space is narrowly defined in western terms. Jürgen Habermas (1929–) was the first to argue that the public sphere is the intentional coming together of people for the primary purpose of engaging in discussions of political import or for expressing opinions about governmental and economic matters. Habermas argues that this type of public sphere first developed in Europe.[46] The appearance of the coffeehouse in the Near and Middle East challenges Habermas's idea that it was Europeans who first redefined the role of public space as a locus for politically charged discourse. An argument can be made that the coffeehouses of the East were the impetus for both a new definition of public space and for this region as the birthplace of a public sphere that would not be observed in Europe until the eighteenth century.

The idea that the life of the coffeehouse represents the first emergence of an identifiable public sphere has recently gained support among scholars, including Uğur Kömeçoğlu. In "The Publicness and Sociabilities of the Ottoman Coffeehouse," Kömeçoğlu suggests that this was precisely the case in Ottoman Turkey, specifically Istanbul, where coffeehouses first appeared in 1550. According to Kömeçoğlu, Ottoman "publicness," or a "public sphere," originated in the Ottoman Empire sometime before Europeans welcomed the coffeehouse as a center for social intercourse and as a defining element of their public domain.[47] Kömeçoğlu explains that coffeehouses rapidly "emerged as a principal institution of the public sphere, a channel and site of public communication, and as an arena linking the socio-cultural with the political."[48] For Kömeçoğlu, the reason coffeehouses succeeded as venues for public discourse was that they were open to all strata of Istanbul society; they were places where men from across the socioeconomic spectrum could assemble to enjoy a drink, conversation, a storyteller, or a musical performer. Istanbul's coffeehouses were also spaces, Kömeçoğlu claims, where men temporarily eschewed social standing and engaged with one another in political debates, openly voicing their anger over the problems they faced in the course of their daily lives, not the least of which were recurring bread shortages. Coffeehouses in Istanbul were recognized sites for the dissemination of rumors and gossip, so it is not surprising that Sultan Murad III and later Sultan Ahmed I (r. 1613–1617) took steps to eradicate them. This supports the notion that an emerging public sphere centered on the coffeehouse is yet another gift of the region to their neighbors on the other side of the Mediterranean Sea.[49] If Kömeçoğlu is correct about the pivotal role of the coffeehouse in the formation of a recognizable public sphere, then the first place to look for its origins is not in 1550s Istanbul but several decades earlier and many hundreds of miles away from the Ottoman capital.

As a place to begin this investigation, Ralph Hattox offers a well-documented description of the role of social life and the coffeehouse in the premodern Arab world.[50] Hattox notes that men of all socioeconomic groups went to neighborhood coffeehouses that catered to a local clientele or to urban shops in cities for both business and pleasure. Like Kömeçoğlu, Hattox accepts the idea that men of all ranks may even have frequented the same shop. However, Hattox's analysis differs from Kömeçoğlu's assertion that coffeehouses were places where men intermingled across the social spectrum.[51] In the Istanbul of which Kömeçoğlu wrote almost exclusively, it seems that associating across social boundaries was an accepted practice in coffeehouses. Hattox, who studied coffeehouses in the Levant and the cities in desert Arabia, found that social custom discouraged fraternizing across social boundaries.[52]

Primary sources from the time corroborate the findings of both Kömeçoğlu and Hattox. Once again, the accounts of travelers provide vivid pictures of how outsiders interpreted life in coffeehouses. After his expeditions at the end of the sixteenth century, the Portuguese explorer Pedro Teixeira, wrote of Baghdad, which he visited in October 1604, as follows: "This part of Baghdad may have three thousand inhabited houses with *succos*[,] that is marts, *caroanceros*, public baths, and workshops of all handicrafts in use among the Moors. Amongst other buildings, as I have said, is a coffee-house."[53] Teixeira continued: "Coffee is . . . prepared and sold in public houses built to that end; wherein all men who desire it meet to drink it, be they mean or great. . . . Only their custom induces them to meet here for conversation, and use this for entertainment."[54] Similarly, George Sandys wrote, "There sit they chatting most of the day, and sip of a drink called Coffa . . . in little China dishes."[55]

Writing in the mid-nineteenth century, Edward William Lane (1801–1876) echoed Teixeira. Lane was a British translator and lexicographer known for his travels in Egypt, where he learned Arabic and took notes about the lives of its inhabitants. He described the consumption of coffee as an important part of the social life of Egyptian "tradesmen" who enjoy "a cup of coffee, which is obtained from the nearest coffee-shop."[56]

The evidence presented above supports an analysis that coffee was a critical component in the development of a public space that was something more than a locus for conducting the business of everyday life. To take a seat in a coffeehouse in Turkey or the Near East was to insert oneself into the debates of the day. Officials in the East were anxious about coffeehouses because they could not control what men discussed. As the next sections reveal, the arrival of coffee in Europe would set in motion a redefining of how people interacted outside their homes.

## Coffeehouses in Venice

In 1546, almost 100 years before Venice's first coffeehouse opened, apprehensions within the city were rising, in part because of conflicts between Ottoman merchants residing there and their Venetian counterparts. Repeated complaints sent to Sultan Rüstem Paşa (ca. 1500–1561) in Constantinople tell of abuses Turkish merchants suffered at the hands of Venetians.[57] Eight years later, it was not just ongoing interpersonal tensions that caused anxiety for the government of Venice. Turkish and Persian traders had begun to threaten Venice's Levantine trade by pushing inward to market fairs in central Italy.[58] By the mid–1570s, as the following example suggests, Ottoman merchants were bringing coffee to Venice. In March of 1575, a Turkish merchant named Huseyn Çelebi bin Haci Hizir bin Ilyas was murdered in Venice, a cup (fincan) for coffee or tea was found among his belongings.[59] And as coffee become more widely available in Venice throughout the rest of sixteenth century, it also was poised to add to civil discord.[60]

Sometime between 1575 and 1630, coffee made its appearance in apothecary shops, where a diverse clientele could obtain coffee.[61] Coffee entered Venetian society by 1647. The evidence suggests that would-be proprietors in Italy neither randomly pulled the notion of the coffeehouse out of their imaginations nor simply recast the drinking houses of their day into establishments that proffered coffee.[62] It seems that the men of Venice met at their favorite apothecary until the appearance of the first coffeehouse of the mid-seventeenth century. Even after coffeehouses opened, apothecary shops remained important centers for the dissemination of information until the eighteenth century,[63]

Perhaps because of unwanted attention from the government and the Holy Office, possibly because apothecaries campaigned vigorously to maintain their position as purveyors of rare products and enticing news, or maybe because the taste of coffee took some practice, a second coffeehouse did not open in Venice until 1683. This one, located in the Piazza San Marco below the arches of the Procuratie Nuove, one of three connected buildings that housed the offices of the Venetian state prosecutors, proved a spark that led to the growing popularity of coffeehouses, despite the reality that they continued to occupy an ambiguous space.[64] A man known simply as Father Paul commented in *The Maxims of the Government of Venice* (1707) that although Venetians sought out the pleasures of the coffeehouse, they did not necessarily linger in the ways observers of coffeehouses in the East had noted.

> The Venetians do not allow any Coffee-houses in their City, that are able to contain great numbers of People. Their Coffee-houses are generally little shops, that will not hold above five or six Persons at a time, and perhaps here are not Seats for above two or three. So that the Company having no where to rest themselves, are gone as soon as they have made an end of drinking their Coffee.[65]

As a side note, the Italian practice of standing at the counter continues today, even though few fear political or religious repercussions.

As this book moves out of Venice, coffee and the coffeehouse had become laden with meanings that will move with them. Simultaneously a luxury product, a window into and an opportunity to imitate the habits of those who lived in stories and in their place of residence/business on the Venetian Rialto, a beverage believed to cure ills and ward off sleep, and the source of anxiety for civil and religious officials, coffee was the catalyst for a new vision of social interaction in public space.

## The British Coffeehouse

In 1685, French merchant Philippe Sylvestre Dufour (1622–1687) wrote, "I will speak for the present of a certain Bean of Arabia called Bon, whereof they make a Drink termed Coffee, which was heretofore in use amongst Arabians, and Egyptians; and which is now a days in very great request amongst the English, French, and Germanes."[66] By the mid- to late seventeenth century, the coffeehouse had moved beyond Italy, made its way to other parts of continental Europe, and crossed the channel into England.

By the time Dufour wrote his treatise on how to make coffee, tea, and chocolate, London's first coffeehouse had been open for almost thirty years, established by Pasqua Rossée, the author of a one-page pamphlet entitled *The Vertue of the Coffee Drink* (ca. 1675). Rossée claimed that coffee is "good against Head-ach," that it was "excellent to prevent and cure the Dropsy, Gout, and Scurvy," that it was "very good to prevent Mis-carryings in Child-bearing Women," and that it would "prevent Drowsiness, and make one fit for business."[67]

London, however, was not the site of the first English encounter with coffee, nor does it seem that Venetian merchants were the first purveyors of British beans. Rather, evidence of coffee drinking in England appears for the first time in the memoirs of the English writer and diarist John Evelyn, a scholar at Balliol College in Oxford.[68] On May 20, 1636, Evelyn wrote in his diary that "there came in my time to the College one Nathaniel Conopios, out of Greece, from Cyril, the Patriarch of Constantinople. . . . He was the first I ever saw drink coffee; which custom came not into England till thirty years after."[69] Thirteen years later, in 1650, the first coffeehouse appeared in Oxford, and it was followed two years later by Rosee's first London coffeehouse.

That coffee drinking would have been introduced to Britain by a member of the educated elite at Oxford illustrates Brian Cowan's assertion that British taste for the drink first developed among a group of men he refers to as *virtuosi*, who participated in "an intellectual culture of curiosity [that] managed to domesticate and civilize a hitherto foreign and suspect drink."[70] The term virtuosi first appeared in 1634, in an English courtesy manual for gentlemen written by the poet Henry Peacham (1546–1634) as a corrective to the "deplorable . . . breeding in generall of our Gentlemen."[71] Peacham declared that men should possess manners that are ""delightful" and worthy of "observation," as exemplified by men "skilled in them," whom "the *Italians* [have] tearmed *Virtuosi*."[72] In preparing his 261-page treatise on the attributes of the proper English gentleman, Peacham drew inspiration from the person of the Italian courtier, defined most notably by Italian Renaissance soldier, diplomat, and writer Baldassare Castiglione (1478–1529) in his *Il cortegiano* (*The Book of the Courtier*), first published in Venice in 1528. For Castiglione, the traits of an ideal courtier included the ability to speak and write well, a knowledge of Latin and Greek, and completion of an education in the humanities.[73] With these traits in mind, Peacham admonished English gentlemen to remember that "learning then is an essential part of Nobilitie."[74]

Possessed of an education that extolled an understanding of classical antiquity and wishing to interact with other elites who had similar interests and knowledge, learned men in England strove to imitate the characteristics of their role models, the virtuosi of the Italian Renaissance.[75] This ideal included a desire to obtain items deemed "rare, novel, surprising, and outstanding in all spheres of life," as the collection of objects of wonder was central to the definition of a true virtuoso.[76] Indeed, in their search for the exceptional and the elusive, seventeenth-century English men of education and looked back to the men of antiquity they so admired. One such figure was the Roman emperor Augustus (63 BCE–19 CE), who reportedly collected and displayed objects he considered "extraordinary and mysterious."[77] By the seventeenth century in England, the ranks of the virtuosi included not just men privileged to have a university education but also men who were a part of making London a place of growing commercial importance.[78] The lives of these men intersect with coffee in their captivation with the unusual, which they learned about from men they deemed "Virtuoso Travelers" for their brave sojourns far from home.[79]

Another of those who wrote about coffee during this time was the English nobleman, writer, and scientist Sir Francis Bacon (1561–1626) whose natural history, the *Sylva sylvarum*, was first published in 1627. In this collection, Bacon looks to antiquity, including the writings of Pliny; to more contemporary observations on the habits of Turks; and to his own experiments to discern coffee's curative properties.[80] Bacon notes that among Turks, "Coffee and Opium are taken down, Tobacco but in smoak."[81] According to Bacon, these items and others such as saffron, ambergris, and mandrake root "both inebriate and provoke sleep."[82] This categorization suggested that coffee belonged among substances that produce some form of intoxication. Writing in the 1640s and 1650s, Oxford physician Thomas Willis countered Bacon's description after watching its effects on his patients, associating it not with inebriation but "with sobriety."[83]

Bacon's musings on coffee hardly seem original, as they reflect, almost literally, the testimonials of early travelers. Yet, as Graham Rees points out, Bacon was careful to note when he borrowed from others and when his conclusions were based on his own experiments and observations.[84] Thus, the *Sylva Sylvarum*, which was written in English, was Bacon's attempt to make scientific study available to a wider seventeenth-century English audience.[85]

In a now-familiar pattern, coffee in England went from a beverage known only through literature to a pleasure pursued in private to the central object in a new social craze, the coffeehouse. Jürgen Habermas argues that before the seventeenth century, there was virtually no distinction between the public and private spheres in the European world.[86] With the rise of trade capitalism in the seventeenth century, a number of changes began taking place, including the advent of conditions conducive to a "new social order," which resulted in the "bourgeois public sphere."[87] A hallmark of this new public space was an opportunity for individuals to come together as a distinct public entity.[88] For Habermas, one of the central institutions of this new order in England was the coffeehouse, as it was a favorite gathering place for men who would come together for political and economic discussions or for debates over works of art and literature—similar to the French *salon* in the latter part of the eighteenth century. Habermas asserts that it was the coffeehouse that "made access to the relevant circles less formal and easier" for a broad swath of middle-class men that included shop owners and artisans. Habermas even goes so far as to suggest that it was the coffeehouse that created English public life by the beginning of the eighteenth century, a time when "London already had 3,000 of them with a core group of regulars."[89]

For Habermas, the coffeehouse was singularly responsible for the transformation of English public space and the transition from the early modern era to the modern era. Habermas correctly identifies the centrality of coffee and the coffeehouse to the remaking of public space in England. He does not, however, include the roles eastern coffeehouses played, nor does he acknowledge the place of apothecaries and Renaissance Italian virtuosi in stirring the desire of Englishmen to drink coffee. While it is true that coffee drinking indelibly changed patterns of social behavior in England, this habit began thousands of miles away and at least 200 years earlier.

The thriving British coffeehouse culture of the mid-seventeenth century, and thus a discernable public sphere owes its existence to the same craving for the luxuries of the East that had permeated Italy for centuries.[90] As Mortimer Epstein (1880–1946) explained in *The Early History of the Levant Company* (1908), luxury goods had been finding their way to England since the Middle Ages through an enduring connection with Italian merchants, first the Florentines, then the Genoese, and by the fifteenth century the Venetians.[91] "Indeed," Epstein notes, "already in the fourteenth century the Venetian merchants in England were sufficiently numerous to be under the government of their own Consul," bringing such luxuries as "gingers, cinnamon, pepper, cloves, nutmegs . . . dates, sugar, currants . . . Tyrian wine," and silk.[92] This trade experienced a decline in the last years of the fifteenth century, in part due to a dispute between King Henry VII (1485–1509) and the rulers of Venice over trade in wine. Henry wanted England to have a share in this profitable import and was therefore unwilling to continue trade in Venetian wine at a level necessary to meet English demand.[93] Unable to secure more favorable terms from the Venetians, the king halted all trade with Venice from 1509 to 1518, when business resumed, albeit at a less lively pace, until 1532. In that year, trade virtually ceased again, leaving Venetian merchants to continue supplying English demand at their own risk. Fearful of unnecessary risk, Venetian ships stopped coming to England entirely in 1587.[94] The departure of Venice as a trading partner meant that English merchants who wanted to trade in goods from the Levant were "forced to go themselves for them." Such ventures were not entirely unfamiliar; in 1581, Queen Elizabeth I (1533–1603) had granted several London merchants a patent to "trade in the dominion of the Great Turk."[95] In 1585, this lucrative trade led to the founding of the Levant Company, followed by the start of the East India Company fifteen years later.[96] In support of this trade, Sir Edward Michelborne of the East India Company proposed a center at Mocha on the Red Sea in 1608, which was viewed as a more hospitable harbor than the one at Aden, which the Portuguese regularly patrolled. In 1609, English traders arrived for the first time in the coffee markets of Yemen that had long been supplying the Ottoman Empire and the lands around the Indian Ocean.[97] Coffee from Mocha could now also feed England's coffee habit, even though the East India Company did not become a major supplier of coffee for Britain until the 1710s.[98]

The answer to the question of what fueled the coffee craze in early modern Britain lies in the merging of culture and commerce. England's pursuit of a lively trade with the East made coffee available, while the virtuosi and the memoirs of travelers fostered a culture of curiosity. In addition, coffee was recognized permissible for consumption in public because it lacked the properties society "[linked] with unreason and illicit sexuality," attributes associated with other foreign drugs, particularly opium.[99] In short, coffee became a beverage respectable members of the middling and upper social strata could drink in public.[100] Before long, English coffeehouses, like those elsewhere, became centers for the production and consumption of news. Some coffeehouse keepers even published newspapers. In coffeehouses, men could hear of the workings of the House

of Commons from a clerk of that body. Journalists and newsletter writers also frequented coffeehouses to hear the news and relay it to their
readers.[101] After food was added to their offerings, English coffeehouses
became sites for private hospitality.[102]

The history presented above suggests that the emerging public sphere
that centered on the coffeehouses of early modern Britain, as Habermas
noted, was most likely the result of a desire to appropriate certain eastern
customs, in the same way that commodities had long been consumed but
in a way that was deemed civilized because it took place in a respectable
environment. In short, a public space arose around the coffeehouse not
just because merchants could provide the beans, master brewers could
prepare it, and men were looking for novel opportunities to interact, but
also because Britain and the rest of Europe were deeply embedded in a
universe of wonder, acquisition, and consumption of the foreign.

The description so far might suggest that the coffeehouse made an
easier transition to Britain than it did elsewhere. This was not the case.
Not all members of English society were thrilled with its arrival. Like
the coffeehouses of Mecca, Constantinople, and Venice, coffeehouses in
Britain raised the anxieties of leaders who argued that they should be
eradicated. This call was no more successful in England than it had been
elsewhere. The futility of efforts to regulate coffeehouses meant that the
task of critiquing them fell to social commentators, who entered the fray
by directing attention to what took place in them:

> He that shall any quarrel here begin, Shall give each man a dish t'
> atone the sin; And so shall he, whose compliments extend So far
> to drink in coffee to his friend; Let noise of loud disputes be quite
> forborne, No maudlin lovers here in corners mourn, But all be brisk
> and talk, but not too much, On sacred things, let none presume to
> touch. Nor profane Scripture, nor sawcily wrong Affairs of state with
> an irreverent tongue.[103]

As this quote suggests, if men were to gather, certain proprieties
should be maintained. Patrons should eschew vociferous arguments,
avoid bemoaning a lost love, not give in to the temptation of talking too
much, lest a loose tongue lead to public criticism of the government.

Twenty years after the opening of the first London café, some elements
of society were still campaigning against them. The following two petitions
claim to speak on behalf of women. As the authors remain anonymous,
however, it is impossible to know for certain who wrote them. It is entirely

possible that the pamphlets were written by men who believed their arguments against coffee would be more successful if they appeared to come from women. What is clear are the accusations that coffee did irreparable damage to English society. The first petition, by someone who identified themselves simply as Well-Willer, is entitled "The Women's Petition Against Coffee" (1674). In it, the author vehemently denounces coffee as a

> Grand Inconvenience accruing to their SEX from the Excessive Use of that Drying, Enfeebling LIQUOR. . . . The Occasion of which Insufferable Disaster, after a Serious Enquiry, and Discussion of the Point by the Learned of the Faculty, we can Attribute to nothing more than the Excessive use of that Newfangled, Abominable, Heathenish Liquor called COFFEE.[104]

The petition ends with a plea that "henceforth the Drinking COFFEE may on severe penalties be forbidden to all Persons under the Age of Threescore."[105]

Well-Willer's appeal must have gone mostly unheeded, as twenty-six years later a shortened version appeared as the "City Wife's Petition Against Coffee," taking the following words from the original petition:

> In our Apprehensions can consist in nothing more than the brisk activity of our Men, who in former Ages were justly esteemed the Ablest performers in Christendom, But to our unspeakable Grief, we find of late a very . . . decay of that true Old English Valour. Our Gallants being in every way Frenchified, that are become meer Cock Sparrows . . . we can attribute nothing more than the Excessive use of that newfangled, abominable, heathenish Liquor called Coffee. . . . For the continual sipping of this pitiful Drink, is enough to bewitch Men.[106]

The author ends with the suggestion that "henceforth the Drinking of COFFEE, may in severe Penalties be forbidden to all Persons under the Age of Threescore."[107]

These objections reveal much about late seventeenth- and early eighteenth-century English society. First, in both appeals, coffee is not just "abominable," it is also "heathenish," to mean it is not the drink of Christians but rather nonbelievers. This could be an allusion to coffee's origins, particularly in light of the assertion that coffee "bewitches" men with a sensuality and exoticism associated most commonly with the East. This may be a stretch. And yet, these appeals do seem to warn against adopting foreign habits, whether of the Muslim world and/or of France (with whom Britain had a long history of acrimony) as a threat to the character of the traditional English male, the results of which would could only be downfall of society. Second, and more pragmatically, the men observed in public abandoning their wives and families in favor of spending hours in cafes drinking coffee with other men were not the only enthusiastic regulars. Inside the coffeehouse, young men could also be found, idling away their time instead of engaging in honest work. As a result, both documents demand that coffee drinking be allowed only for those older than sixty, at which time their working days would likely have ended. In either case, or more likely in combination, the coffee that radically upended the social life of Britain has a similar story in France.

## The Coffeehouse Comes to France

In 1640, Parisians credited the Italians as the first Europeans to possess knowledge of how to brew coffee.[108] One story has it that coffee came to France with Suleiman Aga, whom the Ottoman sultan, Mehmet IV (1052/1642–1105/1693), sent as an ambassador to King Louis XIV (1643–1715) in 1669. According to this account, members of the ambassador's entourage brought enough coffee with them to serve Parisians.[109] The city's first coffeehouse followed just three years later, in 1671.

Jean de La Roque (1661–1745), son of a Marseilles merchant, adds to what is known about the story of coffee and coffeehouses in France. La Roque's *Voyage to Arabia Felix*, written about the travels he undertook from 1708 to 1710, which was published in French in 1716 and published in English translation in 1732, mentions coffee several times.[110] The first of these is La Roque's description of the place in the interior of Yemen where he first encountered what he called "the Coffee-Tree," a plant that grew at the "Foots of the Mountains and little Hills, in the more shady and moist Parts."[111] La Roque was treated to the coffee drink in Aden, a visit that included meetings with both the emir and an official La Roque called the governor. At this meeting, La Roque gave the governor some scarlet cloth, "which he received very agreeably." Then "he invited us very earnestly to trade in his Government, giving us Assurances of his Favour, and speaking to us particularly about Coffee, which is there very excellent, and in great plenty."[112]

La Roque claimed that coffee was something "the French had always before bought of the Turks in the Levant, and sometimes of the English and Dutch."[113] This was the case until his father, Pierre de La Roque, developed a coffee-drinking habit during a journey to Turkey and the Levant in 1644 and began importing the beans into Marseilles, along with other "moveable items for his own use."[114] La Roque stored these objects, which included china cups and cotton muslin napkins edged with gold, silver, and silk thread, in a curiosity cabinet.[115]

Jean de La Roque was aware of the controversies that surrounded coffee throughout the Muslim world and recounted in his narrative the "troubles bred at Mecca and Cairo . . . and since that at Constantinople" due to gatherings in coffeehouses.[116] Given the dates of his adventures, it is unlikely that La Roque witnessed any of that turmoil; he likely learned this information from people he met during his adventures or from the writings of earlier travelers.

La Roque also discussed earlier views of coffee. He acknowledged the contributions of Prospero Alpini's *De medicina aegyptorium* to his understanding of coffee, noting that Alpini's observation of coffee's insomnia-producing chemical properties had since "been . . . discovered and admitted by our best Physicians."[117] Of Sir Francis Bacon, La Roque wrote, "Chancellor Bacon who dy'd in the Year 1626, makes mention of Coffee in his Works, but so superficially, that he seems to have been not well informed."[118] La Roque's account ends with a notation that by the latter part of the seventeenth century coffee had become "every Day more and more in Use in France."[119]

The establishment of coffeehouses in Italy, Britain, and France was mirrored throughout Europe. In Germany, the first coffeehouse was established in Bremen in 1669. The first coffeehouses in Scotland were established in Edinburgh and Glasgow in 1673. Vienna got its first coffeehouse in 1685, and by the late eighteenth century coffeehouses began to appear in Madrid. The coffeehouse crossed the Atlantic Ocean in the second half of the seventeenth century; it was present in Boston in 1670, in New York in 1696, and in Philadelphia in 1703.[120]

Growers in Yemen successfully guarded their monopoly of coffee cultivation until the early seventeenth century. The earliest claim of coffee cultivation outside Arabia comes from India, although this comes mostly from legend. Baba Budan was a follower of the Sufi saint Hazrath Dada Hayath Meer Kalandar, who had arrived in India around 396/1005. In the legend, Budan, an Indian pilgrim to Mecca in the 1600s, smuggled coffee seeds out of Arabia by strapping them to his abdomen, then planted them in Chikmagalur, India, in the foothills of the Mullayanagiri range.[121] By the first decades of the eighteenth century, the Dutch East India Company, founded in 1602 and in operation until 1799, was importing the majority of its coffee from Java. Throughout the eighteenth and nineteenth centuries, the popularity of coffee drinking led to the expansion of coffee growing as part of European colonization in the Caribbean, South and Central America, Africa, and other parts of Asia including Sri Lanka.[122]

## Concluding Thoughts: More on Coffee and Orientalism

"In order to attract custom there are here pretty boys, richly dressed, who serve the coffee and take the money; with music and other diversions," observed Pedro Teixeira of his coffeehouse experience in Baghdad in 1604.[123] In this quote, it is possible to hear not just of the sociability of the coffeehouse but also the early reverberations of Orientalism. Teixeira's observation that the coffeehouse was a place where one could find much more than just a hot drink illustrates an enduring western notion that the "Orient," as Said pointed out, "had been since antiquity a place of romance, exotic beings, haunting memories and landscapes, remarkable experiences."[124] George Sandys, the preacher for the Levant Company, made similar remarks about Levantine social life, presenting the East as a quintessential other. For example, Sandys wrote that women "are not permitted to come into their Temples (yet have they secret places to look in through grates)."[125] Sandys drew a sharp distinction between the respectable women of his country and the women of the Muslim world who lived out their days secluded behind high walls.

> To the publick Bannias, which for excellency of buildings are next to their Mosques. . . . few but frequent them twice in the week, as much for their health, as for delight and cleanliness. The men take them up in the morning, and in the afternoon the Women. But both amongst the Romans did ordinarily frequent them together. . . . The men are attended upon by men, and the Women by Women. In the outer-most room they put off their cloaths, then having Aprons of . . . Linen tyed about their Wastes, they enter the Baths to what degree of heat they please. The Servitors wash them, rub them, stretch out their joynts, and cleanse their skins. . . . But the Women do anoint their bodies with an Oyntment . . . which maketh the skin soft, white, and shining. . . . Much unnatural and filthy lust is said to be

committed daily in the remote Closets of these darksome Bannias, yea Women with Women a thing incredible if former times had not given thereunto both detection and punishment.[126]

This portrayal of women looking through sight holes from a hidden place immediately fashions them as enigmatic in ways that European women could never be.

For Sandys, the otherness of the East began with the questionable conduct of the bathhouses, a site of socialization that long predated the coffeehouse. The source of Sandy's information remains a question as no man would ever have bathed with women. It is also unlikely he ever entered the bath with other men. His information likely came from secondhand reports, which he then embellished with his own imagination. Sandys was not just disconcerted with the "lust" that he claimed had accompanied the life of the bathhouse since Roman times; he seemed particularly bothered by the supposed daily sexual liaisons between women. And yet Sandys wrote with some amazement that all of this bathing had at least one positive outcome: "They have generally the sweetest Children that ever I saw, partly proceeding from their frequent bathings and affected cleanliness."[127]

The words of Sandys, Teixeira, and others reflect another theme of early modern attitudes toward the East, that it was a place of contradictions, a location where buildings dedicated to bodily cleanliness had corners dedicated to moral corruption, where houses of licit coffee drinking were tainted by the presence of alluring young boys to entice customers into coffeehouses.[128] Kömeçoğlu notes that coffeehouses "accommodated a variety of unorthodox sexualities" and were sites where opium was consumed.[129] Further, the observations of westerners conjured images that confirmed for themselves and their audiences that the world of the East was a mysterious place populated by people who were simultaneously a fascinating and dangerous Other. While it was Edward Said who first put forward the theory of Orientalism, what he articulated so eloquently about the relations between East and West had existed for centuries.

The texts I've mentioned here illustrate how travelers' accounts often reveal more about the mentality of the author than they do about the true character of the people they met. As an Englishman and chaplain for the British East India Company, George Sandys would have found the behavior of Turks and Arabs so different from his own life experiences that it is not surprising that he misunderstood what he saw and indulged in exaggeration. From tales such as his Orientalist views were promulgated, and successive generations of travelers participated in a discourse that played a crucial role in reaffirming ancient ideas about an exotic East and helped invent a world that did not actually exist, as Said notes.[130] Westerners embraced coffeehouses in part because they provided new options for socializing but also because they presented an opportunity to appropriate one of the ways of the East into the safety of a world they saw as more cultured.

## CHAPTER 7

# Coffee and Modernity

*Coffee—the favorite drink of the civilized world.*

—Thomas Jefferson, 1824[1]

*Coffee is our bread.*

—Ethiopian Proverb

## The Start of Coffee's Modern Story

After submitting a first draft of this book, a reviewer recommended that the story of coffee not end as it spread out from Europe in the late seventeenth and early eighteenth centuries. This chapter is the result of that suggestion, for which I am grateful. In the course expanding the text, I also benefited from the work of my friend and colleague Jennifer Brinkerhoff, whose book *Institutional Reform and Diaspora Entrepreneurs: The In-Between Difference* was a place to start as I looked back to where my history of coffee began, in Ethiopia, a country where coffee is still an important commercial product and therefore an ongoing economic and political concern.[2] This final chapter begins, however, with a look at the triumph of coffee and the coffeehouse in the Americas. This consideration also includes the story of how the coffee plants that found fertile soil outside Yemen and Ethiopia led to the rise of coffee plantations that produced great wealth for owners and equally great misery for those who labored on them. The chapter then returns to the place of coffee's birth for a discussion of contemporary coffee production and debates about fair trade for farmers and growers, environmental sustainability, and what the future of coffee might be.

## Coffee and Coffeehouses Come to the Americas

In 1624, thirty Dutch families, with the support of the Dutch East India Company established a settlement they called New Amsterdam in what today is the southern tip of Manhattan. They brought tea with them. In 1664, during the second Anglo-Dutch War, the city was lost to the British and renamed New York City. Four years later, in 1668, coffee had begun to replace tea as the preferred morning beverage in New York, and by 1683 the city had become the main port of entry for coffee beans.[3] A year later, in 1669, the first coffeehouse appeared in New York City. A few years later, in 1703, the first coffeehouse in Philadelphia opened.[4] From the beginning, the coffeehouses established in America continued coffeehouse traditions that had long been established.

The travel diary of Dr. Alexander Hamilton (ca. 1667–ca. 1732), a physician who immigrated from Scotland to Annapolis, Maryland in 1738, reveals that by the mid-eighteenth century there were many coffeehouses in New England.[5] On May 30, 1744, Dr. Hamilton left Annapolis and embarked on a journey in New England in the hope of improving his health. For four months, Hamilton recorded an account of the locations he visited and his thoughts on daily life in colonial America, which he later organized into a book he titled *Itinerarium*.[6] Hamilton's reflections include thirty-one references to coffeehouses throughout the region. For example, doctor described a coffeehouse in Philadelphia as a place to make new acquaintances, an activity that, Hamilton also noted, retained a formality that was common in England. He wrote, "In the afternoon I went to the coffee-house, where I was introduced by Dr. Thomas Bond' to several gentlemen of the place, where the ceremony of shaking of hands, an old custom peculiar to the English, was performed with great gravity, and the usual compliments."[7]

On June 18, 1744, Hamilton was in New York City, where visits to the local coffeehouses included a "hit at backgammon" in the late afternoon and chess in the evening.[8] Toward the end of August, when Hamilton was in Whitehall, Rhode Island, he not only disparaged the owner of a coffeehouse, calling him a "queer old dog," but further noted that during the evening he and his companions were "likewise alarmed (not charmed) for half an hour by a man who sang with such a trumpet note that I was afraid he would shake down the walls of the house about us."[9]

Twenty years later, in 1764, the English physicist John Canton

(1718–1772) wrote to Benjamin Franklin, who would have been familiar with the coffeehouses of London from his visits there in 1724–1726, and 1757–1762. Canton noted that "the so-called Club of Honest Whigs," which he had helped form and which was composed primarily of "writers, dissenting clergymen, and men of scientific interests," met "fortnightly on Thursday evenings at St. Paul's Coffeehouse and after 1772 at the London Coffeehouse."[10] Canton mentioned a discussion in the coffeehouse with a Mr. Kinnersley about two experiments he had recently conducted involving electricity.[11] This letter offers evidence that the coffeehouses of eighteenth-century London served as loci for gatherings of intellectuals and nonconformists. This is the role coffeehouses played in colonial America before the Revolutionary War, quite possibly transmitted across the Atlantic Ocean with men such as Benjamin Franklin and others who had visited London. Franklin returned to England again in December 1764 with a petition to King George III (1738–1830) requesting that Pennsylvania be made a proprietary province rather than a colony of the Crown. Franklin remained in England for the next eleven years, likely spending much time in the city's coffeehouses.

That men living in the colonies who retained ties to England, France, and other parts of Europe were instrumental in the popularity of the coffeehouse on the other side of the ocean is illustrated by the rapid spread of these establishments. For example, in 1767, Richard Charlton (d. 1779) opened a coffeehouse "as a tavern" in Williamsburg, Virginia, that hosted George Washington on one of his visits to the city. The business served as a place where customers could purchase grooming services; Charlton was also a barber and a wigmaker.[12] The coffeehouses of these early American cities were an important part of the social and civic lives of urban dwellers.[13] It could even be said that coffeehouses played a role in the founding of a new nation.

Evidence of this comes from an 1767 newspaper article, "Reply to Coffee-House Orators," which Benjamin Franklin wrote using the anonymous signature "A Friend to Both Countries." Franklin chastised "writers of political pamphlets and newspapers, and . . . coffee-house talkers," as well as "haranguers of the populace among the ancients," whom he claimed "sometimes did a great deal of good, at other times a great deal of harm." He declared that "coffee-houses ring with lying reports of [America] being in rebellion" over two acts of the British Parliament, one requiring colonists to quarter British troops and other imposing restraints on trade. Of the latter, Franklin wrote that "several restraints in the Acts of Trade laid on the Commerce of the Colonies, are not only prejudicial to the Colonies, but to the Mother Country," suggesting that both the Colonies and England would be harmed by any restrictions on trade, thereby accusing the unnamed "coffee-house orators" of inciting men to treason. He wrote, "refusal of full compliance . . . is REBELLION" and should be "punished accordingly."[14]

This piece is a useful illustration of the enduring legacy of the coffeehouses of Arabia as loci for volatile political debate. This document clearly suggests that in America, men gathered in coffeehouses not just for the pleasure of disputation but incite their companions to embrace the idea of a rebellion. It seems that the coffeehouse orators were important contributors to the outbreak of the Revolutionary War in April 1775, particularly among men who were unable to read the newspapers and pamphlets that also played important roles in the Revolution. The documentation confirms that the coffeehouses that existed throughout Britain's American colonies became places for wide-ranging social discourse.

A series of resolutions formulated on September 2, 1793, in a Petersburg, Virginia, coffeehouse provide evidence that coffeehouses in the new United States were key elements in the formation of a public domain. The resolutions were directed at the nation's first president, George Washington, and were adopted by the "Inhabitants of the Town of Petersburg and its Vicinity at Mr. Edward's Coffeehouse."[15] A report of the proceedings includes the support of the residents for the president's Proclamation of Neutrality, signed in Philadelphia on April 22, 1793, which reads in part,

> Whereas it appears that a state of war exists between Austria, Prussia, Sardinia, Great Britain, and the United Netherlands, of the one part, and France on the other; and the duty and interest of the United States require, that they should with sincerity and good faith adopt and pursue a conduct friendly and impartial toward the belligerent Powers;
>
> I have therefore thought fit by these presents to declare the disposition of the United States to observe the conduct aforesaid towards those Powers respectfully; and to exhort and warn the citizens of the United States carefully to avoid all acts and proceedings whatsoever, which may in any manner tend to contravene such disposition.[16]

Those who gathered at Mr. Edward's Coffeehouse asserted their belief that US neutrality was essential for "promoting . . . real happiness &

prosperity." They also resolved that any intrusion of foreign powers in the affairs of the US should not be tolerated: "the interference of any foreign power or Minister in the internal Administration of our Government, is an infringement of the Sovereignty of the people . . . and should therefore excite the indignation and reprehension of every Independent American."[17]

The coffeehouses of North America were also contested territory, both readily embraced and caustically condemned, just as they had been elsewhere. Coffeehouse owner Samuel Richardet, who corresponded with several sitting US presidents, offered coffee and a range of services that included "overnight accommodations, meals, beverages, and a reading room supplied with current newspapers from the United States and Europe," at his establishment, which also served as a place where maritime merchants and ship captains might "meet and post information."[18] Yet in 1793, Thomas Boylston Adams (1772–1832) wrote a letter to his mother, Abigail Adams, about the troublesome talk that establishments such as Richardet's inspired. Adams decried how "the Coffee-House, proper only for the resort of Merchants, [has been] converted into a *den of thieves* and Jacobins."[19] The coffeehouse in question and the year of this letter are both worth noting. The young Adams was referring to talk he had heard in New York's Tontine Coffeehouse, which was frequented by those who held pro-French sentiments.[20] During this time, the Jacobins, one of the cruelest political groups in post-Revolution France, had joined with others for what is known as the Reign of Terror, a bloody ten-month period from September 1793 to July 1794 that ended with the execution of government leaders and members of the nobility. Boylston suggests that he felt it would be prudent to monitor coffeehouses for signs of potentially treasonous activities.

Unlike their predecessors elsewhere, the early coffeehouses of the United States were not exclusively the preserves of men. George Washington wrote in his diary in 1771 that "The Coffeehouse, a popular tavern run by a Mrs. Howard, was on Main near the State House" in Annapolis, Maryland.[21] Inventor, manufacturer, and writer Jabez Burns (1805–1876), whose Burn's Roaster, patented in 1864, "revolutionize[d] the coffee-roasting business," railed against women who aspired to participate the coffee business and indeed in any commercial activity, writing that "it pains us to see a woman out of her sphere."[22] Burns was eager to maintain a monopoly on the preparation of coffee beans and was opposed to women's roasting of beans in their homes: "It is preposterous to suppose that household roasting will be continued long in any part of this country, if coffee properly prepared can be had."[23]

## Sourcing Coffee to Feed a Global Demand

The coffee consumed in the first century of nationhood in the United States came primarily from the East and West Indies, although some also came from Brazil, Costa Rica, Java, and Ceylon (today Sri Lanka). At this time, most people purchased the raw beans from their local general store and then roasted and ground them at home.[24] In the early nineteenth century, coffee plants were cultivated in Hawaii, a future US state. Coffee beans first came to Hawaii in 1817 with Don Francisco de Paula Marin, whose first attempt at cultivation was unsuccessful. However, in 1825 Chief Boki (1785–1829), the governor of Oahu, was more successful with plants he had obtained in Brazil.[25] Three years later, in 1828, an American missionary, Samuel Ruggles (1795–1871), brought coffee plants from the Boki estate on Oahu to the Kona region of Hawaii, where the plants flourished. Commercial cultivation of the Arabica bean began in Kona in the 1830s, where today it is still a thriving industry.[26]

Citizens of the new United States participated in the coffee trade. In 1782, future president John Adams (1735–1826), who was serving as the US envoy to the Netherlands, received a letter from Jean Henri David Uhl, a member of the Supreme German Court of the king of Prussia and the husband of one of the owners of the Fredericdorp Plantation in Suriname, a small country along the northeastern coast of South America. Uhl demanded the return of 8,697 pounds of coffee from his wife's plantation that was aboard the "ship of Captain C. G. Weis." According to Uhl, the British had seized a ship from a Dutch convoy that had subsequently been taken by "An American," who had "sold the vessel and its cargo in Martinique."[27] A 1786 entry in George Washington's diary indicates that goods, including coffee, from Suriname did come to the new nation: "I sent my boat to Alexandria for Molasses and Coffee which had been sent to me from Suriname by a Mr. Brandon of that place."[28]

A more direct link may be drawn to US coffee procurement from Mauritius, an island off the southeastern coast of Africa that was a French possession from 1715 to 1810. In a statement dated January 17, 1789, US merchant Stephen Higginson wrote from Boston to John Adams, who at the time was the US ambassador to Great Britain. According to Higginson, in the two years since France had opened trade between the United States and its colonies in Mauritius and India, he and other US merchants had been "going over to Bourbon where the Coffee is raised, and contracting with the planters for what we wanted."[29]

Soon after coffee arrived in Cuba, around 1758, the United States began importing coffee from the island. An 1807 letter to President James Madison, Henry Hill, the former "consul for Cuba," who was writing on behalf of a Mr. Ramage, then the acting vice consul in Havana, expressed his concern over "the quantity of Sugar and coffee smuggled in Neutral vessels [fr]om that Port." Ramage asked Madison to consider adopting measures to prevent such thievery in the future.[30]

A 1795 letter from Marquis de Rouvray (1743–1819) to Alexander Hamilton suggests that another of the locales for coffee importation may have been the island of Santo Domingo. Rouvray, a Frenchman who had served in the American Revolutionary War, moved to Santo Domingo after the war, where he purchased sugar and coffee plantations. The letter mentions a debt from 1790 Rouvray paid to Henri Jacques Guillaume-Clarke, a representative of the Duke of Orleans, to settle a debt incurred by Rouvray's son for a commission as a captain in the Hussars (a cavalry regiment in the British Army formed in 1690) and hints at the possibility that the marquis exported coffee and sugar to the United States from his plantations in the Caribbean.[31]

By the first years of the nineteenth century, US merchants were in the business of exporting coffee and related products. On June 3,1803, Samuel Endicott, master of the *Mount Vernon*, which was bound from Boston to Copenhagen, prepared a manifest for the ship. Endicott's list of cargo that had been imported from the West and East Indies included 34,891 bags of coffee valued at $7,548.20. The ship was also taking sugar, tea, and rum to Denmark.[32]

## Coffee and Exploitation

As the demand for coffee in many parts of the world grew, growers experienced pressure to increase production and importers looked for new sources of the product. These pressures strained the supply from Yemen and stirred merchants to find a way to procure plants they could introduce in regions outside the Yemeni highlands. The circumstances under which Yemen lost its monopoly on coffee growing is not entirely clear. The story of Baba Budan, while entertaining, is probably less accurate than an alternate explanation that Dutch merchants who were already trading in beans smuggled coffee plants out of the port of Mocha in the first decade or so of the seventeenth century. This act of thievery began a wave of coffee growing far from Yemen and Ethiopia and coincides with a time when many European countries, including Britain, France, the Netherlands, Spain, and Portugal, were expanding their colonial influences around the world, suggesting that coffee growing became an important agent of European imperialism around the globe. Among the first wave of these coffee plantations were those established on Java, an island colony that is today part of Indonesia. Plantations on Sumatra and Sulawesi soon followed. Coffee reached India sometime before 1616, the year English traveler Edward Terry (1590–1660) observed that "many of the best people in India who are strict in their religion and drink no wine at all, use a liquor more wholesome than pleasant, they call coffee."[33] In the early 1700s, coffee arrived in Brazil from French Guiana, and from there it moved to Colombia, Costa Rica, Cuba, the Dominican Republic, Guatemala, Honduras, and Suriname.[34] Coffee made it north to Mexico around the end of the eighteenth century, although it would not become an important export crop of that country until approximately 100 years later.[35]

At the beginning of the twentieth century, coffee growing came to Kenya, a country that today has a northern border with Ethiopia. Brought to the area by farmers from Britain and other parts of Europe, coffee crops were introduced in a number of locations in Kenya, with the main region stretching from the slopes of Mount Kenya to just outside the capital of Nairobi.[36] Over time, coffee production expanded to other parts of sub-Saharan Africa, including the Ivory Coast, Uganda, Rwanda, and Tanzania. It also remained an important crop in Ethiopia. Coffee was supposedly taken to Vietnam by French missionaries around the middle of the nineteenth century, but it did not become a profitable export until the early 1980s.[37]

The increasing popularity of coffee was accompanied by a by-product of plantation crops, the suffering of plantation laborers. The misery of those who tended coffee plants and harvested coffee beans was slow to enter the consciousness of the individuals and nations that most benefited from these labors. As the United States continues to struggle with the legacy of slavery and exploitation on its own soil, it cannot be forgotten that citizens of the United States also contributed to the dire conditions laborers in other parts of the world experienced as coffee cultivation facilitated an expansion of the slave trade in places such as the Caribbean.

The numerous coffee plantations western foreigners established on their colonial possessions relied on poorly paid and often mistreated local inhabitants for the backbreaking work of planting, harvesting, and preparing beans for export. While the first slaves were brought from Africa to work on sugar plantations, from the mid-eighteenth century onward additional slaves were needed for coffee.[38] In some instances, as was true of the United States, indentured servants and slaves would be exported to locations in the Caribbean if the supply of indigenous workers was insufficient. These slaves were often victims of horrific treatment. One former slave witnessed men who had been "hung . . . with heads downward, drowned . . . in sacks, crucified . . . on planks, buried . . . alive, crushed . . . with mortars."[39] In response to their harsh treatment, slaves resisted in both nonviolent and violent ways, although the nations of Europe and the United States would not fully abolish slavery until the nineteenth century.[40]

While the abolition of slavery in Europe and the United States in the nineteenth century may have ended the trafficking in slave labor, it did little to improve how the non-Europeans who continued to work on the plantations were perceived and treated. This point is illustrated in a book by Francis Beatty Thurber (1842–1907), a wholesale grocer who was born in Delhi of English parents but made his wealth after immigrating to the United States. In *Coffee: From Plantation to Cup* (1881), Thurber wrote of the "contempt and want of consideration with which the natives [of Java] are treated."[41] However, Thurber's own words cast doubt on the genuineness of his concern for local workers; he asserted that the local population was "miserably poor, ignorant, and degraded." Thurber suggested that the situation of Java's indigenous peoples was attributable to "the effect of the climate," but then said that such a scenario "is hard to determine."[42]

Thurber's views on the impact of climate on humanity were echoed by Edwin Arnold Lester (1832–1904), an English coffee plantation owner who wrote *Coffee: Its Cultivation and Profit* (1886), based on his experiences as a plantation owner in India. Lester noted that "natives of most warm countries—and certainly of Lower India—are physically inferior to the working classes of the invigorating north." He advised "every coffee planter" to purchase a copy of "Mr. Monier Williams' recent volume, 'Modern India,'" to learn how best to manage local laborers.[43] It is evident from Lester's writing that he had little respect for the inhabitants of India. His views seem to echo the climate theory of French philosopher and lawyer Montesquieu (1689–1755). According to Montesquieu, the characters and customs of all humans are much influenced by the geography and the climate of where they live.[44]

Local populations and slaves from Africa were not the only sources of plantation labor. During this time, young men from a variety of countries in search of what they believed would be better lives sought out indentured servitude in the hope of eventually gaining their freedom and living a more prosperous life than they would have had at home. For example, in 1858, Chantau, a fifteen-year-old boy from Shawtaw (Shantou), on the eastern coast of China's Guangdong province, was contracted to work in Havana, Cuba. The contract states that he would be paid "four pesos a month," given "two sets of clothing annually," and provided with "eight ounces of salted meat, 2.5 pounds of sweet potatoes or other nutritious roots and provisions" every month for a term of service lasting ten years. In addition to the specifics of compensation, the agreement stipulated that over time Chantau would repay the money provided for his passage from China. The contract is vague about where Chantau would be working or what work he would do. It is possible that he was ordered to work on the *cafetales* (coffee plantations) owned by his patrons, Señor Don Joaquin Pedroso y Echeveria, Señor Don Luis Pedroso, and Don José María Morales, all of whom lived in Havana and were part of Cuba's century-old coffee business.[45]

The exploitation of those who work for the world's major coffee producers continue to mar the coffee industry today, centuries later, prompting efforts toward greater equity. While these efforts seem to be relatively recent, in fact the first murmurs of what later became movements for fair trade were uttered as early as the mid-1940s. Voices in favor of equity and justice continue as crucial elements of debates about coffee production. Over time, discussion of issues such as equitable pay to farmers, how best to grow coffee in ways that are environmentally sound and sustainable, and fair prices for coffee beans yielded results. To understand this newest chapter in coffee's tale it is necessary to return to Ethiopia, where this book began.

## Fair Trade, Sustainability and Globalization

The enduring popularity of coffee means that new questions are waiting to be explored and debated. One of the most compelling issues is the human and environmental costs of producing coffee. It is important that this book not overlook these issues and how they resonate in the contemporary lives of producers, sellers, and consumers.

Images of a drought-stricken, famine-ravaged Ethiopia are all too often the only pictures people have of the African nation. Ethiopia's distinction as "the birthplace of coffee," a point Ethiopian prime minister Hailemariam Desalegn made at the start of a joint press conference during President Barack Obama's visit to his country in July 2017, is often overlooked, as is consideration of the place of coffee in Ethiopia's present.[46] In the years since the catastrophic events of the mid-1980s, as President Obama noted, the government of Ethiopia has pursued a number of initiatives intended to "[lift] millions of people out of poverty" by improving "food security," an effort that has included working with farmers to encourage them to "plant drought-resistant and higher-yield crops."[47] The coffee industry, a source of great national pride and a crucial element of Ethiopia's economic future, is one place where such changes have been sought.

The Ethiopian Commodity Exchange (ECX; founded 2008) is an important part of Ethiopia's sustainable agriculture initiatives.[48] The goal of the ECX is to "revolutionize Ethiopia's tradition bound agriculture through creating a new marketplace that serves all market actors, from farmers to traders to processors to exporters to consumers." Created in response to "agricultural markets . . . characterized by high costs and high risks of transacting [that forced] much of Ethiopia into global isolation," the ECX also sought to address the factors that compounded the nation's economic challenges. Among the more pressing issues ECX founders identified were the decision of buyers and sellers to engage in commercial transactions only with those they knew. These efforts by farmers to avoid risk had the effect of driving up costs and therefore to consumer prices. In addition, 95 percent of Ethiopia's agricultural output was (and remains) in the hands of small-scale farmers, many of who "came to market with little information and [were] at the mercy of merchants in the nearest and only market they know, unable to negotiate better prices or reduce their market risk." The ECX determined that the most effective remedy for these problems was the creation of a partnership that involved "market actors, Members of the Exchange, and . . . the Government of Ethiopia," which brought together buyers and sellers to ensure quality products, efficient delivery of goods, and prompt payment under the leadership of a board of directors.[49] The performance of the ECX has had mixed reviews. A February 2017 article in *The Economist* notes that despite the ECX's designation as sub-Saharan Africa's "most modern commodity exchange outside Johannesburg," "staple foods" meant to stave off starvation and "reduce price volatility and incentivize farmers to plant crops" constitute only 10 percent of its trade, which is dominated by two export products, coffee and sesame seeds. This may be good news for coffee, which must go through the exchange, but other crops are not as well served.[50] In addition, the ECX does not designate all of its coffee as fair trade, a fact that causes some consumers to avoid purchasing Ethiopian coffee.

For consumers who want to ensure that their coffee is equitably sourced, one of the best places to look is to Fair Trade Certified (formerly Fair Trade USA), which began in the 1940s as TransFair USA. Fair Trade Certified guarantees that all of its products are

> made with respect to people and planet. Our rigorous social, environmental and economic standards work to promote safe, healthy working conditions, protect the environment, enable transparency, and empower communities to build strong, thriving businesses. When you choose products with the Fair Trade label, your day-to-day purchases can improve an entire community's day-to-day lives.[51]

A fair trade label on coffee ensures that the small farmers who grow and harvest coffee have not been subjected to exploitative business practices, that they have received a guaranteed minimum price for their harvest, and that they work directly with importers. The last of these guarantees removes the middlemen who offer farmers cash for their crops at the lowest price point. This is an important part of creating long-term sustainability, as fair trade standards are designed "to ensure that households have the money they need to invest in their lives and their work."[52]

The World Fair Trade Organization, which was founded in 1989, espouses goals similar to those of Fair Trade Certified. Committed to "a world in which trade structures and practices have been transformed to work in favour of the poor and promote sustainable development and justice," the WFTO seeks to "enable producers to improve their livelihoods and communities through fairly traded commodities."[53] As a global network and an advocate for national organizations such as Fair Trade Certified, the WFTO ensures that the interest of artisans and producers, especially small farmers, are the main focus of all of its policies, governance, structures, and decision making.[54]

Efforts to raise awareness about the plight of exploited farmers and artisans continue to gain momentum. Consumers have begun paying more attention to the human and environmental costs of the goods they buy, eat, and drink. In response to pressure from consumers, many restaurants, dining halls, coffeehouses, and grocery stores across the nation, and indeed around the world, now serve and stock goods certified as fair trade compliant.

While many see these efforts as steps in a positive direction, others worry that fair trade products, which are perceived to cost more than the same goods not certified as fair trade, contribute to the food inequalities that exist in every nation on earth. The WFTO has responded to allegations that the products they endorse are out of the reach of significant numbers of the consuming public. It asserts that the supposed higher price tag for their merchandise is one of the greatest myths that surrounds the fair trade movement. Its website states that "most Fair Trade products are competitively priced in relation to their conventional counterparts. Fair Trade Organisations work directly with producers, cutting out middlemen, so they can keep products affordable for consumers and return a greater percentage of the price to the producers."[55]

In some instances, what the WTFO claims is true. Careful shopping at both local markets and large chains does yield opportunities to purchase fair trade items at prices no higher than those that are not certified. And yet, on the same excursion to the market, one cannot help but notice that fair trade chocolate is often more expensive than the average bar made by many well-known brands, in the same way that certified fair trade coffee generally sells for more than its mass-produced counterparts. This disparity presents a genuine challenge for those who would prefer to buy products they know are sustainably produced by farmers earning a just wage but do not have the financial resources to do so. Lack of access to affordable goods that fulfill the conditions of groups such as the WTFO and Fair Trade Certified not only continues the practice of bolstering companies that profit from less attention to human and environmental costs, it also serves as a reminder that historic patterns still resonate today in the postcolonial struggles of people who live in former imperial possessions. While the latter is not the subject of this book, it cannot be ignored that the story told here would be incomplete without a nod to the reality that coffee production plays an important role in the deliberations that surround how best to ensure justice for those who provide for the world's necessities and desires.

## Patterns of Globalization and Socialization

As an agent of globalization, coffee transformed more than just how men and later women expressed their delight in one another's company or their dismay about local and national politics. As the brief discussion in this chapter illuminates, the popularity of coffee also forever altered the interrelationships that have historically existed, and continue to exist, between consumers, producers, and suppliers. In this light, coffee is a lens for thinking about the connections that exist between those who enjoy the beverage and those who make this pleasure possible, an association that invites a consideration of what responsibility, if any, shoppers have to producers and what might be in store for the future of all the products we buy. As consumers are paying closer attention to the source of coffee, they can use the past and the present of coffee as an entry point for bigger questions of what a global market that shuns exploitation and degradation might look like.

As this chapter comes to an end, at least one question persists: what does this book have to do with coffee and socialization in the contemporary era? At the very least, local coffeehouses and national chains continue to play host to all manner of human interchange. Workers in offices and on job sites, students cramming for exams, friends meeting to catch up, and musicians sharing their passion for entertaining others can be found on almost any day or night of the week in a favorite coffeehouse. Still also present today are those who gather with like-minded individuals to decry the problems of their era. In all the reasons that exist for sharing in a cup today can also be found the traditions begun long ago, although most are unaware of their connection to a past shared with people who lived centuries ago on distant continents.

# Just the Grounds

"I never thought I had a food history."[1] A semester of exploring what food and drink mean revealed something very personal to each of the students in my History of Food class in the spring of 2017, from those who felt a strong attachment to the foods, traditions, and rituals of their families to those who had little idea of the place of food in their pasts. For almost everyone in the class, our semester-long sojourn through food and drink led them in the often tasty task of thinking more creatively and critically about their connections to ways their immediate families and distant ancestors nourished their bodies and sustained intimate and societal ties.

For this group of students, among the more surprising revelations was how comestibles often had little to do with keeping people alive. Many in this inquisitive group had little idea that foot soldiers in ancient Rome ground their own wheat and baked their own bread, that during the Middle Ages and into the early modern era civic leaders in Venice used food to reinforce loyalty to the city, or that in the third century of the Common Era Chinese Buddhist monks introduced novel methods of food production such as refining sugar and making butter to India.[2]

Over sixteen weeks, lively discussions ensued about how edibles have been integral to the achievement of political goals, how daily bread and delicacies have been used to reinforce and reshape social and religious hierarchies and power structures, and how many of their own simple pleasures have also been tools of colonialism, oppression, and environmental degradation. We also engaged in conversations about how we might all be inspired to support efforts that advance greater equity for those who satisfy the worlds' appetites in ways that are environmentally sustainable. As the semester unfolded, we also explored the light food history sheds on historical and cultural divergences and convergences; on the political, economic, and colonial ambitions of individuals and groups; and on the values, curiosities, anxieties, and desires of populations over time and across vast expanses of territory. These students also forced me to rethink how the final pages of this book should look, reminding me that all good conclusions both look back to where the work started and suggest what the future might hold.

This book began with the assertion that telling the story of a beverage that still commands the unfaltering devotion of many around the world demands a reckoning with social, cultural, economic, political, legal, and religious history and with the regional histories of areas around the Mediterranean, the interior of the Arab East, the European West, and later parts of Asia and the Americas. In this retelling, I have argued that coffee and coffeehouses were the threads that linked seemingly disparate subjects, revealing their place as a pivot of the history of commercial and social globalization. Throughout this book, coffee preparation, rituals of consumption, anxieties about coffee and coffeehouses, and the social patterns of coffeehouses created have been revealed as the products of eastern soils that changed the role of public space around the globe. I have demonstrated that the human history of coffee and coffeehouses are deeply embedded in centuries of material and cultural trade and exchange and thus cannot be understood apart from these interactions or from the significance of these connections in the lives of the people coffee touched.

From its origins as a plant indigenous to the landscapes of Ethiopia and Yemen, the story of coffee unfolded in the medical tracts of Ibn Sina, in accounts of the late-night rituals of Sufi mystics, and in the narratives of merchants and travelers who engaged their audiences with descriptions of magnificent cities such as Aleppo and the details of how coffee in Arabia was brewed. I traced the journey of coffee along desert trade routes and across the Mediterranean Sea, analyzing its history as a product in a history of commerce that preceded it by centuries. By the early sixteenth century, the story of coffee had become the tale of the coffeehouse, a new institution that sparked observations that were not always complimentary about how central it was to the social lives of men. The coffeehouses of Mecca, Constantinople, Venice, Oxford, Philadelphia, and elsewhere raised the blood pressure of those who drank it for the first time and sharpened the anxieties of civil and religious leaders, another part of a history people from the East and the West share. Once coffee crossed the Mediterranean Sea, it became part of the history of Renaissance and early modern demand, consumption, and acquisition, joining silk, pepper, and forms of artistic expression that reflected the world these goods left behind. Finally, coffee increased the both the profitability of imperial possessions and the misery of their inhabitants, a legacy that remains today in many places. Coffee deserves far more than a footnote in the histories examined in these chapters. It was not simply another luxury good among the many that moved from around the globe in all directions. The history of coffee and coffeehouses is at the heart of the inextricable links that exist between the trade in material goods and the cultural exchanges that accompanied such transactions, demonstrating the efficacy of a single product in inaugurating entirely new social patterns.

The start of this book included the claim that there was still much to tell about the story of coffee. At the end of this book, that assertion remains true. Still in need of careful investigation are the impressions those in the eastern Mediterranean had of the merchants, pilgrims, and travelers who came to their lands from both the western Mediterranean and the eastern ends of the Silk Road.[3] The history I have presented here opens a space for an analysis of stories yet untold, or at least underexamined, in the history of the coffee trade. Most immediately, the economic history of coffee prompts more in-depth examination of commercial agreements and what they might reveal about the gendered nature of trade, starting with Genoese and Venetian women who appear as parties in the maritime trade and other business contracts of their husbands. I suspect there is to more to learn about the roles women may have played in the financial prosperity and stability of their families and communities. Similarly, in pre-Islamic and Islamic Arabia, women sometimes played a part in business matters, as did Muhammad's first wife Khadija and the Prophet's first wife after Khadija's death, the widow Sawdah bint Zam'a. Evidence of women as the owners of merchant warehouses and inns throughout the Mediterranean region offers another place to continue the exploration. Knowledge of the role of Jewish women in trade between East and West is also necessary for a more complete picture. The history of coffee and coffeehouses also invites research on the impact of commercial exchanges on cultural and technological innovations in the parts of the world addressed here and in other places

The history in this book also invites continuing work in the history of foodways. As three members of that spring class contemplated whether a hot dog was a sandwich and another student was looking at how the Meals Ready to Eat (MREs) that sustained her and her family during the camping trips of her childhood were the source of fond memories of family and shared experiences, I was struck by how much remains to be done in the study of the history and meaning of food. I also find myself returning to the science of taste and smell, to the role that the physical properties of food and drink play in the conjuring of culinary memories, the creation of new pleasures, and the recognition of the food aversions that are unique to each person.

Finally, a careful study of the successes and failures of the fair trade movement, starting with the earliest efforts of the 1940s, would perhaps uncover new evidence about the lasting scars in places that still struggle with the transformation from colonial possession to independence, particularly in places that still engage in coffee production. Indeed, this consideration might will begin with a fresh look at how this precarious time was understood by people on both sides of the transition. Within this colonial and postcolonial history lie new voices waiting to be heard and a chance to reconsider more familiar ones, all speaking about a legacy of imperialism that marked both those who had been colonized and people in Europe and the United States as all sides sought to redefine this relationship. In short, I am left contemplating where to turn next, aware that this particular work is equally a conclusion and a commencement.

Coffee continues to fascinate. The coffee of today would likely surprise the drinkers of long ago, who would have given little thought to cooling it over ice, flavoring it with syrups, diluting it with milk products, or processing it to remove its quintessential property, caffeine. This last innovation would probably be the most perplexing to them. The coffeehouses and cafés of Mecca, Istanbul, Venice, London, and New York may no longer disquiet officials, but a large group gathered over a steaming pot or two might lead contemporary onlookers to ponder a time when coffeehouses were suspect, accurately identified with discontentedness and even plots of revolution.

What remains, however, is the desire of coffee drinkers to gather over a cup in places that reflect the sociability of the first coffeehouses. While today most cafés have expanded their offerings to include delicate pastries and in some places more substantial fare, they still serve the same timeless and comforting purposes. With a tantalizing smell that drifts out of open doors and windows, shops and coffeehouses continue to invite us to stop and rest awhile, to take a few moments to connect ourselves to people we a share history with, a history that is not just about the beverage but also about how we came to be social.

# NOTES

Introduction

1. Mark Pendergrast, Uncommon Grounds: The History of Coffee and How It Transformed Our World (New York: Basic Books, 1999), xv.

2. John Ray, A Collection of Curious Travels and Voyages, in Two Tomes, the First Containing Leonhart Rauwolff's Itinerary into the Eastern Countries, translated by Nicholas Staphorst (London: S. Smith and B. Walford, 1693), 92. See also Karl H. Dannenfeldt, Leonhard Rauwolf: Sixteenth-Century Physician, Botanist, and Traveler (Cambridge: Harvard University Press, 1968), 71–73.

3. "The smoking, glowing beans Aleppo sends, and distant Mocha too, a thousand shiploads, never rivaled." Giuseppe Parini, Il Giorno (London: Clarendon, 1921), 7.

4. William Harrison Ukers, All about Coffee (New York: The Tea and Coffee Trade Journal, 1922), 7.

5. Coffee Capsules Direct, accessed July 9, 2018, https://coffeecapsulesdirect.com/favourite-coffee-quotes/.

6. Reuters Staff, "Americans Are Drinking a Daily Cup of Coffee at the Highest Level in Six Years: Survey," Reuters, March 17, 2018, accessed July 3, 2018, https://www.reuters.com/article/us-coffee-conference-survey/americans-are-drinking-a-daily-cup-of-coffee-at-the-highest-level-in-six-years-survey-idUSKCN1GT0KU.

7. "Aims and Scope," Food and Foodways: Explorations in the History and Culture of Human Nourishment, journal website, accessed July 9, 2018, https://www.tandfonline.com/action/journalInformation?show=aimsScope&journalCode=gfof20.

8. While sugar was later imported from the Americas, for purposes of this book I focus on Levantine sugar, which west traveled along the Silk Road from China and was being cultivated in Jordan as early as the eighth century.

9. Natalie Koch, "Geopower and Geopolitics in, of, and for the Middle East," International Journal of Middle East Studies 49, no. 2 (2017): 315.

10. David Abulafia, The Great Sea (New York: Oxford University Press, 2011), xxiii.

11. Richard A. Goldthwaite, Wealth and the Demand for Art in Italy, 1300–1600 (Baltimore: Johns Hopkins University Press, 1993), 1.

12. For more on the role of merchants in evolving notions of science in the early modern era, see Pamela H. Smith and Paula Findlen, eds., Merchants and Marvels: Commerce, Science and Art in Early Modern Europe (New York: Routledge, 2002).

13. Ibn Battutah, The Travels of Ibn Battutah, abridged by Tim Mackintosh-Smith (London: Picador, 2000), vii–ix.

14. Edward Said, Orientalism (New York: Random House, 1979), 1.

15. Elliot Horowitz, "Coffee, Coffeehouses, and the Nocturnal Rituals of Early Modern Jewry," AJS Review 14, no. 1 (1989): 18.

16. Unsurprisingly, coffeehouses began as male-only institutions. In some parts of the Muslim world they remain so.

17. Pendergrast, Uncommon Grounds, 6.

18. Christine A. Jones, "Exotic Edibles: Coffee, Chocolate, and the Early Modern French How-To," Journal of Medieval and Early Modern Studies 43, no. 3 (2013): 623.

19. Pendergrast, Uncommon Grounds, 49.

20. Pendergrast, Uncommon Grounds, 7.

21. Filippo de Vivo, "Pharmacies as Centres of Communication in Early Modern Venice," Renaissance Studies 21, no. 4 (2007): 507–9.

22. Brian Cowan, The Social Life of Coffee: The Emergence of the British Coffeehouse (New Haven, Conn.: Yale University Press, 2005), 235. See also Jürgen Habermas, The Structural Transformation of the Public Sphere: An Inquiry into a Category of Bourgeois Society, translated by Thomas Burger with the assistance of Frederick Lawrence (Cambridge, Mass.: MIT Press, 1991), 5–32.

23. Stephen Greenblatt, Marvelous Possessions: The Wonder of the New World (Chicago: University of Chicago Press, 1991), 22–23.

24. John Ellis, An Historical Account of Coffee, with an Engraving and Botanical Description of the Tree: To Which Are Added Sundry Papers Relative to Its Culture and Use, as an Article of Diet and of Commerce (London: Edward and Charles Dilly, 1774), 14. See also Pendergrast, Uncommon Grounds, 6.

25. Ralph S. Hattox, Coffee and Coffeehouses: The Origins of a Social Beverage in the Medieval Near East (Seattle: University of Washington Press, 1985), 11; Pendergrast, Uncommon Grounds, 6.

26. Hattox, Coffee and Coffeehouses, 12.

27. Ari Ben-Menahem, "The Clockwork Universe," in Historical Encyclopedia of Natural and Mathematical Sciences, vol. 1, edited by Christian Witschel (New York: Springer, 2009), 954.

28. Ukers, All about Coffee, 68.

29. Peter C. Mancall, ed., Travel Narratives from the Age of Discovery: An Anthology (New York: Oxford University Press, 2006), 4–5.

30. Pendergrast, Uncommon Grounds, 8–10.

31. Mahmoud Darwish, Memory for Forgetfulness: August, Beirut, 1986, translated by Ibrahim Muhawi (Berkeley: University of California Press, 1995), 7.

Chapter 1: Desert to Sea

1. Mahmoud Darwish, *Memory for Forgetfulness: August, Beirut, 1986*, translated by Ibrahim Muhawi (Berkeley: University of California Press, 1995), 7.

2. Robert D. Kaplan, *The Revenge of Geography: What the Map Tells Us about Coming Conflicts and the Battle against Fate* (New York: Basic Books, 2012), 24.

3. David Abulafia, *The Great Sea* (New York: Oxford University Press, 2011), xxiii.

4. Abulafia, *The Great Sea*, xxiii.

5. Georg Wilhelm Hegel, *The Philosophy of History* (London: George Bell and

Sons, 1884), 91. See also Miriam Cooke, Erdağ Göknar, and Grant Richard Parker, eds., *Mediterranean Passages: Readings from Dido to Derrida* (Chapel Hill: University of North Carolina Press, 2008), 291 and 95.

6. Hegel, *The Philosophy of History*, 199.

7. Hegel, *The Philosophy of History*, 199.

8. Peregrin Horden and Nicholas Purcell, *The Corrupting Sea: A Study of Mediterranean History* (New Jersey: Blackwell, 2000), 12. The Islamic calendar begins with the Hijra, the flight of Muhammad and his followers from Mecca to Medina to escape persecution in 622 CE, thus 622 CE is 1 AH. Although not exact as Islam follows a lunar calendar, AH (after the Hijra) dates are approximately 622 years earlier than the corresponding Common Era dates.

9. Abulafia, *The Great Sea*, xxiii.

10. William B. F. Ryan, "Decoding the Mediterranean Salinity Crisis," *Sedimentology* 56, no. 1 (2009): 95.

11. D. Garcia-Castellanos, F. Estrada, I. Jiménez-Munt, C. Gorini, M. Fernàndez, J. Vergés, and R. De Vicente, "Catastrophic Flood of the Mediterranean after the Messinian Salinity Crisis," *Nature* 462, no. 7274 (2009): 778–81.

12. Horden and Purcell, *The Corrupting Sea*, 13.

13. Examples that address trade in the Mediterranean region include Robert S. Lopez and Irving W. Raymond, *Medieval Trade in the Mediterranean World* (New York: Columbia University Press, 1961); Mark Angelos, "Women in Genoese Commenda Contracts, 1155–1216," *Journal of Medieval History* 20, no. 4 (1994): 299–331; Calvin B. Hoover, "The Sea Loan in Genoa in the Twelfth Century," *Quarterly Journal of Economics* 40, no. 3 (1926): 495–529; Abulafia, *The Great Sea*; David Abulafia, *The Mediterranean in History* (Los Angeles: J. Paul Getty Museum, 2003); Felipe Fernandez-Armesto and Benjamin Sacks, "The Global Exchange of Food and Drugs," in *The Oxford Handbook of the History of Consumption*, edited by Frank Trentmann (New York: Oxford University Press, 2012); Felipe Fernandez-Armesto, *Pathfinders: A Global History of Exploration* (New York: W. W. Norton, 2013); Horden and Purcell, *The Corrupting Sea*; and Sally McKee, "Women under Venetian Colonial Rule in the Early Renaissance: Observations on Their Economic Activities," *Renaissance Quarterly* 51, no. 1 (1998): 34–67.

14. Fernand Braudel, *The Mediterranean and the Mediterranean World in the Age of Philip II*, vol. 2 (Berkeley: University of California Press, 1996), 1243–44.

15. Abulafia, *The Great Sea*, xxx.

16. Herodotus, *The History*, translated by David Grene (Chicago: University of Chicago Press, 1987), 125.

17. Herodotus, *The History*, 257, 59.

18. Herodotus, *The History*, 257–59.

19. Herodotus, *The History*, 257. For additional discussion of Herodotus's description of the eastern Mediterranean, see Anson F. Rainey, "Herodotus' Description of the East Mediterranean Coast," *Bulletin of the American Schools of Oriental Research* 321 (February 2001): 57–63.

20. Bertram Thomas and B. K. N. Wylie, "A Camel Journey across the Rub' Al Khali," *Geographical Journal* 78, no. 3 (931): 211.

21. Gus W. Van Beek, "Frankincense and Myrrh," *The Biblical Archaeologist* 23, no. 3 (1960): 72–75; and Gus W. Van Beek, "Frankincense and Myrrh in Ancient

South Arabia," *Journal of the American Oriental Society* 78, no. 3 (1958): 142. According to Van Beek, high-quality frankincense grew in a topographically similar region of ancient Somaliland (present-day Somalia).

22. Van Beek, "Frankincense and Myrrh in Ancient South Arabia," 145.

23. Nigel Groom, *Frankincense and Myrrh: A Study of the Arabian Incense Trade* (New York: Longman, 1981), 8.

24. Groom, *Frankincense and Myrrh*, 1–8.

25. Van Beek, "Frankincense and Myrrh."

26. Van Beek, "Frankincense and Myrrh in Ancient South Arabia," 144. Nigel Groom, *Frankincense and Myrrh: A Study of the Arabian Incense Trade* (New York: Longman, 1981), 1. Groom notes that Greeks also used frankincense in their temples but to a lesser degree (6).

27. Theophrastus, *Inquiry into Plants*, translated by Arthur Hort (Cambridge: Harvard University Press, 1916), 322.

28. Groom, *Frankincense and Myrrh*, 7.

29. Groom, *Frankincense and Myrrh*, 6.

30. Groom, *Frankincense and Myrrh*, 6–7.

31. Groom, *Frankincense and Myrrh*, 6–7.

32. Groom, *Frankincense and Myrrh*, 150.

33. Wilfred Harvey Schoff, trans., *The Periplus of the Erythraean Sea: Travel and Trade in the Indian Ocean by a Merchant of the First Century* (New York: Longmans, Green, 1912), 29.

34. Schoff, *The Periplus of the Erythraean Sea*, 22.

35. Schoff, *The Periplus of the Erythraean Sea*, 26.

36. Schoff, *The Periplus of the Erythraean Sea*, 32.

37. Schoff, *The Periplus of the Erythraean Sea*, 35. See also analysis in Van Beek, "Frankincense and Myrrh," 75. See also Van Beek, "Frankincense and Myrrh in Ancient South Arabia," 76. In the southern part of Arabia, Cana/Qana was one of the main ports on the southern coast of the Hadhramaut Kingdom (present-day Yemen) and a key link in the transport of frankincense from Egypt to India. For additional information on the history of the Arabian trade in frankincense and myrrh, see Groom, *Frankincense and Myrrh*.

38. Van Beek, "Frankincense and Myrrh," 78; Schoff, *The Periplus of the Erythraean Sea*, 35.

39. The Catalan Atlas, 1375, is a series of six wooden panels covered in parchment attributed to the Majorcan Jewish cartographer Abraham Cresques. The selection here is a nineteenth-century reproduction of the panel "Europe and the Mediterranean."

40. Schoff, *The Periplus of the Erythraean Sea*, 34–35.

41. Schoff, *The Periplus of the Erythraean Sea*, 35.

42. Groom, *Frankincense and Myrrh*, 1.

43. Groom, *Frankincense and Myrrh*, 1.

44. Van Beek, "Frankincense and Myrrh," 83.

45. Wernerian Club, ed., *Pliny's Natural History in Thirty-Seven Books* (London: George Barclay, 1847), 65 and 147.

46. John W. Eadie and John Peter Oleson, "The Water-Supply Systems of

Nabataean and Roman Humayma, *Bulletin of the American Schools of Oriental Research* 262 (1986): 53

47. Pliny, *Natural History*, translated by W. Rackham, W. H. S. Jones, and D. E. Eichholz (London: William Heinemann, 1949), 293.

48. David Matz, *Daily Life of the Ancient Romans* (Westport, Conn.: Greenwood Press, 2002), xvi–xvii.

49. Gary Paul Nabhan, *Cumin, Camels, and Caravans: A Spice Odyssey* (Berkeley: University of California Press, 2014), 35.

50. Wernerian Club, *Pliny's Natural History*, 291.

51. Pliny, *Natural History*, 289, 295.

52. Nabhan, *Cumin, Camels, and Caravans*, 71–72.

53. Pliny, *Natural History*, 297.

54. Xinru Liu, *The Silk Road in World History* (New York: Oxford University Press, 2010): 1.

55. Liu, *The Silk Road in World History*, 4–5.

56. Liu, *The Silk Road in World History*, 6–8.

57. Liu, *The Silk Road in World History*, 8–9.

58. Liu, *The Silk Road in World History*, 8–9.

59. Liu, *The Silk Road in World History*, 9–10.

60. Marco Polo, *The Travels of Marco Polo*, translated by Ronald Latham (1958; repr. New York: Penguin, 1973), 49.

61. Polo, *The Travels of Marco Polo*, 46.

62. Polo, *The Travels of Marco Polo*, 19, 46.

63. Polo, *The Travels of Marco Polo*, 51. The Mosulin were merchants from Mosul, in Iraq.

64. Polo, *The Travels of Marco Polo*, 138.

65. Polo, *The Travels of Marco Polo*, 176.

66. Polo, *The Travels of Marco Polo*, 309.

67. Polo, *The Travels of Marco Polo*, 310.

68. Percy G. Adams, *Travel Literature and the Evolution of the Novel* (Lexington: University of Kentucky Press, 1983), 39.

69. Yehoshua Frenkel, "Ibn Jubayr (c. 1144–1217): Spanish Arab Traveler and Writer," in *Literature of Travel and Exploration: An Encyclopedia*, edited by Jennifer Speake (New York: Routledge, 2013), 580–81.

70. Katie Gramich, "'Every Hill Has Its History, Every Region Its Romance': Travellers' Constructions of Wales, 1844–1913," in *Travel Writing and Tourism in Britain and Ireland*, edited by Benjamin Colbert (New York: Palgrave MacMillan, 2012), 147.

71. Polo, *The Travels of Marco Polo*, 33.

72. Polo, *The Travels of Marco Polo*, 16–17.

73. Polo, *The Travels of Marco Polo*, 19, 9.

74. Anne E. C. McCants, "Exotic Goods, Popular Consumption, and the Standard of Living: Thinking About Globalization in the Early Modern World," *Journal of World History* 18, no. 4 (2007): 437.

75. McCants, "Exotic Goods, Popular Consumption, and the Standard of Living," 435.

76. McCants, "Exotic Goods, Popular Consumption, and the Standard of Living," 435; Janet L. Abu-Lughod, *Before European Hegemony: The World System A.D. 1250–1350* (New York: Oxford University Press, 1991), 78–80.

77. McCants, "Exotic Goods, Popular Consumption, and the Standard of Living," 435.

78. Immanuel Wallerstein, *The Modern World-System I: Capitalist Agriculture and the Origins of the European World-Economy in the Sixteenth Century* (New York: Academic Press, 1974), 332–333. See also McCants, "Exotic Goods, Popular Consumption, and the Standard of Living," 438–39.

79. Wallerstein, *The Modern World-System I*, 332–33.

80. Joel Mokyr, "Is There Still Life in the Pessimistic Case? Consumption during the Industrial Revolution, 1790–1850," *Journal of Economic History* 48, no. 1 (1988): 73.

81. Kevin H. O'Rourke and Jeffrey C. Williamson, "When Did Globalisation Begin?" *European Review of Economic History* 6, no. 1 (2002): 23.

82. O'Rourke and Williamson, "When Did Globalisation Begin?" 23.

83. McCants, "Exotic Goods, Popular Consumption, and the Standard of Living," 442, 439, 443, 447.

Chapter 2: Sociability, Chemistry, and Coffee's Eastern Origins

1. Virginia Woolf, *A Room of One's Own* (Harmondsworth: Penguin, 1928).

2. "Historical Coffee Quotes," Greenstreetroasters, https://greenstreetroasters.wordpress.com/2012/06/12/historical-coffee-poetry/.

3. Albert Sonnenfeld, "Preface," in *Food: A Culinary History*, edited by Jean-Louis Flandrin and Massimo Montanari, translated by Albert Sonnenfeld (New York: Columbia University Press, 1999), xvi

4. John C. Super, "Food and History," *Journal of Social History* 36, no.1 (2002): 165.

5. Pina Palma, *Savoring Power, Consuming the Times: The Metaphors of Food in Medieval and Renaissance Literature* (Notre Dame, IN: University of Notre Dame Press, 2013), 2.

6. Palma, *Savoring Power, Consuming the Times*, 2, 9.

7. G. Besnard, B. Khadari, M. Fernandez-Mazeucos, A. El Bakkali, N. Arrigo, D. Baali-Cherif, V. Brunini-Bronzini de Caraffa, S. Santoni, P. Vargas, and V. Savolainen, "The Complex History of the Olive Tree: From the Late Quaternary Diversification of Mediterranean Lineages to Primary Domestication in the Northern Levant," *Proceedings of the Royal Society* 280, no. 1756 (2013): 1–2.

8. Besnard et al., "The Complex History of the Olive Tree," 2–4.

9. Arthur J. Arberry, trans., *The Koran Interpreted* (London: Allen and Unwin, 1955), 133.

10. Usāmah Ibn-Munqidh, *An Arab-Syrian Gentleman and Warrior in the Period of the Crusades: Memoirs of Usāmah Ibn-Munqich*, translated by Philip K. Hitti (New York: Columbia University Press, 2000), 163.

11. "i love my country," accessed July 9, 2018, http://maraahmed.com/wp/2011/08/16/i-love-my-country-a-poem-by-nazim-hikmet/.

12. Prospero Alpini, *Medicina Aegyptiorum* (Leiden: Gerard Potuliet, 1745), 272.

13. André Burguierè, *The Annales School: An Intellectual History*, translated by Jane Marie Todd (Ithaca, N.Y.: Cornell University Press, 2009), ix.

14. Claude Lévi-Strauss, *Structural Anthropology*, translated by Claire Jacobson and Brooke Grundfest Schoepf (New York: Basic Books, 1963), 24.

15. Claude Lévi-Strauss, *The Raw and the Cooked* (New York: Harper and Row, 1969), 336.

16. Lévi-Strauss, *The Raw and the Cooked*, 336.

17. Lévi-Strauss, *The Raw and the Cooked*, 335–36.

18. Fernand Braudel, *The Structures of Everyday Life: Civilization and Capitalism, 15th Century–18th Century*, vol. 1, translated by Sian Reynolds (San Francisco: Harper and Row Publishers, 1981), 29.

19. Jean-Louis Flandrin and Massimo Montanari, "Introduction to the Original Edition," in *Food: A Culinary History*, edited by Jean-Louis Flandrin and Massimo Montanari, translated by Albert Sonnenfeld (New York: Columbia University Press, 1999), 3–5.

20. Jean-Louis Flandrin, "The Humanization of Eating Behaviors," in *Food: A Culinary History*, edited by Jean-Louis Flandrin and Massimo Montanari, translated by Albert Sonnenfeld (New York: Columbia University Press, 1999), 18–19.

21. Jean-Louis Flandrin, "The Humanization of Eating Behaviors," 19.

22. Giovanni Della Casa, *Galateo Ovvero De' Costumi* (Florence: Felice Le Monnier, 1949), 44.

23. "The Code of Hammurabi," translated by L. W. King, no. 108, *The Avalon Project*, accessed May 23, 2018, http://avalon.law.yale.edu/subject_menus/hammenu.asp.

24. Dr. Kyle Strode, e-mail message to author, July 21, 2016.

25. Dr. Dan Gretch, e-mail message to author, July 21, 2016.

26. Dr. David Hitt, e-mail message to author, July 20, 2016.

27. Dr. Dan Gretch, e-mail message to author, July 21, 2016. Dr. Gretch added that people have many more receptors for molecules that produce smell than we have taste receptors, which helps explain why people perceive only five tastes but many smells.

28. William Harrison Ukers, *All about Coffee* (New York: The Tea and Coffee Trade Journal, 1922), 54.

29. Mark Pendergrast, *Uncommon Grounds: The History of Coffee and How it Transformed our World* (New York: Basic Books, 1999), 3

30. Philip Mayerson, "The Port of Clysma (Suez) in the Transition from Roman to Arab Rule," *Journal of Near Eastern Studies* 22, no. 2 (1996): 122.

31. Pendergrast, *Uncommon Grounds*, 6.

32. Pendergrast, *Uncommon Grounds*, 6–9.

33. Reginald Smith, "A History of Coffee," in *Coffee: Botany, Biochemistry, and Production of Beans and Beverage*, edited by M. N. and K. C. Wilson (London: Croom Helm, 1985), 1–2.

34. Smith, "A History of Coffee," 1–2.

35. Ukers, *All about Coffee*, 54.

36. Bennett Alan Weinberg and Bonnie K. Bealer, *The World of Caffeine: The Science and Culture of the World's Most Popular Drug* (New York: Routledge, 2002),

9. See also Ralph S. Hattox, *Coffee and Coffeehouses: The Origins of a Social Beverage in the Medieval Near East* (Seattle: University of Washington Press, 1985), 12–13.

37. Hattox, *Coffee and Coffeehouses*, 13.

38. Smith, "A History of Coffee," 1. See also Weinberg and Bealer, *The World of Caffeine*, 9.

39. Weinberg and Bealer, *The World of Caffeine*, 9.

40. Katip Çelebi, *The Balance of Truth*, translated by G. L. Lewis (London: George Allen and Unwin, 1957), 60. 950/1543 refers to the date in both the Islamic calendar and the western calendar. The Islamic calendar begins in 622 (1AH/622), the year Muhammad and his followers fled from Mecca to Medina to escape persecution. Only 593 years separate the dates in Çelebi's text, suggesting that the author may simply have added incorrectly.

41. Edwin Lester Arnold, *Coffee: Its Cultivation and Profit* (London: W. B. Whittingham & Co., 1886), 4.

42. Coffee plants did not leave the region until the seventeenth or eighteenth century, as the Yemenis carefully guarded their plants. How this happened is the subject of some disagreement.

43. Rachel Hajar, "The Air of History (Part IV): Great Muslim Physicians Al Rhazes," *Heart Views: The Official Journal of the Gulf Heart Association* 14, no. 2 (2013): 93.

44. Hajar, "The Air of History," 94.

45. Stefano A. E. Leoni, "Ibn Sīnā, Abū ʿAlī al-Ḥusayn ibn ʿAbd Allāh," in *The Oxford Encyclopedia of the Islamic World*, edited by John Esposito (Oxford: Oxford University Press, 2009).

46. Avicenna, *The Canon of Medicine*, translated by O. Cameron Gruner and Mazar H. Shah (New York: AMS Press, 1973), 497.

47. Prospero Alpini, *Medicina Aegyptiorum* (Leiden: Gerard Potuliet, 1745), 272.

48. Çelebi, *The Balance of Truth*, 62.

49. Philippe Sylvestre Dufour, *The Manner of Making Coffee, Tea, and Chocolate as It Is Used in Most Parts of Europe, Asia, Africa, and America, with Their Vertues* (London: William Crook, 1685), 3.

50. The *Tea and Coffee Trade Journal* is published by Bell Publishing Limited in the United Kingdom. See "About," *Tea & Coffee Trade Journal*, accessed July 9, 2018, http://www.teaandcoffee.net/about/.

51. Ukers, *All about Coffee*, 16.

52. H. A. R. Gibb and J. H. Kramers, "Tasawwuf," in *Shorter Encyclopedia of Islam*, edited by H. A. R. Gibb and J. H. Kramers (Leiden: E. J. Brill, 1974), 580.

53. "Sufism," In *The Oxford Dictionary of Islam*, edited by John L. Esposito (Oxford: Oxford University Press, 2003).

54. "Sufism."

55. Gibb, "Tasawwuf," 579. See also "Sufism."

56. Victoria Clark, *Yemen: Dancing on the Heads of Snakes* (New Haven, Conn.: Yale University Press, 2010), 22.

57. "Sufism."

58. Antony Wild, *Coffee: A Dark History* (New York: W. W. Norton and

Company, 2004), 43–48. See also Pendergrast, *Uncommon Grounds*, 6; and Hattox, *Coffee and Coffeehouses*, 14–17.

59. Elliot Horowitz, "Coffee, Coffeehouses, and the Nocturnal Rituals of Early Modern Jewry," *AJS Review* 14, no. 1 (1989): 18.

60. Hattox, *Coffee and Coffeehouses*, 11.

61. Pendergrast, *Uncommon Grounds*, 6.

62. Wild, *Coffee*, 48.

63. Ukers, *All about Coffee*, 16.

64. Hattox, *Coffee and Coffeehouses*, 12.

65. Wilfred H. Schoff, trans., *The Periplus of the Erythraean Sea: Travel and Trade in the Indian Ocean by a Merchant of the First Century* (London: Longmans, Green, 1912), 34.

66. Clark, *Yemen*, 11.

67. Clark, *Yemen*, 14–15.

68. Clark, *Yemen*, 19–20.

69. Clark, *Yemen*, 20–21.

70. Rich Cohen, "Sugar Love (a Not So Sweet Story)," *National Geographic*, August 2013, accessed May 23, 2018, http://ngm.nationalgeographic.com/2013/08 /sugar/cohen-text.

71. Cohen, "Sugar Love."

72. Sidney W. Mintz, *Sweetness and Power the Place of Sugar in Modern History* (New York: Penguin Books, 1985), 25.

73. Cohen, "Sugar Love."

74. Katherine Strange Burke, "A Note on the Archaeological Evidence for Sugar Production in the Middle Islamic Periods in Bilad Al-Sham," *Mamluk Studies Review* 8, no. 2 (2004): 109.

75. Alain Huetz de Lemps, "Colonial Beverages and the Consumption of Sugar," in *Food: A Culinary History*, edited by Jean-Louis Flandrin and Massimo Montanari, translated by Albert Sonnenfeld (New York: Penguin Books, 2000): 383.

76. De Lemps, "Colonial Beverages and the Consumption of Sugar," 383–84.

## Chapter 3: Coffee Crosses the Mediterranean

1. "Historical Coffee Quotes," accessed July 9, 2018, https://greenstreetroasters .wordpress.com/2012/06/12/historical-coffee-poetry/.

2. Sir Henry Blount, *Voyage into the Levant* (London: Andrew Crooke, 1636), 105.

3. Philippe Sylvestre Dufour, *The Manner of Making Coffee, Tea, and Chocolate as It Is Used in Most Parts of Europe, Asia, Africa, and America, with Their Vertues* (London: William Crook, 1685), 2.

4. Fernand Braudel, *Civilization and Capitalism: 15th Century–18th Century* (New York: Harper and Rowe, 1982), 249–51; Fernand Braudel, *The Mediterranean and the Mediterranean World in the Age of Philip II*, vol. 1, translated by Sian Reynolds (New York: Harper & Row, 1973). See also William Harrison Ukers, *All about Coffee* (New York: The Tea and Coffee Trade Journal, 1922), 68; Christine A. Jones, "Exotic Edibles: Coffee, Chocolate, and the Early Modern French How-To,"

*Journal of Medieval and Early Modern Studies* 43, no. 3 (2013); and Marcy Norton, "Tasting Empire: Chocolate and the European Internalization of Mesoamerican Aesthetics," *American Historical Review* 111, no. 3 (2006).

5. Genevieve Carlton, *Worldly Consumers: The Demand for Maps in Renaissance Italy* (Chicago: University of Chicago Press, 2015), 1–4, quote on 1.

6. Fernand Braudel, *The Structures of Everyday Life: The Limits of the Possible*, trans. Sian Reynold (New York: Harper and Rowe Publishers, 1981), 187–88.

7. Procopius, *La Guerra Gotica* (Rome: Forzani, 1896), 131.

8. Braudel, *Civilization and Capitalism*, 187.

9. Braudel, *Civilization and Capitalism*, 188.

10. Braudel, *The Structures of Everyday Life*, 188.

11. Gary Paul Nabhan, *Cumin, Camels, and Caravans: A Spice Odyssey* (Berkeley: University of California Press, 2014), 45, 162–68.

12. Nabhan, *Cumin, Camels, and Caravans*, 164–65. Nabhan notes that evidence includes carbonized pomegranate skins found among the ruins of Jericho.

13. At its height, Islamic Spain encompassed most of present-day Spain and Portugal.

14. Nabhan, *Cumin, Camels, and Caravans*, 163–68.

15. Nabhan, *Cumin, Camels, and Caravans*, 170.

16. Henri Pirenne, *Economic and Social History of Medieval Europe* (London: Routledge and Kegan Paul, 1936), 26–39.

17. "*I mercanti importano pure sale, pepe e altre spezie (. . .) a soddisfare o il bisogno o il piacere degli uomini*" (merchants also import salt, pepper, and other spices . . . to satisfy the need or pleasure of men). Bonvesin da la Riva, *Le Meraviglie di Milano: De Magnalibus Mediolani*, edited by Guiseppe Pontiggia (Milano: Bompiani, 1974), 33–34, quote on 33. Bonvesin della Riva belonged to a relatively new penitential order founded around the beginning of the twelfth century in Lombardy.

18. Ibn Battutah, *The Travels of Ibn Battutah*, abridged by Tim Mackintosh-Smith (London: Picador, 2000), 3, x. Battutah's family was Lawatah in origin, a subgroup of the larger Berber people who had migrated from Libya to Morocco centuries before Battutah's birth.

19. Ibn Battutah, *The Travels of Ibn Battutah*, x–xi.

20. Ibn Battutah, *The Travels of Ibn Battutah*, 6.

21. Gene Brucker, *Renaissance Florence* (Berkeley: University of California Press, 1969), 70. The Bardi family went bankrupt in the mid-fifteenth century, when they fell victim to bankruptcy, first for supporting Edward III of England against the French in the Hundred Years' War (1337–1453) and then for providing financial assistance to the government of Florence during a war with its long-standing rival.

22. Brucker, *Renaissance Florence*, 54–55.

23. Brucker, *Renaissance Florence*, 70.

24. Francesco Balducci Pegolotti, *La pratica della mercatura scritta da Francesco Balducci Pegolotti* (Lisbon: Lucca, 1766), 81–82, 42–43.

25. Pegolotti, *La pratica della mercatura scritta da Francesco Balducci Pegolotti*, 44–46.

26. Pegolotti, *La pratica della mercatura scritta da Francesco Balducci Pegolotti*, 346, 350–51.

27. When Mongol emperor Berdi Beg was assassinated by his brother in 1359, the empire experienced a downward spiral that ended in its collapse nine years later.

28. Christopher I. Beckwith, *Empires of the Silk Road: A History of Central Eurasia from the Bronze Age to the Present* (Princeton, N.J.: Princeton University Press, 2009), 194–96.

29. Karl H. Dannenfeldt, *Leonhard Rauwolf, Sixteenth Century Physician, Botanist, and Traveler* (Cambridge, Mass.: Harvard University Press, 1968), 32.

30. "Epistle Dedicatory," in John Ray, *A Collection of Curious Travels and Voyages, in Two Tomes, the First Containing Leonhart Rauwolff's Itinerary into the Eastern Countries,* translated by Nicholas Staphorst (London: S. Smith and B. Walford, 1693), n.p. This source includes a 1693 English translation of Leonhard Rauwolf, Aigentliche beshreibung de Raisz so er vor diser zeit gegen Auffgang inn die Morganlander . . . selbs volbracht (1583).

31. Dannenfeldt, *Leonhard Rauwolf,* 32.

32. Ray, *A Collection of Curious Travels and Voyages,* 88.

33. Ray, *A Collection of Curious Travels and Voyages,* 86–87.

34. Aleppo was actually the final location for the Venetian colony, which was first established in Damascus in the thirteenth century and subsequently moved to Tripoli, Syria, in 1545. It relocated to Aleppo in the mid-sixteenth century.

35. Luca Molà, *The Silk Industry of Renaissance Venice* (Baltimore, Md.: Johns Hopkins University Press, 2000), 57. See also Dannenfeldt, *Leonhard Rauwolf,* 59–62.

36. Ray, *A Collection of Curious Travels and Voyages,* 92.

37. Ray, *A Collection of Curious Travels and Voyages,* 92.

38. Ray, *A Collection of Curious Travels and Voyages,* 92.

39. Ralph S. Hattox, *Coffee and Coffeehouses: The Origins of a Social Beverage in the Medieval Near East* (Seattle: University of Washington Press, 1985), 27.

40. Ray, *A Collection of Curious Travels and Voyages,* 92. See also Dannenfeldt, *Leonhard Rauwolf,* 68–72.

41. Ray, *A Collection of Curious Travels and Voyages,* 92.

42. Ray, *A Collection of Curious Travels and Voyages,* 121–22.

43. Ray, *A Collection of Curious Travels and Voyages,* 274.

44. Dannenfeldt, *Leonhard Rauwolf,* 167.

45. Ray, *A Collection of Curious Travels and Voyages,* 38.

46. Ray, *A Collection of Curious Travels and Voyages,* 64.

47. Prospero Alpini, *De Plantis Aegypti* (Patavi: Typis P. Frambotti, 1640), 63.

48. Tsugitaka Sato, *Sugar in the Social Life of Medieval Islam* (Leiden: Brill, 2014), 175.

49. Quoted in Danilo Reato, *La bottega del caffè: I caffè Veneziani tra 700 e 900* (Venezia: Arsenale Editrice Venezia, 1991), 13. Translation in Danilo Reato, *The Coffee-House: Venetian Coffee-Houses from the 18th to the 20th Century,* translated by Danilo Reato (Venice: Arsenale Editrice, 1991), 13.

50. Reato, *La bottega del caffè,* 13

51. Reato, *La bottega del caffè,* 14.

52. Anthony Sherley, Robert Sherley, and Thomas Sherley, *The Three Brothers, or the Travels and Adventures of Sir Anthony, Sir Robert and Sir Thomas Sherley* (London: Hurst, Robinson, and Co., 1825), 38.

53. William Biddulph, *Travels into Africa, Asia, and to the Black Sea*

(Amsterdam: Theatrum Orbis Terrarum Ltd., 1968), 65. This quote is from the original 1609 text of Biddulph's *Travels*, published in facsimile from the original housed at the Bodleian Library, Oxford University. The fin-ion Biddulph refers to is the small cup used to drink coffee. It is perhaps a mistranslation of the Turkish word *fincan* for the same item.

54. Biddulph, *Travels into Africa, Asia, and to the Black Sea*, 66.

55. Biddulph, *Travels into Africa, Asia, and to the Black Sea*, 64.

56. Richard Bannister, "Sugar, Coffee, Tea, and Cocoa, Their Origin, Preparation, and Uses," *Journal of the Society of Arts* 38, no. 1979 (1890): 1002.

57. Mel White, "Socotra: Yemen's Legendary Island," *National Geographic*, June 2012, http://ngm.nationalgeographic.com/2012/06/socotra/white-text.

58. George Sandys, *Sandy's Travels* (London: John Williams, 1673), 51.

59. Sandys, *Sandy's Travels*, 51–52.

60. Pietro Della Valle, *Viaggi di Pietro Della Valle* (Brighton: G. Gancia, 1853), 124.

61. Pedro Teixeira, *The Travels of Pedro Teixeira with His "Kings of Harmuz" and Extracts from His "Kings of Persia"* (London: Hakluyt Society, 1802). 62.

62. Teixeira, *The Travels of Pedro Teixeira*, 121.

63. Teixeira, *The Travels of Pedro Teixeira*, 121.

64. Dannenfeldt, *Leonhard Rauwolf*, 3–4.

65. Dannenfeldt, *Leonhard Rauwolf*, 4–5.

66. Jean-Louis Flandrin and Massimo Montanari, eds., *Food: A Culinary History from Antiquity to the Present*, translated by Albert Sonnenfeldt (New York: Penguin Books, 2000), 360. See also Markman Ellis, *The Coffee House: A Cultural History* (London: Weidenfeld & Nicolson, 2004), Kindle location 1752.

67. Cemal Kafadar, "A Death in Venice (1575): Anatolian Muslim Merchants Trading in the Serenissima," *Journal of Turkish Studies* 10 (1986): 216.

68. Eric Dursteler, "Commerce and Coexistence: Veneto-Ottoman Trade in the Early Modern Era," *Turcica* 34 (2002): 111.

69. Heinrich Eduard Jacob, *Coffee: The Epic of a Commodity*, translated by Eden Paul and Cedar Paul (New York: The Viking Press, 1935), 55; Bennett Alan Weinberg and Bonnie K. Bealer, *The World of Caffeine* (New York: Routledge, 2002), 64.

70. Horatio F. Brown, "The Venetians and the Venetian Quarter in Constantinople to the Close of the Twelfth Century," *Journal of Hellenic Studies* 40, no. 1 (1920): 68–70.

71. Alfred E. Lieber, "Eastern Business Practices and Medieval European Commerce," *Economic History Review* 21, no. 2 (1968): 236.

72. Anna Comnena, *The Alexiad*, translated by E .R. A. Sewter (London: Penguin Books, 1969), 11.

73. Brown, "The Venetians and the Venetian Quarter," 70.

74. Jonathan Riley-Smith, *The Crusades: A History*, 3rd ed. (New York: Bloomsbury Academic, 2014), 48–49.

75. Riley-Smith, *The Crusades*, 50–51, 373.

76. Joanne M. Ferraro, *Venice: History of the Floating City*, (New York: Cambridge University Press, 2012), 41.

77. Terri L. Weese and Lynn Bohs, "Eggplant Origins: Out of Africa, into the Orient," *Taxon* 59, no. 1 (2010): 49; Ferraro, *Venice*, 45.

78. Jared Diamond, *Guns, Germs, and Steel: The Fates of Human Societies* (New York: W. W. Norton and Company, 1999), 115.

79. Pliny, *Natural History*, 160.

80. Pliny, *Natural History*, 192.

81. Edward Said, *Orientalism* (New York: Random House, 1979), 2.

82. Said, *Orientalism*, 1.

83. Said, *Orientalism*, 1.

84. Said, *Orientalism*, 1–2.

85. John L. Esposito, "Coffee and Coffeehouses," in *The Islamic World Past and Present*, vol. 1, edited by John L. Esposito (New York: Oxford University Press, 2004), 108.

## Chapter 4: Coffee and the World of Commodities

1. Anonymous, A Cup of Coffee: Or, Coffee in Its Colours (London, 1663).

2. Yuval Noah Harari, *Sapiens: A Brief History of Humankind* (New York: HarperCollins, 2015), ix.

3. Harari, *Sapiens*, 35–36.

4. Angela Nuovo and Francesco Ammannati, "Investigating Book Prices in Early Modern Europe: Questions and Sources," *JLIS.it* 8, no. 3 (2017): 6.

5. Richard A. Goldthwaite, *Wealth and the Demand for Art in Italy, 1300–1600* (Baltimore, Md.: Johns Hopkins University Press, 1993), 155. See also Nuovo and Ammannati, "Investigating Book Prices in Early Modern Europe," 6–7.

6. Iain MacLeod Higgins, ed., *The Book of John Mandeville* (Indiananapolis, Ind.: Hackett Publishing Company, 2011), 39. Ascoparcz is another term Mandeville used to refer to the indigenous people of Arabia.

7. Frank Trentmann, ed., *The Oxford Handbook of the History of Consumption* (Oxford: Oxford University Press, 2012), 3.

8. Frank Trentmann, "Introduction," in *The Oxford Handbook of the History of Consumption*, edited by Frank Trentmann (Oxford: Oxford University Press, 2012), 1–19, See also John Brewer and Roy Porter, eds., *Consumption and the World of Goods* (New York: Routledge, 1993).

9. Richard A. Goldthwaite, "The Empire of Things: Consumer Demand in Renaissance Italy," in *Patronage, Art, and Society in Renaissance Italy*, edited by F. W. Kent and Patricia Simons with J. D. Eade (Oxford: Clarendon Press, 1987), 156.

10. Goldthwaite, "The Empire of Things," 157.

11. Goldthwaite, *Wealth and the Demand for Art in Italy, 1300–1600*, 1.

12. Evelyn Welch, *Shopping in the Renaissance: Consumer Cultures in Italy, 1400–1600* (New Haven, Conn.: Yale University Press, 2005), 3–6.

13. Goldthwaite, *Wealth and the Demand for Art in Italy, 1300–1600*, 40.

14. Pietro Casola, *Canon Pietro Casola's Pilgrimage to Jerusalem in the Year 1494*, edited by M. Margaret Newett (Manchester: University of Manchester Press, 1907), 129.

15. Nuovo and Ammannati, "Investigating Book Prices in Early Modern Europe," 6–7. See also Goldthwaite, *Wealth and the Demand for Art in Italy, 1300–1600*, 1; and Carlton, *Worldly Consumers*, 1–4.

16. Evelyn Welch, *Shopping in the Renaissance*, 8.

17. Welch, *Shopping in the Renaissance*, 19–23.

18. For more about women and business in early modern Venice and Milan, see Monica Chojnacka, *Working Women of Early Modern Venice* (Baltimore, Md.: Johns Hopkins University Press, 2001); Laura Deleidi, "Donne milanesi della prima metà del cinquecento: la memoria degli atti notarili," *Società e Storia* 18 (1994); and Jeanette M. Fregulia, "Widows, Legal Rights, and the Mercantile Economy in Early Modern Milan," *Early Modern Women: An Interdisciplinary Journal* 3 (2008).

19. Christine A. Jones, "Exotic Edibles: Coffee, Chocolate, and the Early Modern French How-To," *Journal of Medieval and Early Modern Studies* 43, no. 3 (2013): 623.

20. Pamela H. Smith and Paula Findlen, *Merchants and Marvels: Commerce, Science and Art in Early Modern Europe* (New York: Routledge, 2002), 3–9. See also Stephen Greenblatt, *Marvelous Possessions: The Wonder of the New World* (Chicago: University of Chicago Press, 1991).

21. Joyce Appleby, *Shores of Knowledge: New World Discoveries and the Scientific Imagination* (New York: W. W. Norton, 2013), 5–7. For more information on Arab and Muslim contributions to European science and technology, see Sameen Ahmed Khan, "Medieval Arab Contributions to Optics," *Digest of Middle East Studies* 25, no. 1 (2016) : 19–35; and George Saliba, "Islamic Reception of Greek Astronomy," *Proceedings of the IAU Symposium* 260 (2009): 149–65.

22. Jones, "Exotic Edibles," 623. See also Deborah Howard, "Venice and the Mamluks," in *Venice and the Islamic World, 828–1797*, edited by Stefano Carboni (New York: The Metropolitan Museum of Art, 2007), 81.

23. Miriam Cooke, Erdağ Göknar, and Grant Richard Parker, eds., *Mediterranean Passages: Readings from Dido to Derrida* (Chapel Hill: University of North Carolina Press, 2008), 125.

24. Cooke, Göknar, and Parker, *Mediterranean Passages*, 128.

25. *Ar-Rihla* can mean both a journey that seeks religious enlightenment within Islam, as in the case of the hajj, or, more generally, a travel narrative.

26. Bernhard Bischoff, "The Study of Foreign Languages in the Middle Ages," *Speculum* 36, no. 2 (1961): 209–24, esp. 212.

27. Saliba, "Islamic Reception of Greek Astronomy," 162–65; Bischoff, "The Study of Foreign Languages in the Middle Ages," 216.

28. Welch, *Shopping in the Renaissance*, 303.

29. Martin Jacobs, *Reorienting the East, Jewish Travelers to the Medieval Muslim World* (Philadelphia: University of Pennsylvania Press, 2014), 4–6. While Jacobs's focus is on Jewish travelers, he notes the influence of the writings of Ibn Jubayr in the late twelfth century and the account of Ibn Battutah in the fourteenth century (25). See also Bischoff, "The Study of Foreign Languages in the Middle Ages," 217.

30. Bischoff, "The Study of Foreign Languages in the Middle Ages," 217.

31. Jacobs, *Reorienting the East*, 31–32.

32. Jacobs, *Reorienting the East*, 34.

33. Jacobs, *Reorienting the East*, 34.

34. Jacobs, *Reorienting the East*, 119–20.

35. Ibn Battutah, *The Travels of Ibn Battutah*, abridged by Tim Mackintosh-Smith (London: Picador, 2002), 286.

36. Jacobs, *Reorienting the East*, 157.

37. William Biddulph, *The Trauels of Certaine Englishmen into Africa, Asia, Troy, Bythinia, Thracia, and to the Blacke Sea and into Syria, Cilicia, Pisidia, Mesopotamia, Damascus, Canaan, Galile, Samaria, Iudea, Palestina, Ierusalem, Iericho, and to the Red Sea: And to Sundry Other Places* (London: Th. Haveland, 1609), 65.

38. Biddulph, *The Trauels of Certaine Englishmen*, 66.

39. Howard, "Venice and the Mamluks," 85.

40. Vasco da Gama, *A Journal of the First Voyage of Vasco Da Gama, 1497–1499*, translated by E. G. Ravenstein (London: The Hakluyt Society, 1898), 24.

41. Bischoff, "The Study of Foreign Languages in the Middle Ages," 217.

42. Patrick Collinson, *The Reformation: A History* (New York: The Modern Library, 2003), 41.

43. Nuovo and Ammannati, "Investigating Book Prices in Early Modern Europe," 3.

44. Higgins, *The Book of John Mandeville*, 77.

45. Higgins, *The Book of John Mandeville*, xiv.

46. Higgins, *The Book of John Mandeville*, xiv.

47. Higgins, *The Book of John Mandeville*, 77.

48. Higgins, *The Book of John Mandeville*, 91.

49. Higgins, *The Book of John Mandeville*, 29.

50. Mancall, *Travel Narratives from the Age of Discovery*, 7.

51. Higgins, *The Book of John Mandeville*, 163.

52. Greenblatt, *Marvelous Possessions*, 9. Here Greenblatt is speaking about European travelers to the New World, although the same might also be said of travelers to the East.

53. Greenblatt, *Marvelous Possessions*, 16–20. See also Mancall, *Travel Narratives from the Age of Discovery*, 8–9. Anthropologists have also ventured into this territory; see, for example, Clifford Geertz, *The Interpretation of Cultures* (New York: Basic Books, Inc., 1973).

54. Higgins, *The Book of John Mandeville*, 96.

55. Carlo Ginzburg, *The Cheese and the Worms: The Cosmos of a Sixteenth-Century Miller*, translated by John and Anne Tedeschi (Baltimore, Md.: Johns Hopkins University Press, 1992), 128, xii, 30, and 41. The Qur'an was first published in translation in Venice in 1547.

56. Pietro Della Valle, *Viaggi di Pietro Della Valle* (Brighton: G. Gancia, 1853), 76.

57. Munqidh quoted in Janet Abu-Lughod, *Before European Hegemony: The World System A.D. 1250–1350* (New York: Oxford University Press, 1991), 107.

58. Maria Pia Rossignani, "Milan: Discovery of Frankincense Lumps in a Roman Burial Tomb," in *Profumi d'Arabia: Atti del Covengo*, edited by Alessandra Avanzini (Rome: L'Erma di Bretschneider, 1997), 147.

59. H. D. Schepelern, "The Museum Wormianum Reconstructed: A Note on the Illustration of 1655," *Journal of the History of Collection* 2, no. 1 (1990): 81.

60. Rosamond E. Mack, *Bazaar to Piazza: Islamic Trade and Italian Art, 1300–1600* (Berkeley: University of California Press, 2002), 1. For a look at the historic and cultural contexts of Venice's relationship with the Islamic world, see Carboni, *Venice and the Islamic World*.

61. Mack, *Bazaar to Piazza*, 8.

62. Mack, *Bazaar to Piazza*, 10–11.

63. Mack, *Bazaar to Piazza*, 51–52, 71.

64. Mack, *Bazaar to Piazza*, 157–58.

65. Mack, *Bazaar to Piazza*, 171–72 (quote on 171).

66. Jones, "Exotic Edibles: Coffee, Chocolate, and the Early Modern French How-To," 623.

67. William Harrison Ukers, *All about Coffee* (New York: The Tea and Coffee Trade Journal, 1922), 68.

68. Mark Pendergrast, *Uncommon Grounds: The History of Coffee and How It Transformed Our World* (New York: Basic Books, 1999), 8–10.

69. Jones, "Exotic Edibles," 623.

70. "Hartlib Papers," University of Sheffield, accessed May 24, 2018, https://www.sheffield.ac.uk/library/cdfiles/hartlib.

71. Samuel Hartlib to Robert Boyle, n.d. [September 1687?], in T. Birch, ed., *The Works of the Honourable Robert Boyle*, 2nd ed., vol. 6 (London, 1772), 94–95, accessed May 24, 2018, https://www.hrionline.ac.uk/hartlib/view?docset=additional&docname=BOYLE_25&termo=transtext_coffee#highlight.

72. J. P. Griffin, "Venetian Treacle and the Foundation of Medicines Regulation," *British Journal of Clinical Pharmacology* 58, no. 3 (2004): 317–18.

73. Griffin, "Venetian Treacle," 317.

74. Griffin, "Venetian Treacle," 317.

75. Samuel Hartlib to John Worthington, April 20, 1659, in J. Crossley, ed., *The Diary and Correspondence of Dr. John Worthington*, vol. 13 (Manchester: Chetham Society, 1847), 120, accessed May 24, 2018, https://www.hrionline.ac.uk/hartlib view?docset=additional&docname=WORTH_05&termo=transtext_coffee#highlight.

76. Entry for August 15, 1683, in *The Diary of John Evelyn* (London: MacMillan, Limited, 1908), 357.

77. Gary Paul Nabhan, *Cumin, Camels, and Caravans: A Spice Odyssey* (Berkeley: University of California Press, 2014), 45, 170.

78. Massimo Montanari, "Introduction," in *A Cultural History of Food in the Medieval Age*, edited by Massimo Montanari (New York: Berg, 2012), 5, 8.

79. Craig Clunas, "Modernity Global and Local: Consumption and the Rise of the West," *American Historical Review* 104, no. 5 (1997): 1508.

80. Felipe Fernandez-Armesto and Benjamin Sacks, "The Global Exchange of Food and Drugs," in *The Oxford Handbook of the History of Consumption*, edited by Frank Trentmann (New York: Oxford University Press, 2012), 132–133.

Chapter 5: Anxieties about Coffee

1. Katip Çelebi, *The Balance of Truth*, translated by G. L. Lewis (London, George Allen and Unwin, Ltd., 1957), 60.

2. Richard Bannister, "Sugar, Coffee, Tea, and Cocoa, Their Origin, Preparation, and Uses," *Journal of the Society of Arts* 38, no. 1979 (1890): 1003.

3. Siegfried R. Waldvogel, "Caffeine—A Drug with a Surprise," *Angewandte Chemie* 42, no. 6 (2003): 604.

4. Waldvogel, "Caffeine—A Drug with a Surprise," 604.

5. "Coffee and Coffeehouses," excerpted at *Oxford Islamic Studies Online*, edited by John L. Esposito, accessed April 6, 2015, http://www.oxfordislamicstudies.com/article/opr/t243/e76?_hi=1&_pos=1.

6. Alexander Knysh, *Islam in Historical Perspective* (New York: Routledge, 2017), 133–134.

7. Muhammad Asad, trans., *The Message of the Qur'an* (England: The Book Foundation, 2003), 761.

8. Asad, *The Message of the Qur'an*, 218.

9. Asad, *The Message of the Qur'an*, 224.

10. Asad, *The Message of the Qur'an*, 59.

11. Asad, *The Message of the Qur'an*, 187.

12. "Intoxicants," in *The Oxford Dictionary of Islam*, edited by John L. Esposito, quoted at *Oxford Islamic Studies Online*, accessed July 23, 2015, http://www.oxfordislamicstudies.com/article/opr/t125/e1058?_hi=2&_pos=1.

13. Ralph S. Hattox, *Coffee and Coffeehouses: The Origins of a Social Beverage in the Medieval Near East* (Seattle: University of Washington Press, 1985), 3.

14. Juan Eduardo Campo, "Dietary Rules," in *The Oxford Encyclopedia of the Islamic World*, vol. 1, edited by John Esposito (New York: Oxford University Press, 1995), 375–377. Qat is a leafy narcotic that was chewed for its wakeful properties before and after the introduction of coffee.

15. Alan Bennett Weinberg and Bonnie K. Bealer, *The World of Caffeine: The Science and Culture of the World's Most Popular Drug* (New York: Routledge, 2000), 16–17.

16. Campo, "Dietary Rules," 375–77.

17. Ralph Hattox, *Coffee and Coffeehouses* (Seattle: University of Washington Press, 1985), 29–31.

18. Hattox, *Coffee and Coffeehouses*, 27.

19. Knysh, *Islam in Historical Perspective*, 13–14. See also Gary Paul Nabhan, *Cumin, Camels, and Caravans: A Spice Odyssey* (Berkeley: University of California Press, 2014), 45, 108–109. See also Karen Armstrong, *Islam: A Short History* (New York: Modern Library, 2002); and F. E. Peters, *The Children of Abraham: Judaism, Christianity, Islam* (Princeton, N.J.: Princeton University Press, 2005).

20. Hattox, *Coffee and Coffeehouses*, 31–40. Hattox offers a concise summary of the case from a distillation of the sources.

21. Hattox, *Coffee and Coffeehouses*, 32–33.

22. Hattox, *Coffee and Coffeehouses*, 35–38.

23. Hattox, *Coffee and Coffeehouses*, 35.

24. Hattox, *Coffee and Coffeehouses*, 32–40.

25. Hattox, *Coffee and Coffeehouses*, 37–38.

26. Hattox, *Coffee and Coffeehouses*, 40–41. See also Mark Pendergrast, *Uncommon Grounds: The History of Coffee and How It Transformed Our World* (New York: Basic Books, 1999), 6–7.

27. Uriel Heyd, *Ottoman Documents on Palestine, 1552–1615: A Study of the Firman According to the Mühimme Defteri* (Oxford: Clarendon Press, 1960), xv.

28. Heyd, *Ottoman Documents on Palestine*, xv.

29. More accurately spelled "*qadi*" (Arabic spelling: قاضي); the term refers to a Muslim judge who makes rulings according to Shari'a law.

30. Heyd, *Ottoman Documents on Palestine*, 160–61.

31. Heyd, *Ottoman Documents on Palestine*, 160–61.

32. Heyd, *Ottoman Documents on Palestine*, 160–62.

33. Heyd, *Ottoman Documents on Palestine*, 161–62. *The Oxford Dictionary of Islam* defines *waqf* generally as the endowment of a property for the sole benefit of a particular philanthropy with the intention of prohibiting any use or disposition of the property outside that specific purpose. The most typical kinds of waqf are religious (mosques and real estate that exclusively provides revenue for mosque maintenance and service expenses); and philanthropic support for the poor and the public at large by funding such institutions and activities as libraries, scientific research, education, health services, and care of animals and the environment. "Waqf," in *The Oxford Dictionary of Islam*, edited by John L. Esposito, excerpted at *Oxford Islamic Studies Online*, accessed May 18, 2015, http://www.oxfordislamic studies.com/article/opr/t125/e2484?_hi=4&_pos=1.

34. In 1571, Pope Pius V united Catholic maritime states with the intent of challenging Ottoman control over the eastern Mediterranean. The Holy League included the papal states, Spain, Naples, and Sicily under the rule of the House of Habsburg, the republics of Genoa and Venice, the Grand Duchy of Tuscany, the duchies of Savoy Parma and Urbino, and the Knights of Malta.

35. Hattox, *Coffee and Coffeehouses*, 102.

36. Çelebi, *The Balance of Truth*, 60–62.

37. Çelebi, *The Balance of Truth*, 60–62.

38. John L. Esposito, "Coffee and Coffeehouses," in *The Islamic World Past and Present*, vol. 1, edited by John L. Esposito (New York: Oxford University Press, 2004), 108

39. Esposito, "Coffee and Coffeehouses," 108.

40. Heyd, *Ottoman Documents on Palestine*, 160–61.

41. Weinberg and Bealer, *The World of Caffeine* (New York: Routledge, 2000), 67–68.

42. Brian P. Levack, *The Witch-Hunt in Early Modern Europe* (New York: Routledge, 2016), 108.

43. Levack, *The Witch-Hunt in Early Modern Europe*, 216.

44. Paul Grendler, "The Roman Inquisition and the Venetian Press, 1540–1605," *Journal of Modern History* 47, no. 1 (1975): 51.

45. Grendler, "The Roman Inquisition and the Venetian Press, 1540–1605," 49.

46. Angela Nuovo, "Private Libraries in Sixteenth-Century Italy," in *Early Printed Books as Material Objects. Proceedings of the Conference Organized by the Ifla Rare Books and Manuscripts Section*, edited by Bettina Wagner and Marcia Reed (Berlin: De Gruyter Saur, 2010), 231.

47. Grendler, "The Roman Inquisition and the Venetian Press, 1540–1605," 49.

48. Grendler, "The Roman Inquisition and the Venetian Press, 1540–1605," 49.

49. Grendler, "The Roman Inquisition and the Venetian Press, 1540–1605," 53.

50. Angela Nuovo, "A Lost Arabic Koran Rediscovered," *The Library* 12, no. 4 (1990): 273–274; Arjan Van Dijk, "Early Printed Qur'ans: The Dissemination of the Qur'an in the West," *Journal of Qur'anic Studies* 7, no. 2 (2008): 136.

51. Grendler, "The Roman Inquisition and the Venetian Press, 1540–1605," 62.

52. Grendler, "The Roman Inquisition and the Venetian Press, 1540–1605," 63–64.

53. Markman Ellis, *The Coffee-House: A Cultural History* (London: Orion Publishing, 2004), 82.

54. Ellis, *The Coffee-House: A Cultural History* 84.

55. Vincenzo Bellondi, *Documenti e aneddoti di storia veneziana (810–1854)* (Florence: Librato Editore, 1902), 155–57.

56. Filippo de Vivo, "Pharmacies as Centres of Communication in Early Modern Venice," *Renaissance Studies* 21, no. 4 (2007): 505–507. See also John Jeffries Martin, *Venice's Hidden Enemies: Italian Heretics in a Renaissance City* (Berkeley: University of California Press, 1993).

57. De Vivo, "Pharmacies as Centres of Communication in Early Modern Venice," 508–509.

58. Mark Pendergrast, *Uncommon Grounds: The History of Coffee and How It Transformed Our World* (New York: Basic Books, 1999), 7.

59. William Harrison Ukers, *All about Coffee* (New York: The Tea and Coffee Trade Journal, 1922), 954.

60. Ellis, *The Coffee-House*, 259.

61. Paolo Sarpi, *The Maxims of the Government of Venice. In an Advice to the Republik, How It Ought to Govern Itself, Both Inwardly and Outwardly, in Order to Perpetuate Its Dominion* (London: J. Morphew, 1707), 15.

62. Bellondi, *Documenti e aneddoti di storia veneziana*, 215.

63. Bannister, "Sugar, Coffee, Tea, and Cocoa," 1002–1003.

64. "By the King. A Proclamation for the Suppression of Coffee-Houses" (1675), accessed May 24, 2018, https://www.staff.uni-giessen.de/~g909/tx/suppress.htm.

65. Brian Cowan, *The Social Life of Coffee: The Emergence of the British Coffeehouse* (New Haven, Conn.: Yale University Press, 2005), 25.


Chapter 6: Coffee and New Patterns of Socialization

1. Francis Bacon, *The Vertues of Coffee* (London: W. G. for John Playford, 1663).

2. William Harrison Ukers, *All about Coffee* (New York: The Tea and Coffee Trade Journal, 1922), 61.

3. Ralph S. Hattox, *Coffee and Coffeehouses: The Origins of a Social Beverage in the Medieval Near East* (Seattle: University of Washington Press, 1985), 96–97.

4. Yu Lu, *The Classic of Tea*, translated by Francis Ross Carpenter (Boston: Little, Brown, and Company, 1974), 11.

5. Lu, *The Classic of Tea*, 11.

6. Lu, *The Classic of Tea*, 11.

7. Lu, *The Classic of Tea*, 11–12. Little is known about Bodhi Dharma, although legend has it that he was a Buddhist monk who lived between the fifth and sixth centuries of the Common Era who first brought Buddhism to China.

8. Rachel Laudan, *Cuisine and Empire Cooking in World History* (Berkeley: University of California Press, 2013), 122.

9. Lu, *The Classic of Tea*, 60, 13–17.

10. Lu, *The Classic of Tea*, 77–87.

11. Lu, *The Classic of Tea*, 90–95.

12. Lu, *The Classic of Tea*, 111.

13. Lu, *The Classic of Tea*, 118.

14. Lu, *The Classic of Tea*, 116. The Tang Dynasty (618–907) ruled during Lu's time.

15. Laudan, *Cuisine and Empire Cooking in World History*, 127–28.

16. Laudan, *Cuisine and Empire Cooking in World History*, 127–29.

17. Laudan, *Cuisine and Empire Cooking in World History*, 122–31.

18. Laudan, *Cuisine and Empire Cooking in World History*, 125–26; Ina McCabe Baghdiantz, *A History of Global Consumption: 1500–1800* (New York: Routledge, 2014), 142.

19. Beat Kümin, "Eating Out in Early Modern Europe," in *A Cultural History of Food in the Early Modern Age*, edited by Beat Kümin (New York: Berg, 2012), 94.

20. Laudan, *Cuisine and Empire Cooking in World History*, 91. See also Hattox, *Coffee and Coffeehouses*, 32–40.

21. Paul Freedman, "Eating Out," in *A Cultural History of Food in the Renaissance*, edited by Ken Albala (New York: Berg, 2012), 102, 111.

22. Freedman, "Eating Out," 111.

23. Francesco Colonna, *Hypnerotomachia Poliphili* (1499) (Padova: Antenore, 1980), 92. See also Freedman, "Eating Out," 109–111.

24. Freedman, "Eating Out," 111.

25. Beat Kümin, "Eating out in Early Modern Europe," 88.

26. Jean-Robert Pitte, "The Rise of the Restaurant," in *Food: A Culinary History from Antiquity to the Present*, edited by Jean-Louis Flandrin and Massimo Montanari (New York: Penguin Books, 1999), 474. Boulanger provoked a lawsuit from the Parisian caterer's guild, as he sold more substantive fare than simply the rich broth, *bouillons*, to which such shops were limited. In the end, according to Pitte, Boulanger prevailed and others soon followed his example.

27. Julian Coman, "Origins of First 'Restaurant' Challenged after 200 Years," *The Telegraph*, September 3, 2000, accessed May 24, 2008, http://www.telegraph .co.uk/news/worldnews/1353970/Origins-of-first-restaurant-challenged-after -200-years.html.

28. Pitte, "The Rise of the Restaurant," 472–73. For more about the rise of the restaurant, see Rebecca Spang, *The Invention of the Restaurant: Paris and Modern Gastronomic Culture* (Cambridge, Mass.: Harvard University Press, 2000).

29. Laudan, *Cuisine and Empire Cooking in World History*, 122.

30. Lu, *The Classic of Tea*, 122.

31. Lu, *The Classic of Tea*, 142.

32. Ina Baghdiantz McCabe, *A History of Global Consumption: 1500–1800* (New York: Routledge, 2014), 142.

33. Bennett Alan Weinberg and Bonnie K. Bealer, *The World of Caffeine: The Science and Culture of the World's Most Popular Drug* (New York: Routledge, 2000), 39.

34. "An Exact Description of the Growth, Quality, and Vertues of the Leaf Tee, Alias Tay, Drawn up for Satisfaction of Persons of Quality and the Good of the Nation in General," 1664 broadside, accessed July 2, 2018, https://quod.lib.umich .edu/e/eebo/A42427.0001.001?rgn=main;view=toc.

35. "An Exact Description of the Growth, Quality, and Vertues of the Leaf Tee."

36. Kümin, "Eating Out in Early Modern Europe," 89.

37. Freedman, "Eating Out," 112–13. See also Pitte, "The Rise of the Restaurant," 471.

38. Kümin, "Eating Out in Early Modern Europe," 89.

39. Kümin, "Eating Out in Early Modern Europe," 89.

40. Hattox, *Coffee and Coffeehouses*, 89.

41. Hattox, *Coffee and Coffeehouses*, 89–90. Hattox's argument finds support in Uğur Kömeçoğlu, "The Publicness and Sociabilities of the Ottoman Coffeehouse," *Javnost—The Public: Journal of the European Institute for Communication and Culture* 12, no. 2 (2005): 5–22.

42. Ibn Battutah, *The Travels of Ibn Battutah*, abridged by Tim Mackintosh-Smith (London: Picador, 2002), 1, 97.

43. Battutah, *The Travels of Ibn Battutah*, 98.

44. Busbecq quoted in Peter C. Mancall, ed., *Travel Narratives from the Age of Discover: An Anthology* (New York: Oxford University Press, 2006), 366. For more about Busbecq, see 363.

45. Al-Tamgruti quoted in Mancall, *Travel Narratives from the Age of Discovery*, 376.

46. Kömeçoğlu, "The Publicness and Sociabilities of the Ottoman Coffeehouse," 17–18. Problematizing Habermas and others, Kömeçoğlu focuses on role of the coffeehouse in creating an Ottoman public sphere as a space for entertainment and as a site of struggle against Ottoman absolutism. See also Hattox, *Coffee and Coffeehouses*, 92–111.

47. Kömeçoğlu, "The Publicness and Sociabilities of the Ottoman Coffeehouse," 6, 17–18.

48. Kömeçoğlu, "The Publicness and Sociabilities of the Ottoman Coffeehouse," 5–6.

49. Kömeçoğlu, "The Publicness and Sociabilities of the Ottoman Coffeehouse," 9. Closures ceased during the reign of Ottoman sultan Murad IV (1623–1640).

50. Hattox, *Coffee and Coffeehouses*, 92.

51. Hattox, *Coffee and Coffeehouses*, 94.

52. Hattox, *Coffee and Coffeehouses*, 76–77.

53. Pedro Teixeira, *The Travels of Pedro Teixeira with His "Kings of Harmuz" and Extracts from His "Kings of Persia"* (London: Hakluyt Society, 1802), 62.

54. Teixeira, *The Travels of Pedro Teixeira*, 62.

55. George Sandys, *Sandy's Travels* (London: John Williams, 1673), 51–52.

56. Edward William Lane, *An Account of the Manners and Customs of the Modern Egyptians* (London: John Murray, 1860), 152. Lane was among those Edward Said described as an Orientalist. He altered his translation of *One Thousand and One Nights* to reflect the Victorian mores of his day.

57. Cemal Kafadar, "A Death in Venice (1575): Anatolian Muslim Merchants Trading in the Serenissima," *Journal of Turkish Studies* 10 (1986): 199.

58. Halil Inalcik, "Capital Formation in the Ottoman Empire," *Journal of Economic History* 29, no. 1 (1969): 113. See also Kafadar, "A Death in Venice (1575)," 199.

59. Kafadar, "A Death in Venice (1575)," 213–16.

60. Jean-Louis Flandrin, "Introduction: The Early Modern Period," in *Food: A Culinary History from Antiquity to the Present*, edited by Jean-Louis Flandrin and Massimo Montanari (New York: Penguin Books, 2000), 360. See also Kafadar, "A Death in Venice (1575)," 192.

61. Filippo de Vivo, "Pharmacies as Centres of Communication in Early Modern Venice," *Renaissance Studies* 21, no. 4 (2007): 515.

62. Christine A. Jones, "Exotic Edibles: Coffee, Chocolate, and the Early Modern French How-To," *Journal of Medieval and Early Modern Studies* 43, no. 3 (2013): 623.

63. De Vivo, "Pharmacies as Centres of Communication in Early Modern Venice," 520.

64. Ferraro, *Venice*, 222. For the Piazza San Marco, see Markham Ellis, *The Coffee House: A Cultural History* (London: Orion Publishing, 2004), Kindle location 1768.

65. Paolo Sarpi, *The Maxims of the Government of Venice: In an Advice to the Republick, How It Ought to Govern Itself, Both Inwardly and Outwardly, in Order to Perpetuate Its Dominion* (London: J. Morphew, 1707), 15.

66. Philippe Sylvestre Dufour, *The Manner of Making Coffee, Tea, and Chocolate as It Is Used in Most Parts of Europe, Asia, Africa, and America, with Their Vertues* (London: William Crook, 1685), 2–3.

67. Pasqua Rosee, *The Vertue of the Coffee Drink* (London, [1666?]).

68. Brian Cowan, *The Social Life of Coffee: The Emergence of the British Coffeehouse* (New Haven, Conn.: Yale University Press, 2005), 25. See also David Brandon, *Life in a 17th Century Coffee Shop* (Gloucestershire: The History Press, 2007), 9.

69. John Evelyn, *The Diary of John Evelyn* (London: MacMillan, 1908), 6.

70. Brian Cowan, "Public Spaces, Knowledge, and Sociability," in *The History of Consumption*, edited by Frank Trentmann (New York: Oxford University Press, 2012), 253.

71. Henry Peacham, *Peacham's Compleat Gentleman, 1634* (London: Clarendon Press, 1906), n.p. ("To My Reader").

72. Peacham, *Peacham's Compleat Gentleman*, 105.

73. Information synthesized from Baldassare Castiglione, *Il Cortegiano* (Firenze: G. C. Sansoni, 1894). For an English translation, see Baldassare Castiglione, *The Book of the Courtier*, translated by George Anthony Bull (New York: Penguin Books, 1967).

74. Peacham, *Peacham's Compleat Gentleman*, 18.

75. Cowan, *The Social Life of Coffee*, 10–11.

76. Cowan, *The Social Life of Coffee*, 10–11.

77. Wolfram Koeppe, "Heilbrunn Timeline of Art History: Collecting for the Kunstkammer," Metropolitan Musume of Art, http://www.metmuseum.org/toah/.

78. Cowan, *The Social Life of Coffee*, 2.

79. Cowan, *The Social Life of Coffee*, 11–17.

80. Guido Giglioni, "Mastering the Appetites of Matter: Francis Bacon's Sylva Sylvarum," in *The Body as Object and Instrument of Knowledge: Embodied*

*Empiricism in Early Modern Science*, edited by Charles T. Wolfe and Ofer Gal (Springer Netherlands, 2010), 149.

81. Francis Bacon, *Sylva Sylvarum or a Natural History in Ten Centuries* (London: W. Rawley, 1626), 155.

82. Bacon, *Sylva Sylvarum*, 155.

83. Cowan, *The Social Life of Coffee*, 25.

84. Graham Rees, "An Unpublished Manuscript by Francis Bacon: *Sylva Sylvarum* Drafts and Other Working Notes," *Annals of Science* 34, no. 4 (1981): 377.

85. Giglioni, "Mastering the Appetites of Matter," 149.

86. Jürgen Habermas, *The Structural Transformation of the Public Sphere: An Inquiry into a Category of Bourgeois Society*, translated by Thomas Burger with the assistance of Frederick Lawrence (Cambridge, Mass.: MIT Press, 1991), 5–12.

87. Habermas, *The Structural Transformation of the Public Sphere*, 14, 27.

88. Habermas, *The Structural Transformation of the Public Sphere*, 27.

89. Habermas, *The Structural Transformation of the Public Sphere*, 32–33, quote on 33.

90. Brian Cowan, "An Open Elite: The Peculiarities of Connoisseurship in Early Modern England," *Modern Intellectual History* 1, no. 2 (2004): 154–156.

91. Mortimer Epstein, *The Early History of the Levant Company* (London: George Routledge & Sons, 1908), 1.

92. Epstein, *The Early History of the Levant Company*, 1–3.

93. Epstein, *The Early History of the Levant Company*, 3.

94. Epstein, *The Early History of the Levant Company*, 3–5.

95. Epstein, *The Early History of the Levant Company*, 5, 16.

96. Cowan, *The Social Life of Coffee*, 56. For English trade with Venice and the East, see Epstein, *The Early History of the Levant Company*, 1–66.

97. Cowan, "An Open Elite," 58.

98. Cowan, "An Open Elite," 66.

99. Cowan, "An Open Elite," 32.

100. Cowan, "An Open Elite," 32.

101. Cowan, "An Open Elite," 172–73.

102. Cowan, "An Open Elite," 181.

103. Ukers, *All about Coffee*, 108.

104. A Well-Willer, *The Women's Petition against Coffee* (London, 1674).

105. A Well-Willer, The Women's Petition against Coffee.

106. The City-Wife's Petition against Coffee (London, 1700).

107. The City-Wife's Petition against Coffee.

108. Felipe Fernandez-Armesto and Benjamin Sacks, "The Global Exchange of Food and Drugs," in *The Oxford Handbook of the History of Consumption*, edited by Frank Trentmann (New York: Oxford University Press, 2012), 138–139.

109. Markman Ellis, *The Coffee House: A Cultural History* (London: Orion Publishing, 2004), Kindle location 1704.

110. Ellis, *The Coffee House*, Kindle location 590.

111. Jean de La Roque, *A Voyage to Arabia Felix* (London: E. Symon, 1732), 237.

112. La Roque, *A Voyage to Arabia Felix*, 43–44, quote on 44.

113. La Roque, *A Voyage to Arabia Felix*, 2.

114. La Roque, *A Voyage to Arabia Felix*, 34.

115. La Roque, *A Voyage to Arabia Felix*, 341–42.

116. La Roque, *A Voyage to Arabia Felixx*, 326.

117. La Roque, *A Voyage to Arabia Felix*, 290.

118. La Roque, *A Voyage to Arabia Felix*, 292.

119. La Roque, *A Voyage to Arabia Felix*, 294.

120. For the more complete list, see Ellis, *The Coffee House*, Kindle location 5335.

121. Muzaffar Assadi, "Threats to Syncretic Culture: Baba Budan Giri Incident," *Economic and Political Weekly* 34, no. 14 (1999): 746.

122. Bhaswati Bhattacharya, "Local History of a Global Commodity: Production of Coffee in Mysore and Coorg in the Nineteenth Century," *Indian Historical Review* 40, no. 1 (2014): 69.

123. Teixeira, *The Travels of Pedro Teixeira*, 62.

124. Edward Said, *Orientalism* (New York: Random House, 1979), 1.

125. Sandys, *Sandy's Travels.*, 43.

126. Sandys, *Sandy's Travels*, 54.

127. Sandys, *Sandy's Travels*, 54.

128. Sandys, *Sandy's Travels*, 52. See also Hattox, *Coffee and Coffeehouses*, 108–111.

129. Kömeçoğlu, "The Publicness and Sociabilities of the Ottoman Coffeehouse," 15–16.

130. Said, *Orientalism*, 1.

## Chapter 7: Coffee and Modernity

1. "Coffee," The Thomas Jefferson Foundation, accessed July 9, 2018, https://www.monticello.org/site/research-and-collections/coffee.

2. Jennifer M. Brinkerhoff, Institutional Reform and Diaspora Entrepreneurs: The In-Between Difference (New York: Oxford University Press, 2016).

3. William Harrison Ukers, *All about Coffee* (New York: The Tea and Coffee Trade Journal, 1922), 115.

4. Markman Ellis, *The Coffee House: A Cultural History* (London: Orion Publishing, 2004), Kindle location 5334.

5. This Alexander Hamilton is not to be confused with the better-known Alexander Hamilton (1757–1802), a framer of the United States Constitution who was killed following a famous 1804 duel with Aaron Burr (1756–1836) and is today the subject of the Broadway sensation *Hamilton*.

6. "The Other Alexander Hamilton Visits Newport, 1744." New England Historical Society, accessed April 17, 2017,

7. "Itinerarium [of Alexander Hamilton]," loc. 60, Early American Digital Archives, accessed April 15, 2017, http://eada.lib.umd.edu/text-entries/itinerarium/.

8. "Itinerarium," loc. 161.

9. "Itinerarium," loc. 503.

10. "From Benjamin Franklin to John Canton, 14 March 1764," National Archives, Founders Online, accessed May 23, 2018, http://founders.archives.gov/documents/Franklin/01-11-02-0024.

11. "From Benjamin Franklin to John Canton."

12. George Washington, "Diary Entry: 4 May 1768," National Archives,

Founders Online, accessed May 23, 2018, http://founders.archives.gov/documents
/Washington/01-02-02-0003-0013-0004.

13. Ukers, *All about Coffee*, 115–16.

14. Benjamin Franklin, "Reply to Coffee-House Orators, [9 April 1767],"
National Archives, Founders Online, accessed May 23, 2018, http://founders
.archives.gov/documents/Franklin/01-14-02-0055. Benjamin Franklin, who lived in
England for twenty-one years in the period 1724–1775 and considered himself an
Anglophile, hoped that the American colonies and Britain could co-exist and
worked to find a compromise until the eve of the American Revolution. However,
after the Crown passed the Stamp Act of 1767, he did so as an American rather than
as the neutral he had been up to that point. When he returned to the colonies in
1775, he took a leadership role in planning the Revolution. See Jonathan R. Dull,
*Benjamin Franklin and the American Revolution* (Lincoln: University of Nebraska
Press, 2010), 30–32.

15. "Resolutions from Petersburg, Virginia, Citizens, 2 September 1793,"
National Archives, Founders Online, accessed May 23, 2018, https://founders
.archives.gov/documents/Washington/05-14-02-0012.

16. "The Proclamation of Neutrality 1793," Yale University Law School, Avalon
Project, Documents in Law, History and Diplomacy, accessed May 23, 2018, http://
avalon.law.yale.edu/18th_century/neutra93.asp.

17. "Resolutions from Petersburg, Virginia, Citizens."

18. "To Thomas Jefferson from Samuel Richardet, 12 October 1802," National
Archives, Founders Online, accessed May 23, 2018, https://founders.archives.gov
/documents/Jefferson/01-38-02-0447.

19. "Thomas Boylston Adams to Abigail Adams, 10 August 1793," National
Archives, Founders Online, accessed May 23, 2018, https://founders.archives.gov
/documents/Adams/04-09-02-0254.

20. "Thomas Boylston Adams to Abigail Adams," footnote 1.

21. George Washington, "Diary Entry: 23 September 1771," National Archives,
Founders Online, accessed May 23, 2018, http://founders.archives.gov/documents
/Washington/01-03-02-0001-0022-0023. The Main Street mentioned in this quote is
now Church Street.

22. Ukers, *All about Coffee*, 625 (first quote), 627. Mark Pendergrast, *Uncommon
Grounds: The History of Coffee and How It Transformed Our World* (New York: Basic
Books, 1999), 58 (second quote). The second quote is from *Spice Mill*, a trade publi-
cation Burns started in 1878.

23. Ukers, *All about Coffee*, 836.

24. Pendergrast, *Uncommon Grounds*, 46–49.

25. "Hawaii Coffee History," http://www.hawaiicoffeeassoc.org/history, n.d.,
accessed July 2, 2018.

26. "Hawaii Coffee History-Kona Coffee History," accessed July 2, 2018, https://
espressocoffeeguide.com/gourmet-coffee/asian-indonesian-and-pacific-coffees
/hawaii-coffee/kona-coffee-history/, n.d.

27. "John Henri David Uhl to John Adams: A Translation, 1 July 1782," National
Archives, Founders Online, accessed July 2, 2018, https://founders.archives.gov
/?q=uhl%20to%20adams&s=1111311111&sa=&r=2&sr=.

28. George Washington, "Diary Entry: 15 September 1786," National Archives,

Founders Online, accessed May 23, 2018, https://founders.archives.gov/documents
/Washington/01-05-02-0001-0003-0015.

29. "Enclosure Stephen Higginson to John Adams, 17 January 1789," National
Archives, Founders Online, accessed May 23, 2018, https://founders.archives.gov
/documents/Jefferson/01-14-02-0356. Bourbon, now Réunion, is an island located
approximately 110 miles southwest of Mauritius.

30. "To James Madison from Henry Hill, 27 February 1807," National Archives,
Founders Online, accessed July 2, 2018, https://founders.archives.gov/?q=james%20
madison%20to%20henry%20hill%201807%20sugar&s=1111311111&sa=&r=8&sr=.

31. "To Alexander Hamilton from Marquis De Rouvray, 15 August 1795,"
National Archives, Founders Online, accessed July 3, 2018, https://founders
.archives.gov/?q=rouvray&s=1111311111&sa=&r=6&sr=.

32. "Ready to Sail: The Manifest," National Archives at Boston, accessed May 23,
2018, https://www.archives.gov/boston/exhibits/mount-vernon/manifest.html.

33. Ukers, *All about Coffee*, 82.

34. Francis Beatty Thurber, *Coffee: From Plantation to Cup. A Brief History of
Coffee Production and Consumption* (New York: American Grocer Publishing
Association, 1881), 105. See also "Coffee Origins: World Map of Coffee Growing
Regions," accessed July 2, 2018, coffeeresearch.org, http://www.coffeeresearch.org
/coffee/originsmap.htm.

35. Thurber, *Coffee*, 105.

36. "Coffees from Africa and Arabia," Coffee Review, accessed July 3, 2018,
https://www.coffeereview.com/coffee-reference/coffee-categories/geographic
-origins/coffees-from-africa-and-arabia/kenya/.

37. Chris Summers, "How Vietnam Became a Coffee Giant," *BBC News
Magazine*, January 24, 2014, accessed July 3, 2018, https://www.bbc.com/news
/magazine-25811724.

38. Pendergrast, *Uncommon Grounds*, 17–18.

39. Quoted in Pendergrast, *Uncommon Grounds*, 18.

40. David Richardson, "Shipboard Revolts, African Authority, and the Atlantic
Slave Trade, *William and Mary Quarterly*, 58, no. 1 (2001): 69.

41. Thurber, *Coffee*, 67.

42. There's so much to the logistics of bringing people in to a place with limited
access.

43. Edward Lester Arnold, *Coffee: Its Cultivation and Profit* (London: W. B.
Whittingham & Co., 1886), 35.

44. Charles-Louis de Secondat, Baron de Montesquieu, *The Spirit of Laws*, vol. 1
(London: T. C. Hamsard, 1823), 19.

45. "Chinese Coolie Contract Regarding Work in Cuba, 1858," *Early America
Digital Archive*, accessed May 23, 2018, http://eada.lib.umd.edu/text-entries
/chinese-coolie-contract-regarding-work-in-cuba-1858/.

46. "Remarks by President Obama and Prime Minister Hailemariam Desalegn
of Ethiopia in a Joint Press Conference," July 27, 2015, accessed May 23, 2018, https://
obamawhitehouse.archives.gov/the-press-office/2015/07/27/remarks-president
-obama-and-prime-minister-hailemariam-desalegn-ethiopia.

47. "Remarks by President Obama and Prime Minister Hailemariam Desalegn."

48. Many thanks to Dr. Jennifer M. Brinkerhoff, for pointing me to the Ethiopian Commodity Exchange website.

49. "Company Profile," Ethiopian Commodity Exchange, accessed May 23, 2018, http://www.ecx.com.et/CompanyProfile.aspx#AU.

50. "Ethiopia's State-of-the-Art Commodity Exchange," *The Economist*, February 2, 2017, accessed May 23, 2018, https://www.economist.com/news/finance -and-economics/21716036-not-transformative-its-founders-hoped-ethiopias-state -art-commodity.

51. "What Is Fair Trade?" Fair Trade Certified, accessed May 23, 2018, https:// www.fairtradecertified.org/why-fair-trade.

52. "Income Sustainability," Fair Trade Certified, accessed July 9, 2018, https:// www.fairtradecertified.org/impact/income-sustainability.

53. "Vision and Mission," World Fair Trade Organization, accessed May 23, 2018, http://www.wfto.com/about-us/vision-and-mission.

54. "Vision and Mission."

55. "Fair Trade Myths," World Fair Trade Organization, accessed May 23, 2018, https://wfto.com/fair-trade/fair-trade-myths.

Conclusion

1. Declaration made by several students at the end of my History of Food course, spring 2017.

2. Rachel Laudan, *Cuisine and Empire Cooking in World History* (Berkeley: University of California Press, 2013), 76, 118–119; Joanne M. Ferraro, *Venice: History of the Floating City* (New York: Cambridge University Press, 2012), 115–16.

3. While these sources are rare, Amin Maalouf, *The Crusades through Arab Eyes*, translated by Jon Rothschild (New York: Schocken Books, 1984) demonstrates the value of making an effort to find them.

# BIBLIOGRAPHY

Abulafia, David. *The Great Sea*. New York: Oxford University Press, 2011.

Abulafia, David, ed. *The Mediterranean in History*. Los Angeles: J. Paul Getty Museum, 2003.

Abu-Lughod, Janet L. *Before European Hegemony: The World System A.D. 1250–1350*. New York: Oxford University Press, 1991.

Adams, Percy G. *Travel Literature and the Evolution of the Novel*. Lexington: University of Kentucky Press, 1983.

Albala, Ken, ed. *The Food History Reader: Primary Sources*. New York: Bloomsbury, 2014.

Alpini, Prospero. *Medicina aegyptiorum*. Leiden: Gerard Potuliet, 1745.

Alpini, Prospero. *De plantis Aegypti*. Patavi: Typis P. Frambotti, 1640.

Angelos, Mark. "Women in Genoese Commenda Contracts, 1155–1216." *Journal of Medieval History* 20, no. 4 (1994): 299–231.

Antaki, Dawud ibn 'Umar. *The Nature of the Drink Kauhi and the Berry of Which It Is Made, Described by an Arabian Phisitian*. Translated by Edward Pococke. Oxford: Henry Hall, 1659.

Anthony Sherley, Robert Sherley, and Thomas Sherley, *The Three Brothers, or the Travels and Adventures of Sir Anthony, Sir Robert and Sir Thomas Sherley*. London: Hurst, Robinson, and Co., 1825.

Antonielli, L., and G. Chittolini. *Storia Della Lombardia: Dalle origini al seicento*. Vol. 1. Roma-Bari: Editori Laterza, 2003.

Appleby, Joyce. *Shores of Knowledge: New World Discoveries and the Scientific Imagination*. New York: W. W. Norton, 2013.

Arano, Luisa Cogliati. *The Medieval Health Handbook: Tacuinum Sanitatis*. Translated by Oscar Ratti and Adele Westbrook. New York: George Braziller, 1976.

Arberry, Arthur J., trans. *The Koran Interpreted*. Oxford: Oxford University Press.

Armstrong Karen. *Islam: A Short History*. New York: Modern Library, 2002.

Arnold, Edwin Lester. *Coffee: Its Cultivation and Profit*. London: W. B. Whittingham & Co., 1886.

Asad, Muhammad, trans. *The Message of the Qur'an*. England: The Book Foundation, 203.

Assadi, Muzaffar. "Threats to Syncretic Culture: Baba Budan Giri Incident." *Economic and Political Weekly* 34, no. 14 (1999): 746–48.

Astuti, G., and G. Scriba. *Rendiconti Mercantili Inediti Del Cartolare Di Giovanni Scriba. Pubblicati Con Introduzione E Commento Dal Guido Astuti. Con 5 Tavole Fuori Testo*. L'Istituto giuridico della R. Univ., 1933.

Avicenna. *The Canon of Medicine.* Translated by O. Cameron Gruner and Mazar H. Shah. New York: AMS Press, 1973.

Ayvazoğlu, Beşir. *Turkish Coffee Culture.* Ankara: Republic of Turkey Ministry of Culture and Tourism, 2011.

Bacon, Francis. *Sylva Sylvarum or a Natural History in Ten Centuries.* London: W. Rawley, 1626.

Bacon, Francis. *The Vertues of Coffee.* London: W. G. for John Playford, 1663.

Badoer, Giacomo. *Il Libro Dei Conti Di Giacomo Badoer (Constantinopli 1436–1440).* Rome: Libreria dello Stato, 1956.

Baghdiantz, Ina McCabe. *A History of Global Consumption: 1500–1800.* New York: Routledge, 2014.

Bannister, Richard. "Sugar, Coffee, Tea, and Cocoa, Their Origin, Preparation, and Uses." *Journal of the Society of Arts* 38, no. 1979 (1890): 997–1016.

Battutah, Ibn. *The Travels of Ibn Battutah.* Abridged by Tim Mackintosh-Smith. London: Picador, 2000.

Beckwith, Christopher I. *Empires of the Silk Road: A History of Central Eurasia from the Bronze Age to the Present.* Princeton, NJ: Princeton University Press, 2009.

Bellondi, Vincenzo. *Documenti e aneddoti d storia Veneziana (1810–1854).* Florence: Librato Editore, 1902.

Ben-Menahem, Ari. "The Clockwork Universe." In *Historical Encyclopedia of Natural and Mathematical Sciences,* vol. 1, edited by Christian Witschel, 911–1722. New York: Springer, 2009.

Ben-Yehoshua, Shimshon, Carole Borowitz, and Lumír Ondřej Hanuš. "Frankincense, Myrrh, and the Balm of Gilead: Ancient Spices of Southern Arabia and Judea." *Horticultural Reviews* 39 (2012): 1–76.

Besnard, G., B. Khadari, M. Navascues, M. Fernandez-Mazeucos, A. El Bakkali, N. Arrigo, D. Baali-Cherif, V. Brunini-Bronzini de Caraffa, S. Santoni, P. Vargas, and V. Savolainen. "The Complex History of the Olive Tree: From Late Quaternary Diversification of Mediterranean Lineages to Primary Domestication in the Northern Levant." *Proceedings of the Royal Society* 280, no. 1756 (2013).

Bhattacharya, Bhaswati. "Local History of a Global Commodity: Production of Coffee in Mysore and Coorg in the Nineteenth Century." *Indian Historical Review* 40, no. 1 (2014): 67–86.

Biddulph, William. *The Trauels of Certaine Englishmen into Africa, Asia, Troy, Bythinia, Thracia, and to the Blacke Sea and into Syria, Cilicia, Pisidia, Mesopotamia, Damascus, Canaan, Galile, Samaria, Iudea, Palestina, Ierusalem, Iericho, and to the Red Sea: And to Sundry Other Places.* London: Th. Haveland, 1609.

Biddulph, William. *Travels into Africa, Asia, and to the Black Sea.* Amsterdam: Theatrum Orbis Terrarum Ltd., 1968.

Birch, T., ed., *The Works of the Honourable Robert Boyle.* 2nd ed. Vol. 6. London, 1772.

Bischoff, Bernhard. "The Study of Foreign Languages in the Middle Ages." *Speculum* 36, no. 2 (1961): 209–24.

Blount, Henry. *Voyage into the Levant*. London: Andrew Crooke, 1636.

Boivin, Nicole, and Dorian Q. Fuller. "Shell Middens, Ships, and Seeds: Exploring Coastal Subsistence, Maritime Trade and the Dispersal of Domesticates in and around the Ancient Arabian Peninsula." *Journal of World Prehistory* 22 (2009): 113–180.

Brandon David. *Life in a 17th Century Coffee Shop*. Gloucestershire: The History Press, 2007.

Braudel, Fernand. *Civilization and Capitalism: 15th Century–18th Century*. New York: Harper and Rowe, 1982.

Braudel, Fernand. *The Mediterranean and the Mediterranean World in the Age of Philip II*. Vol. 1. Translated by Sian Reynolds. New York: Harper & Row, 1973.

Braudel, Fernand. *The Mediterranean and the Mediterranean World in the Age of Philip II*. Vol. 2. Berkeley: University of California Press, 1996.

Braudel Fernand Braudel, *The Structures of Everyday Life: Civilization and Capitalism, 15th Century–18th Century*. Vol. 1. Translated by Sian Reynolds. San Francisco: Harper and Row Publishers, 1981.

Braudel, Fernand. *The Structures of Everyday Life: The Limits of the Possible*. Translated by Sian Reynolds. San Francisco: Harper and Rowe Publishers, 1981.

Brewer, John, and Roy Porter, eds. *Consumption and the World of Goods*. New York: Routledge, 1993.

Brinkerhoff, Jennifer M. *Institutional Reform and Diaspora Entrepreneurs: The In-Between Difference*. New York: Oxford University Press, 2016.

Brown, Horatio F. "The Venetians and the Venetian Quarter in Constantinople to the Close of the Twelfth Century." *The Journal of Hellenic Studies* 40, no. 1 (1920): 68–88.

Brucker, Gene. *Renaissance Florence*. Berkeley: University of California Press, 1969.

Brucker, Gene. *The Society of Renaissance Florence: A Documentary Study*. Toronto: University of Toronto Press, 1998.

Bruscoli, Francesco Guidi. *Bartolomeo Marchionni "homen de grossa Fazenda" (ca. 1450–1530): Un Mercanti Fiorentino a Lisbona e l'empero portoghese*. Florence: Leo S. Olschki Editore, 2014.

Burguierè, André. *The Annales School: An Intellectual History*. Translated by Jane Marie Todd. Ithaca: Cornell University Press, 2009.

Burke, Katherine Strange. "A Note on the Archaeological Evidence for Sugar Production in the Middle Islamic Periods in Bilad Al-Sham. *Mamluk Studies Review* 8, no. 2 (2004): 109–18.

Camporesi, Piero. *Bread of Dreams: Food and Fantasy in Early Modern Europe*. Translated by David Gentilcore. Chicago: University of Chicago Press, 1989.

Campo, Juan Eduardo. "Dietary Rules." In *The Oxford Encyclopedia of the Islamic*

*World.* Vol. 1, edited by John Esposito. New York: Oxford University Press, 1995.

Carboni, Stefano. *Venice and the Islamic World, 828–1797.* New York Metropolitan Museum of Art, 2007.

Carlton, Genevieve. *Worldly Consumers: The Demand for Maps in Renaissance Italy.* Chicago: University of Chicago Press, 2015.

Casola, Pietro. *Canon Pietro Casola's Pilgrimage to Jerusalem In the Year 1494.* Edited by M. Margaret Newett. Manchester: Manchester University Press, 1907.

Castiglione, Baldassare. *Il Cortegiano.* Firenze: G. C. Sansoni, 1894.

Castiglione, Baldassare. *The Book of the Courtier.* Translated by George Anthony Bull. New York: Penguin Books, 1967.

Cavallo, Sandra, and David Gentilcore. "Introduction: Spaces, Objects and Identities in Early Modern Italian Medicine." In *Spaces, Objects and Identities in Early Modern Italian Medicine,* edited by Sandra Cavallo and David Gentilcore. Malden, Mass: Blackwell

Çelebi, Katip. *The Balance of Truth.* Translated by G. L. Lewis. London: George Allen and Unwin, Ltd, 1957.

Chojnacka, Monica. *Working Women of Early Modern Venice.* Baltimore, Md.: Johns Hopkins University Press, 2001.

Clark, Victoria. *Yemen: Dancing on the Heads of Snakes.* New Haven, Conn.: Yale University Press, 2010.

Clifford, M. N., and K. C. Wilson, eds. *Coffee: Botany, Biochemistry and Production of Beans and Beverage.* London: Croom Helm, 1985.

Clunas, Craig. "Modernity Global and Local: Consumption and the Rise of the West." *American Historical Review* 104, no. 5 (1997): 1497–1511.

Cohen, Elizabeth S. "Evolving the History of Women in Early Modern Italy: Subordination and Agency." In *Spain and Italy, Politics, Society, and Religion,* edited by Thomas James Dandelet and John A. Marino. The Medieval and Early Modern Iberian World. Boston: Brill, 2007.

Cohen, Rich. "Sugar Love (a Not So Sweet Story)." *National Geographic,* August 2013. Accessed May 23, 2018. http://ngm.nationalgeographic.com/2013/08/sugar /cohen-text.

Collinson, Patrick. *The Reformation: A History.* New York: The Modern Library, 2003.

Colonna, Francesco. *Hypnerotomachia Poliphili.* Padova: Antenore, 1980.

Comnena, Anna. *The Alexiad.* Translated by E .R. A. Sewter. London: Penguin Books, 1969.

Cooke, Miriam, Erdağ Göknar, and Grant Richard Parker, eds. *Mediterranean Passages: Readings from Dido to Derrida.* Chapel Hill: University of North Carolina Press, 2008.

Cowan, Brian. "An Open Elite: The Peculiarities of Connoisseurship in Early Modern England." *Modern Intellectual History* 1, no. 2 (2004): 151–83.

Cowan, Brian. "Public Spaces, Knowledge, and Sociability." In *The History of Consumption*, edited by Frank Trentmann. New York: Oxford University Press, 2012.

Cowan, Brian. *The Social Life of Coffee: The Emergence of the British Coffeehouse.* New Haven, Conn.: Yale University Press, 2005.

Crawford, John. "History of Coffee." *Journal of the Statistical Society of London* 15, no. 1 (1852): 50–58.

Crossley, J., ed. *The Diary and Correspondence of Dr. John Worthington.* Vol. 13. Manchester: Chetham Society, 1847. Accessed May 24, 2018. https://www .hrionline.ac.uk/hartlib/view?docset=additional&docname=WORTH _05&termo=transtext_coffee#highlight.

Da Gama, Vasco. *A Journal of the First Voyage of Vasco Da Gama, 1497–1499.* Translated by E. G. Ravenstein. London: The Hakluyt Society, 1898.

Dani, Ahmad Hasan. "Significance of the Silk Road to Human Civilization: Its Cultural Dimensions." *Senri Ethnological Studies* 32 (1992): 21–26.

Dannenfeldt, Karl H. *Leonhard Rauwolf, Sixteenth-Century Physician, Botanist, and Traveler.* Cambridge: Harvard University Press, 1968.

Darwish, Mahmoud. *Memory for Forgetfulness: August, Beirut, 1986.* Translated by Ibrahim Muhawi. Berkeley: University of California Press, 1995.

De Lemps, Alain Huetz. "Colonial Beverages and the Consumption of Sugar." In *Food: A Culinary History*, edited by Jean-Louis Flandrin and Massimo Montanari. Translated by Albert Sonnenfeld. New York: Penguin Books, 2000.

De Vivo, Filippo. "Pharmacies in Early Modern Venice." *Renaissance Studies* 21, no. 1 (2007): 505–21.

Deleidi, Laura. "Donne milanesi della prima metà del cinquecento: la memoria degli atti notarili." *Societá e Storia* 18 (1994): 279–314.

Della Casa, Giovanni. *Galateo Ovvero De' Costumi.* Florence: Felice Le Monnier, 1949.

Della Valle, Pietro. *Viaggi di Pietro della Valle.* Brighton: G. Gancia, 1853.

Diamond, Jared. *Guns, Germs, and Steel: The Fates of Human Societies.* New York: W. W. Norton, 1999.

DuFour, Philippe Sylvestre. *The Manner of Making Coffee, Tea, and Chocolate as It Is Used in Most Parts of Europe, Asia, Africa, and America, with Their Vertues.* London: William Crook, 1685.

Dursteler, Eric. "Commerce and Coexistence: Veneto-Ottoman Trade in the Early Modern Era." *Turcica* 34 (2002): 105–33.

Dursteler, Eric R. *Venetians in Constantinople: Nation, Identity, and Coexistence in the Early Modern Mediterranean.* Baltimore, Md.: Johns Hopkins University Press, 2006.

Eadie, John W. and John Peter Oleson, "The Water-Supply Systems of Nabataean and Roman Humayma. *Bulletin of the American Schools of Oriental Research* 262 (1986): 49–76.

Eaton, Charles le Gai, ed. *The Book of Hadith*. London: The Book Foundation, 2008.

Edens, Christopher and Garth Bawden. "History of Tayma and the Hejazi Trade During the First Millennium B.C." *Journal of the Economic and Social History of the Orient* 32, no. 1 (1989): 48–103.

Edwards, David N. "Ancient Egypt in the Sudanese Middle Nile: A Case of Mistaken Identity?" In *Ancient Egypt in Africa*, edited by Donald O'Connor and Andrew Reid. Portland, Ore.: Cavendish Publishing, 2003.

Ellis, John. *An Historical Account of Coffee, with an Engraving and Botanical Description of the Tree: To Which Are Added Sundry Papers Relative to Its Culture and Use, as an Article of Diet and of Commerce*. London: Edward and Charles Dilly, 1774.

Ellis, Markman. *The Coffee House: A Cultural History*. London: Orion Publishing, 2004.

Epstein, Mortimer. *The Early History of the Levant Company*. London: George Routledge & Sons, 1908.

Epstein, Steven A. *An Economic and Social History of Later Medieval Europe, 1000–1500*. New York: Cambridge University Press, 2009.

Epstein, Steven A. *Wills and Wealth in Medieval Genoa, 1150–1250*. Cambridge, Massachusetts: Harvard University Press, 1984.

"Ethiopia's State-of-the-Art Commodity Exchange." *The Economist*, February 2, 2017. Accessed May 23, 2018. https://www.economist.com/news/finance-and -economics/21716036-not-transformative-its-founders-hoped-ethiopias -state-art-commodity.

Esposito, John L., ed. *The Islamic World Past and Present*. Vol. 1. New York: Oxford University Press, 2004.

Evelyn, John. *The Diary of John Evelyn*. London: MacMillan, 1908.

Faroqhi, Suraiya. *Pilgrims and Sultans: The Hajj under the Ottomans, 1517–1683*. New York: I. B. Tauris, 1994.

Fernandez-Armesto, Felipe. *Pathfinders: A Global History of Exploration*. New York: W. W. Norton, 2013.

Fernandez-Armesto, Felipe, and Benjamin Sacks. "The Global Exchange of Food and Drugs." In *The Oxford Handbook of the History of Consumption*, edited by Frank Trentmann. New York: Oxford University Press, 2012.

Ferraro, Joanne M. *Venice: History of a Floating City*. New York: Cambridge University Press, 2012.

Findlen, Paula. "Possessing the Past: The Material World of the Italian Renaissance." *American Historical Review* 103, no. 1 (1998): 83–114.

Flandrin, Jean-Louis, and Massimo Montanari, eds. *Food: A Culinary History from Antiquity to the Present*. Translated by Albert Sonnenfeld. New York: Penguin Books, 2000.

Flandrin, Jean-Louis, and Massimo Montanari. "Introduction to the Original Edition." In *Food: A Culinary History*, edited by Jean-Louis Flandrin and

Massimo Montanari. Translated by Albert Sonnenfeld. New York: Columbia University Press, 1999.

Flandrin, Jean-Louis. "The Humanization of Eating Behaviors," in *Food: A Culinary History*, edited by Jean-Louis Flandrin and Massimo Montanari. Translated by Albert Sonnenfeld. New York: Columbia University Press, 1999.

Flandrin, Jean-Louis. "Introduction: The Early Modern Period." In *Food: A Culinary History*, edited by Jean-Louis Flandrin and Massimo Montanari. New York: Penguin Books, 2000.

Freedman, Paul. "Eating Out." In *A Cultural History of Food in the Renaissance*, edited by Ken Albala. New York: Berg, 2012.

Fregulia, Jeanette M. "Widows, Legal Rights, and the Mercantile Economy in Early Modern Milan." *Early Modern Women: An Interdisciplinary Journal* 3 (2008): 233–238.

Frenkel, Yehoshua. "Ibn Jubayr (c. 1144–1217): Spanish Arab Traveler and Writer." In *Literature of Travel and Exploration: An Encyclopedia*, edited by Jennifer Speake. New York: Routledge, 2013.

Friedlander, Shems. *The Whirling Dervishes*. Albany, New York: State University of New York Press, 1992.

Garcia-Castellanos, D., F. Estrada, I. Jiménez-Munt, C. Gorini, M. Fernàndez, J. Vergés, and R. De Vicente. "Catastrophic Flood of the Mediterranean after the Messinian Salinity Crisis." *Nature* 462, no. 7274 (2009): 778–781.

Gautier, Alban. "Eating out in the Early and High Middle Ages." In *A Cultural History of Food in the Medieval Age*, edited by Massimo Montanari. New York: Berg, 2012.

Geertz, Clifford. *The Interpretation of Cultures*. New York: Basic Books, 1973.

Gibb, H. A. R., and J. H. Kramers. "Tasawwuf." In *Shorter Encyclopedia of Islam*, edited by H. A. R. Gibb and J. H. Kramers. Leiden: E. J. Brill, 1974.

Giglioni, Guido. "Mastering the Appetites of Matter: Francis Bacon's Sylva Sylvarum." In *The Body as Object and Instrument of Knowledge: Embodied Empiricism in Early Modern Science*, edited by Charles T. Wolfe and Ofer Gal. Springer Netherlands, 2010.

Ginzburg, Carlo. *The Cheese and the Worms: The Cosmos of a Sixteenth Century Miller*. Translated by John and Anne Tedeschi. Baltimore, Md.: Johns Hopkins University Press, 1992.

Goitein, S. D. *A Mediterranean Society the Jewish Communities of the World as Portrayed in the Documents of the Cairo Geniza: Cumulative Indices*. 7 vols. Berkeley: University of California Press, 1971.

Goldthwaite, Richard A. "The Empire of Things: Consumer Demand in Renaissance Italy." In *Patronage, Art, and Society in Renaissance Italy*, edited by F. W. Kent and Patricia Simons with J. D. Eade. Oxford: Clarendon Press, 1987.

Goldthwaite, Richard A. *Private Wealth in Renaissance Florence: A Study of Four Families*. Princeton, N.J.: Princeton University Press, 1968.

Goldthwaite, Richard A. *Wealth and the Demand for Art in Italy, 1300–1600.* Baltimore, Md.: Johns Hopkins University Press, 1993.

Goody, Jack. *Food and Love: A Cultural History of East and West.* New York: Verso, 1998.

Gramich, Katie. "'Every Hill Has Its History, Every Region Its Romance': Travellers' Constructions of Wales, 1844–1913." In *Travel Writing and Tourism in Britain and Ireland,* edited by Benjamin Colbert. New York: Palgrave MacMillan, 2012.

Greenblatt, Stephen. *Marvelous Possessions: The Wonder of the New World.* Chicago: University of Chicago Press, 1991.

Grendler, Paul. "The Roman Inquisition and the Venetian Press, 1540–1605." *Journal of Modern History* 47, no. 1 (1975): 48–65.

Griffin, J. P. "Venetian Treacle and the Foundation of Medicines Regulation." *British Journal of Clinical Pharmacology* 58, no. 3 (2004): 317–25.

Groom, Nigel. *Frankincense and Myrrh: A Study of the Arabian Incense Trade.* New York: Longman, 1981.

Habermas, Jürgen. *The Structural Transformation of the Public Sphere An Inquiry into a Category of Bourgeois Society.* Translated by Thomas Burger with the assistance of Frederick Lawrence. Cambridge, Mass.: MIT Press, 1991.

Hajar, Rachel. "The Air of History (Part IV): Great Muslim Physicians Al Rhazes." *Heart Views: The Official Journal of the Gulf Heart Association* 14, no. 2 (2013): 93–95.

Harari, Yuval Noah. *Sapiens: A Brief History of Humankind.* New York: HarperCollins, 2015.

Hattox, Ralph S. *Coffee and Coffeehouses: The Origins of a Social Beverage in the Medieval Near East.* Seattle: University of Washington Press, 1985.

Hegel, Georg Wilhelm. *The Philosophy of History.* London: George Bell and Sons, 1884.

Herodotus. *The History.* Translated by David Grene. Chicago: University of Chicago Press, 1987.

Heyd, Uriel. *Ottoman Documents on Palestine, 1552–1615: A Study of the Firman According to the Mühimme Defteri.* Oxford: Clarendon Press, 1960.

Higgins, Iain MacLeod, ed. *The Book of John Mandeville.* Indianapolis, Ind.: Hackett Publishing Company, 2011.

Hoover, Calvin B. "The Sea Loan in Genoa in the Twelfth Century." *Quarterly Journal of Economics* 40, no. 3 (1926): 495–529.

Horden, Peregrin, and Nicholas Purcell. *The Corrupting Sea: A Study of Mediterranean History.* Oxford: Blackwell, 2000.

Horowitz, Elliot. "Coffee, Coffeehouses, and the Nocturnal Rituals of Early Modern Jewry." *AJS Review* 14, no. 1 (1989): 17–46.

Howard, Deborah. "Venice and the Mamluks." In *Venice and the Islamic World,*

*828–1797*, edited by Stefano Carboni. New York: The Metropolitan Museum of Art, 2007.

Ibn-Munqidh, Usāmah. *An Arab-Syrian Gentleman and Warrior in the Period of the Crusades: Memoirs of Usāmah Ibn-Munqich*. Translated by Philip K. Hitti. New York: Columbia University Press, 2000.

Inalcik, Halil. "Capital Formation in the Ottoman Empire." *Journal of Economic History* 29, no. 1 (1969): 97–140.

Ishaq. *The Life of Muhammad*. Translated by A. Guillaume. New York: Oxford University Press, 1955.

Jardine, Lisa. *Worldly Goods: A New History of the Renaissance*. New York: W. W. Norton, 1996.

Jacob, Heinrich Eduard. *Coffee: The Epic of a Commodity*. Translated by Eden Paul and Cedar Paul. New York: Viking Press, 1935.

Jacobs, Martin. *Reorienting the East, Jewish Travelers to the Medieval Muslim World*. Philadelphia: University of Pennsylvania Press, 2014.

Jones, Christine A. "Exotic Edibles: Coffee, Chocolate, and the Early Modern French How-To." *Journal of Medieval and Early Modern Studies* 43, no. 3 (2013): 623–53.

Kafadar, Cemal. "A Death in Venice (1575): Anatolian Muslim Merchants Trading in the Serenissima." *Journal of Turkish Studies* 10 (1986): 191–218.

Kaplan, Robert D. *The Revenge of Geography: What the Map Tells Us about Coming Conflicts and the Battle against Fate*. New York: Random House, 2012.

Khan, Sameen Ahmed. "Medieval Arab Contributions to Optics." *Digest of Middle East Studies* 25, no. 1 (2016): 19–35.

Knysh, Alexander. *Islam in Historical Perspective*. New York: Routledge, 2017.

Koch, Natalie. "Geopower and Geopolitics in, of, and for the Middle East." *International Journal of Middle East Studies* 49, no. 2 (2017): 315–318. Kömeçoğlu, Uğur. "The Publicness and Sociabilities of the Ottoman Coffeehouse." *Javnost—The Public: Journal of the European Institute for Communication and Culture* 12, no. 2 (2005): 5–22.

Kömeçoğlu, Uğur. "The Publicness and Sociabilities of the Ottoman Coffeehouse." *Javnost-The Public: Journal of the European Institute for Communication and Culture* 12, no. 2 (2005): 5–22.

Krusinski, Father J. T. *The History of the Late Revolutions of Persia*. London: J. Pemberton, 1733.

Kümin, Beat. "Eating out in Early Modern Europe." In *A Cultural History of Food in the Early Modern Age*, edited by Beat Kümin. New York: Berg, 2012.

La Roque, Jean de. *A Voyage to Arabia Felix*. London: E. Symon, 1732.

Lane, Edward William. *An Account of the Manners and Customs of the Modern Egyptians*. London: John Murray, 1860.

Laudan, Rachel. *Cuisine and Empire Cooking in World History*. Berkeley: University of California Press, 2013.

Leoni, Stefano A. E. "Ibn Sīnā, Abū ʿAlī al-Ḥusayn ibn ʿAbd Allāh." In *The Oxford Encyclopedia of the Islamic World*, edited by John Esposito. Oxford: Oxford University Press, 2009.

Levack, Brian P. *The Witch-Hunt in Early Modern Europe*. New York: Routledge, 2016.

Lévi-Strauss, Claude. *The Raw and the Cooked*. New York: Harper and Row, 1969.

Lévi-Strauss, Claude. *Structural Anthropology*. Translated by Claire Jacobson and Brooke Grundfest Schoepf. New York: Basic Books, 1963.

Lieber, Alfred E. "Eastern Business Practices and Medieval European Commerce." *Economic History Review* 21, no. 2 (1968): 230–43.

Liu, Xinru. *The Silk Road in World History*. New York: Oxford University Press, 2010.

Lopez, Robert S. *Studi Sull'economia Genovese New Medio Evo*. Edited by Federico Patetta and Mario Chiaudano. Turin: S. Lattes and C. Editori, 1936.

Lopez, Robert S., and Irving W. Raymond. *Medieval Trade in the Mediterranean World*. New York: Columbia University Press, 1961.

Lu, Yu. *The Classic of Tea*. Translated by Francis Ross Carpenter. Boston: Little, Brown, and Company, 1974.

Maalouf, Amin. *The Crusades through Arab Eyes*. New York: Schocken Books, 1989.

Mack, Rosamond E. *Bazaar to Piazza: Islamic Trade and Italian Art, 1300–1600*. Berkeley: University of California Press, 2002.

Malecka, Anna. "How Turks and Persians Drank Coffee: A Little-Known Document of Social History by Father J. T. Krusinski." *Turkish Historical Review* 6 (2015): 175–93.

Mancall, Peter C., ed. *Travel Narratives from the Age of Discovery: An Anthology*. New York: Oxford University Press, 2006.

Martin, John Jeffries. *Venice's Hidden Enemies: Italian Heretics in a Renaissance City*. Berkeley: University of California Press, 1993.

Matz, David. *Daily Life of the Ancient Romans*. Westport, Conn.: Greenwood Press, 2002.

Mayerson, Philip. "The Port of Clysma (Suez) in the Transition from Roman to Arab Rule." *Journal of Near Eastern Studies* 22, no. 2 (1996): 119–126.

McCabe, Ina Baghdiantz. *A History of Global Consumption: 1500–1800*. New York: Routledge, 2014.

McCants, Anne E. C. "Exotic Goods, Popular Consumption, and the Standard of Living: Thinking about Globalization in the Early Modern World." *Journal of World History* 18, no. 4 (2007): 433–62.

McKee, Sally. "Women under Venetian Colonial Rule in the Early Renaissance: Observations on Their Economic Activities." *Renaissance Quarterly* 51, no. 1 (1998): 34–67.

Millar, Fergus. "Caravan Cities; the Roman near East and Long Distance Trade by Land." *Bulletin of the Institute of Classical Studies of the University of London* 42, no. 71 (1998): 119–37.

Mintz, Sidney W. *Sweetness and Power the Place of Sugar in Modern History*. New York: Penguin Books, 1985.

Mokyr, Joel. "Is There Still Life in the Pessimistic Case? Consumption during the Industrial Revolution, 1790–1850." *Journal of Economic History* 48, no. 1 (1988): 69–92.

Molà, Luca. *The Silk Industry of Renaissance Venice*. Baltimore, Md.: Johns Hopkins University Press, 2000.

Montanari, Massimo. "Introduction." In *A Cultural History of Food in the Medieval Age*, edited by Massimo Montanari. New York: Berg, 2012.

de Montesquieu, Charles-Louis de Secondat. *The Spirit of Laws*. 2 vols. London: T. C. Hamsard, 1823.

Munqidh, Usamah ibn. *Observations of the Crusaders (1188)*. Oxford: Oxford University Press.

Nabhan, Gary Paul. *Cumin, Camels, and Caravans: A Spice Odyssey*. Berkeley: University of California Press, 2014.

Norton, Marcy. "Tasting Empire: Chocolate and the European Internalization of Mesoamerican Aesthetics." *American Historical Review* 111, no. 3 (2006): 660–91.

Nuovo, Angela, and Francesco Ammannati. "Investigating Book Prices in Early Modern Europe: Questions and Sources." *JLIS.it* 8, no. 3 (2017): 3–25.

Nuovo, Angela. "A Lost Arabic Koran Rediscovered." *The Library* XII, no. 4 (1990): 273–94.

Nuovo, Angela. "Private Libraries in Sixteenth-Century Italy." In *Early Printed Books as Material Objects: Proceedings of the Conference Organized by the Ifla Rare Books and Manuscripts Section*, edited by Bettina Wagner and Marcia Reed, 229–40. New York: De Gruyter Saur, 2010.

O'Rourke, Kevin H., and Jeffrey G. Williamson. "When Did Globalisation Begin?" *European Review of Economic History* 6, no. 1 (2002): 23–50.

Palma, Pina. *Savoring Power, Consuming the Times: The Metaphors of Food in Medieval and Renaissance Literature*. Notre Dame, Ind.: University of Notre Dame Press, 2013.

Parini, Giuseppe. *Il Giorno*. London: Clarendon, 1921.

Peacham, Henry. *Peacham's Compleat Gentleman, 1634*. London: Clarendon Press, 1906.

Pegolotti, Francesco Balducci. *La pratica della mercatura scritta da Francesco Balducci Pegolotti*. Lisbon: Lucca, 1766.

Pendergrast, Mark. *Uncommon Grounds: The History of Coffee and How It Transformed Our World*. New York: Basic Books, 1999.

Peters, F. E. *The Children of Abraham: Judaism, Christianity, Islam*. Princeton, N.J.: Princeton University Press, 2005.

Pirenne, Henri. *Economic and Social History of Medieval Europe*. London: Routledge and Kegan Paul, 1936.

Plautus. *The Comedies of Plautus*. Edited by Henry Thomas Riley. London: George Bell and Sons, 1894.

Pliny. *Natural History*. Translated by H. Rackham, W. H. S. Jones, and D. E. Eichholz. London: William Heinemann, 1949.

Pitte, Jean-Robert. "The Rise of the Restaurant." In *Food: A Culinary History from Antiquity to the Present*, edited by Jean-Louis Flandrin and Massimo Montanari. New York: Penguin Books, 1999.

Polo, Marco. *The Travels of Marco Polo*. Translated by Ronald Latham. 1958; repr., New York: Penguin, 1976.

Procopius. *La Guerra Gotica*. Rome: Forzani, 1896.

Rainey, Anson F. "Herodotus' Description of the East Mediterranean Coast." *Bulletin of the American Schools of Oriental Research* 321 (February 2001): 57–63.

Ray, John. *A Collection of Curious Travels and Voyages, in Two Tomes, the First Containing Leonhart Rauwolff's Itinerary into the Eastern Countries*. London: S. Smith and B. Walford, 1693.

Reato, Danilo. *The Coffee-House: Venetian Coffee-Houses from the 18th to the 20th Century*. Translated by Danilo Reato. Venice: Arsenale Editrice, 1991.

Rees, Graham. "An Unpublished Manuscript by Francis Bacon: *Sylva Sylvarum* Drafts and Other Working Notes." *Annals of Science* 34, no. 4 (1981): 377–412.

Richardson, David. "Shipboard Revolts, African Authority, and the Atlantic Slave Trade. *William and Mary Quarterly*, 58, no. 1 (2001): 69–92.

Riley-Smith, Jonathan. *The Crusades: A History*. 3rd ed. New York: Bloomsbury Academic, 2014.

Riva, Bonvesin della. *Le Meraviglie di Milano: De Magnalibus Mediolani*. Edited by Guiseppe Pontiggia. Milano: Bompiani, 1974.

Rossignani, Maria Pia. "Milan: Discovery of Frankincense Lumps in a Roman Burial." In *Profumi d'Arabia, Atti del Covengo*, edited by Alessandra Avanzini. Rome: L'Erma de Bretschneider, 1997.

Rowland, Ingrid. *The Culture of the High Renaissance*. Cambridge: Cambridge University Press, 1998.

Ryan, William B. F. "Decoding the Mediterranean Salinity Crisis." *Sedimentology* 56, no. 1 (2009): 95–136.

Said, Edward. *Orientalism*. New York: Random House, 1979.

Saliba, George. "Islamic Reception of Greek Astronomy." *Proceedings of the IAU Symposium* 260 (2009): 149–65.

Sandys, George. *A Relation of a Journey Begun in Ano Domi 1610*. London: Philip Chetwin, 1670.

Sandys, George. *Sandy's Travels*. London: John Williams, 1673.

Sarpi, Paulo. *The Maxims of the Government of Venice. In an Advice to the Republick, How It Ought to Govern Itself, Both Inwardly and Outwardly, in Order to Perpetuate Its Dominion*. London: J. Morphew, 1707.

Sato, Tsugitaka. *Sugar in the Social Life of Medieval Islam*. Leiden: Brill, 2014.

BIBLIOGRAPHY

Schepelern, H. D. "The Museum Wormianum Reconstructed: A Note on the Illustration of 1655." *Journal of the History of Collection* 2, no. 1 (1990): 81–85.

Schoenholt, Donald N. "Globalization Blues: Part 2." *Tea and Coffee Trade Journal,* April 2016, 38–40.

Schoff, Wilfred Harvey, trans. *The Periplus of the Erythraean Sea: Travel and Trade in the Indian Ocean by a Merchant of the First Century.* New York: Longmans, Green, 1912.

Sherley, Anthony, Robert Sherley, and Thomas Sherley. *The Three Brothers, or the Travels and Adventures of Sir Anthony, Sir Robert and Sir Thomas Sherley.* London: Hurst, Robinson, and Co., 1825.

Smith, Reginald F. "A History of Coffee." In *Coffee: Botany, Biochemistry, and Production of Beans and Beverage,* edited by M. N. Clifford and K. C. Wilson, 1–12. London: Croom Helm, 1985.

Spang, Rebecca. *The Invention of the Restaurant: Paris and Modern Gastronomic Culture.* Cambridge, Mass.: Harvard University Press, 2000.

Summers, Chris. "How Vietnam Became a Coffee Giant," *BBC News Magazine,* January 24, 2014. Accessed July 2, 2018. https://www.bbc.com/news /magazine-25811724.

Super, John C. "Food and History." *Journal of Social History* 36, no. 1 (2002): 165–178.

Teixeira, Pedro. *The Travels of Pedro Teixeira with His "Kings of Harmuz" and Extracts from His "Kings of Persia."* London: Hakluyt Society, 1902.

Thomas, Bertram, and B. K. N. Wyllie. "A Camel Journey across the Rub' Al Khali." *Geographical Journal* 78, no. 3 (1931): 209–38.

Thurber, Francis Beatty. *Coffee: From Plantation to Cup. A Brief History of Coffee Production and Consumption.* New York: American Grocer Publishing Association, 1881.

Trentmann, Frank, ed. *The Oxford Handbook of the History of Consumption.* New York: Oxford University Press, 2012.

Ukers, William Harrison. *All About Coffee.* New York: The Tea and Coffee Trade Journal, 1922.

Van Beek, Gus W. "Frankincense and Myrrh." *The Biblical Archaeologist* 23, no. 3 (1960): 69–95.

Van Beek, Gus W. "Frankincense and Myrrh in Ancient South Arabia." *Journal of the American Oriental Society* 78, no. 3 (1958): 141–52.

Van Dijk, Arjan. "Early Printed Qur'ans: The Dissemination of the Qur'an in the West." *Journal of Qur'anic Studies* 7, no. 2 (2008): 136–43.

Waldvogel, Siegfried R. "Caffeine—A Drug with a Surprise." *Angewandt Chemie* 42, no. 6 (2003): 604–5.

Wallerstein, Immanuel. *The Modern World-System I: Capitalist Agriculture and the Origins of the European World-Economy in the Sixteenth Century.* New York: Academic Press, 1974.

Weese, Terri L., and Lynn Bohs. "Eggplant Origins: Out of Africa, into the Orient." *Taxon* 59, no. 1 (2010): 49–56.

Weinberg, Bennett Alan, and Bonnie K. Bealer. *The World of Caffeine: The Science and Culture of the World's Most Popular Drug*. New York: Routledge, 2000.

Welch, Evelyn. *Shopping in the Renaissance: Consumer Cultures in Italy, 1400–1600*. New Haven, Conn.: Yale University Press, 2005.

Wernerian Club, ed. *Pliny's Natural History in Thirty-Seven Books*. London: George Barclay, 1847.

White, Mel. "Socotra: Yemen's Legendary Island." *National Geographic*, June 2012. Accessed May 24, 2018. http://ngm.nationalgeographic.com/2012/06/socotra /white-text.

Wild, Antony. *Coffee: A Dark History*. New York: W. W. Norton, 2004.

Woolf, Virginia. *A Room of One's Own*. Harmondsworth: Penguin, 1928.

# INDEX

71–72; and globalization, 158, 160; as idea, 57–58; as inebriant, 135; as intoxicant, 8; medicinal uses, 8, 14, 38, 66, 70, 96–97, 134, 160; and modern consumerism, 158; origins of, 45, 48; origins of, legends, 47–48; preparation of, 42, 66, 100, 160; as stimulant, 8, 104, 106

coffee, cultivation of, 140, 141; Brazil, 150, 152; Ceylon (Sri Lanka), 150; Colombia, 152; Costa Rica, 150, 152; Cuba, 151, 152; Dominican Republic, 152; East Indies, 150; Ethiopia, 46, 48, 145, 152, 160; and European colonization, 142; Guatemala, 152; Hawaii, 150; Honduras, 152; indentured servitude, 154; India, 141–42, 152, 153; Ivory Coast, 152; Java, 142, 150, 152 153; Kenya, 152; labor conditions, 152–54; Mauritius, 150–51; Mexico, 152; Rwanda, 152; Santo Domingo, 151; and the slave trade, 152–53, 154; spread of, 12, 55, 150, 151–52; Sulawesi, 152; Sumatra, 152; Suriname, 150, 152; Tanzania, 152; Uganda, 152; West Indies, 150; Yemen, 141, 160

coffee, cultural presence: in art, 7–8; association with Arabs and Turks, 97–98; and colonization, 46, 55; compared to wine, 106–7; literary consumption, 91–92; in literature, 29, 66, 68–69; resistance to, 11–12, 12, 108–9

coffee, geographically: across the Islamic world, 105; appearance of, 106; arrival in England, 119, 133–34; arrival in Europe, 72–73, 115, 118; in colonial America, 146; European colonies, 55; in France, 140–41; New York City, 146; Paris, 123; spread of, 28, 57, 72–73, 80, 95, 105;

coffee and religion: See also Qur'an; Islam; and Catholicism, 116; contention in Islamic law, 105–7; in

religious ritual, 8, 11; Sufi traditions, 8, 11, 14, 107, 160

coffee culture, 11, 14, 15, 91–92; artistic history, 7; Central America, 6; Egypt, 14; in England, 134–36; England, 137–38; India, 6; Indonesia, 6; literary history, 7; London, 15; South America, 6; spread of, 11, 14, 15, 91–92, 112; written word, 7

*Coffee: From Plantation to Cup* (Thurber, 1881), 153

coffeehouses, 8–9, 36; Aleppo, Syria, 66, 69, 70; and the American Revolution, 148; in Arabia, 124, 128–29; Baghdad, 131, 142; British women, 138–39; in colonial America, 12, 141, 146–50; Constantinople, 69; contemporary, 158; Egypt, 69, 110, 131–32; in England, 120, 134–35, 138; and the evening of social differences, 136; in France, 140; Germany, 141; intellectual stimulation and entertainment, 113–14, 146–47; Istanbul, 130–31; the Levant, 110; and masculinity, 114, 128–29, 139–40; Mecca, 66, 107–9; and merchants, 7; Morocco, 114; in the Muslim world, 7, 10, 108–14, 130–31 new forms of social interactions, 12, 36, 71–72, 108–14, 120–21, 124, 146–47 (*see also* coffeehouses: as third space); Ottoman Empire, 108–13; and political discourse, 147–49; resistance to, 5, 103–4, 106, 108–10, 116, 120, 138–40, 149; Scotland, 141; similarities to teahouses, 127–28; social good, 5; spread across Europe, 141; spread of, 14, 80; as third space, 127, 128–29, 160; Venice, 119, 132–33; Vienna, 141; and women, 114

*Coffee: Its Cultivation and Profit* (Lester, 1886), 153–54

colonialism: expansion, 7; and place, 5–6

Hattox, Ralph, 131
Hebron, 22
Helena, mother of Emperor
   Constantine, 85
Henry VII, King, 137
Herodotus, 22–23
Hikmet, Nâzım, 40
Himyarite kingdom, 45
Hugh of Vermandois, 75

I

Ibn Battutah, 61–62, 86–87, 129; travel
   writings, 7
Ibn Jubayr, Muḥammad ibn Aḥmad,
   83–84
Ibn Sina, 11, 14, 50, 51, 64, 66, 68, 97–98,
   160
Il cortegiano (1528), 134
Index librorum prohibitorum, 117
India, 12, 27, 31, 55, 56, 61, 62, 65
industrial revolution, 81–82
"Inhabitants of the Town of Petersburg
   and its Vicinity at Mr. Edward's
   Coffeehouse," 148–49
Islam, 8, 26, 46. See also Qur'an; indi-
   vidual locations; jurisprudence
   regarding coffee, 105–7, 109; resis-
   tance to coffee and coffeehouses,
   107–12
Islam, Classical Age of, 18
Islam's Golden Age, 59–60
Israel, 27
Italy, Murano, 22
Itinerarium (Hamilton), 146
itinerary literature, 86–87. See also
   pilgrimages; travel literature

J

Jericho, 35
Jordan: Petra, 10–11, 26–27; Wadi Rum,
   27, 28f

K

Ka'aba, 108

Khair BeyIslam, 12
Kömeçoğlu, Uğur, 130–31, 143

L

Lane, Edward William, 131–32
languages, 84
La Roque, Jean de, 140–41
Leechbook of Bald, 97
legal aspects, 8
legends: the angel Gabriel, 47; Hadji
   Omar, the dervish, 46–47; Kaldi
   of Ethiopia, 46, 48; King Solomon,
   47; Muhammad, 47; the Yemeni
   priest, 46
Leonardo, da Vinci, 90
the Levant, 5, 10, 13, 75, 83
Levant Company, 70, 137, 142
Lévi-Strauss, Claude, 41–42
luxury goods, history of, 11, 33, 79–82,
   100, 136
Lu Yü, 124–26

M

Mandeville, John, 33
Marin, Francisco de Paula, 150
the marvelous, 83
The Maxims of the Government of
   Venice (1707), 133
Mecca, 4, 66, 70, 104, 107–8; closure
   of coffeehouses, 108–9; closure
   of coffeehouses (1511), 12
Medici family, 75
medieval Europe, 60
the Mediterranean Sea, 5, 6, 10, 26f;
   geology, 19–20; names for, 17–19
the Mediterranean world, 21–22;
   language, 21
Menocchio, 91
merchants, 11, 83. See also Venetian
   merchants; and Arabic, 84
Meshullam of Volterra, 87
Moluccas, 31
Mongol Empire, invasions by, 63
monopods, 33
Morosini, Gianfrancesco, 69

Morosini family, 75
Muhammad, 105–6
Mühimme Defteri, 110–11
Murad III, 111
Murad IV, 112
*Musei wormiani historia*, 93, 94f

## N

Nabataeans, 10, 26–27
Naples, 63
New Amsterdam. *See* New York City
New Testament, 39
New York City, 146
North Africa, 75

## O

Octavian, 18
Odoric of Pordenone, 89
olives and olive oil, 39–41; as medicine, 41
olive tree, 40f
Order to the Cadi and the Bey of Gaza, 111–12
Order to the Cadi of Jerusalem, 110–11
Orientalism, 8, 11, 13, 67, 76–77, 124, 139, 142–44
others, descriptions of, 86–87, 90–91, 96, 100
Ottoman Empire, 5, 108; control over sacred sites, 87–88

## P

Paganini, Paganino, 117
Pallavicini family, 75
Pegolotti, Francesco Balducci, 62–63, 83
pepper, 34
Persia, 75
personal narratives, 88
Peter the Hermit, 75
petroglyphs, 28f
Phoenicians, 10, 18, 23, 98, 99
pilgrimages, 85–86, 88
Pococke, Edward, 97–98
Polo, Marco, 31

polyvalence of food, 39–41
Pope Clement VIII, 115–16
Pope Urban II, 74
*La pratica della mercatura* (Pegolotti), 62, 83
Prester John, 88, 90
printed word, 12, 88
Proclamation of Neutrality, 148–49
Procopius of Caesarea, 58–59
Protestant Reformation, 116
pseudo-Arabic styles in art, 93
public spaces, 9; bath houses, 142–43; coffee as transformative of, 136; Eastern Mediterranean, 129–30, 131–32; Europe, 130

## Q

Qian, Zhang, 30
Qur'an, 39, 105; first printed copy in Arabic, 117; nabidh, 106; Surah 5:90, 106; Surah 6:118, 105; Surah 6:145, 105; Surah 36, 105, 106

## R

Rauwolf, Leonhard, 64–68, 89
Rāzī, Abū Bakr Muhammad ibn Zakarīyā. *See* Rhazes
Red Sea, 27
Renaissance: curiosity, 80; public dining, 126–27; rise of consumerism, 6–7, 80; universe of the marvelous, 7
"Reply to Coffee-House Orators" (Franklin, 1767), 147–48
restrictions on consumption: drink, 104; food, 104; Islamic, 104–6; Jewish, 104; Qur'anic, 105–6
Rhazes, 8, 11, 50, 51
Rialto, 11
Richardet, Samuel, 149
Roman Catholic Church: banning of coffee, 12; condemnation of apothecaries, 12
Roman Empire, 18, 27, 98–99
Roman Inquisition, 116–19